WORLD AIR POWER

JOURNAL

CONTENTS

Military Aviation Review

International

NH-90 full-scale development

The development phase of NATO's NH-90 multi-role helicopter received the go-ahead on 26 April when West Germany formally took a 21.7 per cent share in the programme. As this was slightly below the one-quarter planned, France and Italy have each raised their stakes to 36.3 per cent, and the Netherlands has opted for 5.7 per cent. Thus only four nations remain in NH-90, their plans being to fly a prototype by early 1994 and start deliveries in 1998. Engine choice is expected to settle upon two Rolls-Turboméca RTM322 turboshafts. Long-term requirements could be for as many as 732 NH-90s, but that is probably optimistic in the current East-West political climate. France has declared a need for 210 (150 army and 60 navy), Italy for 214 (150 army and 64 naval) and the Netherlands 24 naval versions. The West German army requires 120, the navy 50, and the air force between 64 and 114.

NATO sees reduced threat

Ministers of the NATO nations meeting during May officially declared the Warsaw Pact non-effective for its long-supposed prime purpose of threatening NATO with a surprise attack. Whilst agreeing that arms levels could be reduced in certain categories as a result, NATO remains wary of the USSR, whose forces 'are still impressive' and continue to undergo modernisation, according to General Vigleik Eide, Chairman of the Military Committee. A US call for France to re-join the military structure of NATO was rejected in Paris, however.

Western Europe

DENMARK:
S-61 update

Improved navigation systems for Denmark's eight SAR-assigned Sikorsky S-61A helicopters were secured in April by a contract placed with GEC Ferranti for navigation and air data computers linked to new displays and processors. Information will be presented on a monochrome screen, complete with coastlines and air traffic control areas relative to the helicopter's position, and the database includes locations and heights of all oil rigs in potential search areas.

GREECE:
Mirage dissatisfaction

Thomson-CSF engineers continued their assessment of reported problems with the RDM radar aboard Greece's Dassault Mirage 2000s during the spring months, deliveries of 40 aircraft on order having been halted at Greece's request last October with the 28th. It is alleged that RDM does not meet operational requirements, with the result that the 'all-weather interceptors' are unable to fly at night.

ITALY:
First Harrier II order

Having recently agreed with Spain and the US Marine Corps on joint development of a Harrier II+ variant with AN/APG-65 nose radar, Italy became the first to place an order when it received a formal letter of offer from the US for two TAV-8B trainers late in May. Final details of the tri-national project had not been concluded at the time, but Italy has had the confidence to begin training its first Harrier pilots in the USA. A total of 16 Harriers is required, to be based at the existing naval helicopter station at Luni.

NH500s received

Helicopter pilot training for all three armed services is receiving an overdue modernisation following delivery on 27 May of the first of 50 Nardi-MDH NH500E light helicopters. These are going to 72° Stormo at Frosinone – the Scuola Volo Elicotteri, or School of Helicopter Flying – as replacements for ageing Bell 47G/OH-13s and AB.204s. Selection of a new training helicopter was delayed from the mid-1970s, resulting in the IAF buying ex-US Army Bell OH-13s from a scrapyard and rebuilding them for a second lease of life.

Dornier 228 order

News was released during April of an order placed by the army's aviation branch for eight Dornier Do 228 turboprop twins, including two with survey equipment for the Instituto Geografico Militare. Hitherto, the IGM has used a Piaggio P.166 provided by the IAF.

SWEDEN:
Last Viggen

On 29 June, Saab delivered the 329th and last Viggen, ending a production run which began with the prototype's first flight on 8 February 1967. All have been delivered to the Swedish air force, in the form of 108 AJ 37 attack aircraft, 28 SF 37s and 26 SH 37s for reconnaissance, 18 Sk 37 trainers and, in the 'second generation', 149 JA 37 interceptors.

SWITZERLAND:
Vampire trainers withdrawn

De Havilland Vampire T.Mk 55 trainers were withdrawn from instructional service with the Swiss air force in June following delivery of the first of 20 replacement BAe Hawks. Switzerland is the last country to use the Vampire, the prototype of which flew in September 1943, but a few single-seat FB.Mk 6s are being maintained in service as target tugs for a little longer, pending arrival of more Pilatus PC-9s.

UNITED KINGDOM:
Tornado GR.Mk 4 update plans

Despite cancellation of its new-build Mk 4s, the RAF is proceeding with a mid-life update (MLU) for the majority of Mk 1s in service. Details revealed in May indicated that 165 surviving aircraft from the 229 due to have been delivered by 1991 will be converted to Mk 4s: 70 by BAe from 1992/3 onwards; 15 by joint BAe and RAF working parties at RAF stations; and 80 by the winner of a tender competition. A further 25 late-production GR.Mk 1s will be updated later. MLU features include terrain-reference navigation, FLIR, wide-angle HUD and other new avionics. An upgrade for the Tornado F.Mk 3 interceptor was also given the go-ahead in May, following finalisation of a feasibility study. Work is due to begin at BAe's Warton plant in 1994.

Blue Vixen flight trials

GEC Ferranti Blue Vixen pulse-Doppler radar became airborne in a Sea Harrier FRS.Mk 2 for the first time on 24 May when XZ439 conducted a flight lasting over an hour from BAe's Dunsfold flight-test centre. The radar was operated successfully at heights up to 40,000 ft. XZ439 is the second of two Mk 1s converted to the new standard, and first flew in March 1989, although the radar has already been air-tested in BAe One-Eleven and 125 aircraft.

All surviving 38 Sea Harrier Mk 1s are due to be converted and will be joined by 10 new Mk 2s ordered in March 1990.

Hawk gets wingtip 'Winders

A first flight was made in April of wingtip Sidewinder rails on BAe's Hawk 100 aerodynamic test and demonstrator aircraft, ZA101. Export customers Abu Dhabi, Brunei, South Korea and Saudi Arabia have specified the additional weapons points for Hawk 100s and/or single-seat Hawk 200s. The maiden flight was undertaken at Warton, to where all Hawk final assembly and flight-test was transferred from Dunsfold in 1989.

Bolshoi Arrows

The RAF's Red Arrows aerobatic team made its first visit to the Soviet Union in June when displays were given in Kiev over the weekend of 23rd-24th. The nine red Hawks (plus spare) were led by Squadron Leader Tim Miller in his final season as 'Red 1' before handing over to Adrian Thurley. Plans to display elsewhere, including Moscow, failed to materialise.

WEST GERMANY:
First Tornado ECR accepted

Some four months late as the result of software integration problems, the first ECR (Electronic Combat and Reconnaissance) version of the Panavia Tornado for the Luftwaffe was handed over at Manching late in April in the course of trials at the military aircraft experimental unit, Wehr-technischedienststelle 61 (WTD 61). Deliveries to two new squadrons – within Jagdbombergeschwader 32 at Lechfeld, and JBG 38 at Jever – were due to begin shortly afterwards. IOC will not be attained for some months, as the Texas Instruments AGM-88A HARM anti-radar missiles cannot be fired until new software has been installed in the missile control unit computer. A four-month test of HARM ended in the USA in April when naval Tornado 4529 fired three missiles against targets in the China Lake test range, California.

Eastern Europe

CZECHOSLOVAKIA:
Forces running down

Implications of the 15 per cent reduction in military spending planned by the Czech government for the financial year 1990-91 were understood to involve disposal of 51 of the current total of 417 air force aircraft. The USSR has promised to remove 20 of 105 combat aircraft based on Czech soil by the end of 1990.

EAST GERMANY:
Unwanted 'Fulcrums'

Among topics raised by the East and West German defence ministers during their meeting in May was the delivery to the GDR of MiG-29 'Fulcrums' from 52 on order. Up to that time, 20 had been received, including two tandem-seat trainers, the East Germans intimating that cancellation of the remainder of the order was

WORLD
AIR POWER
JOURNAL

Aerospace Publishing Ltd

Published quarterly by
Aerospace Publishing Ltd
179 Dalling Road
London W6 0ES
UK

ISSN 0959-7050

Published under licence in USA
and Canada by Airtime Publishing
Inc., 10 Bay Street, Westport, CT
06880, USA

Editorial Offices:
WORLD AIR POWER
JOURNAL
Aerospace Publishing Ltd
179 Dalling Road
London W6 0ES
UK

Publisher: Stan Morse
Editors: David Donald
        Jon Lake
Production Editor: Trisha Palmer
Design: Barry Savage
Typesetting: SX Composing Ltd
Origination and printing by
    Imago Publishing Ltd
Printed in Spain

Europe Correspondent:
  Paul Jackson
Washington Correspondent:
  Robert F. Dorr
USA West Coast Correspondent:
  René J. Francillon
Asia Correspondent:
  Pushpindar Singh
Australia Correspondent:
  Greg Maggs
Switzerland Correspondent:
  Peter Gunti

**World Air Power Journal
is published quarterly
and is available by
subscription**

**SUBSCRIPTION AND BACK
NUMBERS:**

**UK and World (except USA
and Canada) write to:
Aerospace Publishing Ltd
FREEPOST
MARLBOROUGH
Wilts SN8 2BR
UK**

**(No stamp required if posted
within the UK)**

**USA and Canada, write to:
Airtime Publishing Inc.
10 Bay Street
Westport, CT 06880
USA**

**Prevailing subscription rates
available on request.
Single issues and back issues
(subject to availability):
Delivery Mainland USA, Alaska
and Hawaii: $16.00 (US) each
Delivery Canada: $20.00 (Can)
each**

**Please enclose payment with
your order. Visa and
MasterCard accepted. Please
include your card number,
expiration date and signature.**

The publishers would like to thank
Wing Commander R. V. Morris,
O/C No. 14 Squadron RAF, for his
enthusiastic and generous help in
the preparation of the Tornado
feature.

Left: NH90 took a further step towards fruition with the go-ahead announcement. The type is to be developed for both assault and naval duties.

Above: The last JA37 was handed over to the Swedish air force, ending the production of the fighter. Saab production is now switching to the Gripen.

not possible. With moves towards German integration proceeding, some observers were predicting that the unified state of Germany might be tempted to standardise on the MiG-29 as a Phantom replacement, instead of waiting for the later-generation (and far more expensive) EFA but it seems more likely that most Soviet-supplied equipment will be returned or destroyed.

HUNGARY:

Strength reductions planned

Reviewing the strength of its armed forces shortly after coming to power in May, the democratic government of Hungary pledged cuts in the air force from 99 to 61 interceptors and 79 to 66 attack helicopters, while retaining 11 strike aircraft.

SOVIET UNION:

MiG-27s transfer to navy

Concern was expressed by Norway at intelligence reports confirming the move of some 45 MiG-27 'Flogger-J' dedicated nuclear strike aircraft from Debrecen in Hungary to a base on the Kola peninsula. This is the first insertion of tactical strike aircraft close to the Norwegian border and presents a further worrying feature to NATO in that the aircraft have been re-assigned to the naval aviation force. The USSR is attempting to have naval aircraft excluded from CFE arms-reduction agreements, but its already substantial land-based naval air force has recently been augmented by Tu-26 'Backfire' and Su-24 'Fencer' bombers from the air arm.

'Mystic' achievements

International height and speed records in the 16-22 tonne class were claimed for the Myasischchev M-17 'Mystic' equivalent to the Lockheed U-2/TR-1. During a flight on 28 March which was not immediately announced, design bureau chief test pilot, Vladimir Arkhippenko, achieved 21990 m (71,785 ft) and two days later flew at 558 km/h (347 mph) around a 100-km (62-mile) circuit. Despite its obvious military potential, the 'Mystic' apparently remains a civil aircraft for earth resources exploration and pollution control, and of two built one has been retired to a museum. There are unconfirmed reports of a twin-engined version, which, if proved to exist, could be the expected Soviet parallel to Lockheed's TR-1.

Despite withdrawing the T.Mk 55 trainers from service, the Swiss air force continues to operate de Havilland Vampires in the shape of the FB.Mk 6. Based at Sion, these aircraft serve as target tugs.

A commemorative scheme from Belgium, celebrating 70 years for 42 Smaldeel/Escadrille at Bierset. The unit flies the Mirage 5BR on reconnaissance duties, and has the two-seat 5BD for training.

Another 'special' scheme is worn by this 8 Smaldeel/Escadrille Mirage 5BA, marking the FAB/BLu's 20 years of Mirage 5 operations. Like its sister squadron, 8 Sm/Esc also flies the 5BD two-seater.

Middle East

BAHRAIN:

Falcons delivered

The tiny Arabian Gulf archipelago of Bahrain was re-aligning its air defences in mid-1990 following delivery in March of its first General Dynamics F-16 Fighting Falcons. Before the end of September, the Bahrain Amiri Air Force was due to have completed acceptances of eight F-16Cs and four tandem-seat F-16Ds, considerably upgrading its combat arm, hitherto based on a dozen Northrop F-5 Tiger IIs.

EGYPT:

Albatros gift

EAF training began at Bilbeis in April on Aero L-39 light jets presented to the EAF by Libya. Although Colonel Khadaffi had grandiosely promised 'a wing' of L-39s, Egypt in fact received 20 wings and 10 fuselages – somewhat less than it might have been led to believe. Official presentation of all 10 L-39s took place on 23 March, the aircraft being used to assist older L-29 Delfins in basic instruction prior to student pilots' Dassault-Dornier/Alpha Jet stage. This would imply that the EAF has found it necessary to introduce an intermediate aircraft between the EMBRAER/Kader Tucano and the Alpha Jet.

IRAN:

Agusta-Bell order

Reports in April of the sale to Iran of 12 Agusta-Bell 212 utility helicopters suggest that Italy's ban on sales to that country (because of involvement in the Gulf War) is at an end. Equally, the US government has

The end is drawing near for the RAF's Buccaneer force, scheduled for replacement by Tornados released from RAF Germany. Major overhauls are still being undertaken, as evidenced by this No. 208 Squadron aircraft seen prior to painting.

not invoked its power of veto on the sale of a US design to a country with which relations are far from friendly. At the same time, Iraq may have gained a small batch of AB 212AS shipborne helicopters held up by Italy for the duration of hostilities. Iran's army appears to be receiving spares to keep at least some of its Italian-built Boeing Vertol CH-47C Chinooks airworthy, as evidenced by their use for relief work following the June earthquake in northern regions.

SAUDI ARABIA:
Sikorsky Desert Hawk deliveries

On 1 April 1990, Sikorsky completed delivery of 12 S-70A-1 Desert Hawks (modified UH-60 Black Hawk) to the Royal Saudi Land Forces Army Aviation Command (RSLFAAC). The first lot of six S-70A-1s was delivered by C-5 Galaxy in January, the second on 1 April. The helicopters had been ordered by the Saudis under FMS (foreign military sales) in May 1988.

The Desert Hawk is powered by a 1,900-hp General Electric T700-GE-701A engine. This makes it similar to the US Army's UH-60L, which replaced the original UH-60A squad assault helicopter (powered by an earlier version of the same engine) on the Stratford, Connecticut production line in October 1989.

The Desert Hawk is equipped with 15 troop seats and Racal Jaguar 5 frequency-hopping radio. A significant part of the programme is a blade erosion protection system consisting of polyurethane tape and a spray-on coating. The 12 S-70A-1s, together with 15 Bell 406CS also currently being delivered, will be based at King Khalid Military City north of Riyadh. The Bell aircraft are specialised versions of the OH-58D Kiowa Warrior.

The Saudi purchase of Sikorsky and Bell helicopters is part of the kingdom's ambitious *Al'mana* plan to develop an army aviation service based on the American pattern. On 18-22 June 1990, the US Army – which acts as agent for the FMS helicopters – held a low-key conference on procurement by Saudi Land Forces. Reporters were excluded even from unclassified sessions.

In addition to the Desert Hawks, Saudi Arabia is purchasing a VIP transport version of the Black Hawk, scheduled for delivery in December 1990.

The transport Black Hawk is in final assembly at Sikorsky's West Palm Beach, Florida, facility. With most systems in common with the S-70A-1, it is actually closer in its mission fit to the US Marine Corps VH-60 executive transport which carries President Bush as 'Marine One'.

The *Al'mana* plan is expected to result in Saudi purchases of a significant number of additional Desert Hawk-type aircraft, to be manufactured in the United Kingdom by Westland. It is understood that Riyadh has committed for purchase of 80 WS-70A Desert Hawks from the Westland production line at Yeovil, Somerset. The Saudi land forces are expected to use these aircraft in the assault role with the GIAT M621 20-mm cannon and Forges Zeebrugge 19-tube rocket launcher, which can handle various anti-vehicle and anti-personnel rockets.

YEMEN:
United air force

The armed forces of North and South Yemen were technically dissolved on 22 May when the two states achieved their long-planned unification. Building of combined services is now under way, and it will be interesting to see which, if any, air force equipment is discarded. South Yemen re-equipped with Soviet aircraft from 1969 onwards, while its counterpart's allegiances varied between West and East, resulting in a front-line force of Northrop F-5Es, MiG-21 'Fishbeds' and Sukhoi Su-22 'Fitters'. However, the status of the former SYAF is uncertain, as the majority of its equipment was destroyed in a 1986 coup and may not have been replaced.

Far East

CHINA:
Fighter modernisations abandoned

Chinese attempts to gain Western technology for much-needed enhancement of ageing combat aircraft received a double blow in the spring with apparent abandonment of both the Q-5K Kong Yun and J-8 III. Cessation of the Q-5K attack aircraft was announced in Paris during April, France's Thomson-CSF/Sextant Avionique having been previously commissioned to add a laser-ranger, HUD, INS, air data sensor, radio altimeter and revised instrumentation to the basic Q-5. A prototype flew on 17 September 1988 and up to 600 in-service A-5s were to have been similarly modified.

AEW Nimrod avionics obtained

In a surprise announcement in June, the UK firm of GEC revealed that it was negotiating with China for the possible sale of 16 radar systems from the abandoned RAF Nimrod AEW.Mk 3 programme. The radars, comprising 11 from the aircraft converted, plus spares and test units, were bought back by the manufacturer when the project was cancelled in favour of a Boeing E-3D Sentry purchase in December 1986. Contrary to received opinion, the equipment was not entirely useless, but merely did not have the performance demanded by the UK. GEC remains convinced that

extra expenditure can bring the system up to specification, although even in its present state, it represents an improvement on China's zero AEW capability. Both Shaanxi Y-8 (An-12 'Cub') and Ilyushin Il-18 'Coot' are under consideration as platforms for the radar's nose and tail antennas, although it is unlikely that more than 10 aircraft will be converted.

MALAYSIA:
Tornado dropped

Unofficial, but believable, reports entered circulation in May, suggesting that Malaysia had abandoned its protracted negotiations for the purchase of a dozen attack and reconnaissance Panavia Tornados from the UK. Priority then switched to a simpler fighter-attack package to include either Dassault Mirage 2000s or GD F-16 Fighting Falcons, evaluation having begun even before the Tornado's fate became known. As part of this less costly solution, however, Malaysia is in the market for some 20-32 light attack aircraft or armed trainers, for which the BAe Hawk is favoured. The new aircraft are required to replace refurbished McDonnell Douglas A-4PTM Skyhawks, 36 of which have been offered for sale, with interest expressed by Argentina and Chile.

PAKISTAN:
More Mirages

Protracted negotiations with Australia, for the purchase of surplus Dassault Mirage IIIOs, were completed on 24 April when announcement was made in Canberra of the sale of 50 aircraft, plus spares and a flight simulator. The PAF, which currently operates over 80 Mirage IIIs and non-radar Mirage 5s, appears to have gained the package for the bargain price of $36 million, compared with the minimum of $79 million originally demanded by the RAAF. Pakistan proposes to refurbish the aircraft before placing them in service or selling a few to other countries (such as Chile, which is interested in 10), but the Mirages are in generally good shape, having undergone an interim refurbishment (including new wings) in the early 1980s as the result of delays in ordering F-18 Hornets.

Among the less common F-16 users is the Dutch air force's Testgroep, which flies the Fighting Falcon from Volkel on tactical evaluation duties. The unit performs trials with new weapons and systems.

Jaguar GR.Mk 1s from Nos 6 and 41 Squadrons prepare to leave Coltishall for Oman. The hastily-applied sand scheme is for operations in the Gulf region in support of UN activity following the Iraqi invasion of Kuwait. Four of the aircraft are recce-configured.

The Tornado ECR has begun to be delivered to the Luftwaffe. In addition to an internal reconnaissance system, the ECR has a sensitive receiver system to allow it to operate in the defence suppression role, armed with AGM-88 HARM anti-radar missiles.

THAILAND:
Airbus ordered

The first military contract for the European Airbus was placed by Thailand, which requires an A310-324 to be delivered in September 1991 for Wing 6 at Don Muang as a VIP transport. West Germany is thinking of buying four A310s for 1992 delivery as replacements for a similar number of Boeing 707s, but might delay two until the end of the decade, when the A340 will be available.

SRI LANKA:
SLAF in action

SLAF aircraft were called to action on 26 June in an attempt to lift a two-week siege by Tamil guerrillas of a government fort at Jaffna. Missions were reportedly flown by helicopters firing rockets and machine-guns and by light bombers – presumed to be the Bell 412s of No. 4 Squadron and COIN SIAI-Marchetti SF-260TP Warriors of No. 1 Squadron respectively. Civilians were warned by leaflet to flee before the attacks began, but reports that napalm was used were denied by the SLAF.

Africa

ANGOLA:
Airlift saves UNITA

Fighting for the first time without South African help, UNITA rebels narrowly avoided defeat by Angola's Marxist government forces when a covert CIA airlift brought US weapons from Kamina in Zaïre to an airstrip at the rebels' stronghold at Jamba. Government troops were forced to withdraw from attacks against the for-

ward base at Mavinga after a decisive battle on 6-7 May, UNITA villages having earlier come under attack from Cuban-flown Su-22 'Fitters' and various MiGs dropping phosphorus and chemical weapons. Aircraft claims by UNITA during the campaign included an Mi-25 'Hind' on 25 February; a CASA 212 Aviocar on 27 March; and an Mi-17 'Hip-H' and Mi-25 'Hind' both on 29 March. The CIA airlift was undertaken by civil-registered Lockheed L-100 Hercules of Tepper Aviation and began disastrously on 27 November with the crash of one aircraft on a night approach to Jamba. Two more L-100s were subsequently brought in.

Australasia

AUSTRALIA:
Final Hornet delivered

Manufacture of the McDonnell Douglas F/A-18 Hornet in Australia ended on 16 May – on time and on budget – when ASTA handed over its 73rd aircraft. Together with two built in the US, these make up the 57 F/A-18A and 18 tandem-seat F/A-18B fighters ordered in 1981 for A$2,427 million. The current cost of the 75 aircraft is now over $A4,000 million, but that is due to inflation and currency rate changes outside the manufacturer's control.

F-111 update plans

Talks began in May between the RAAF and Rockwell concerning a proposed upgrade for two squadrons of F-111Cs which would keep the force operational until 2010. Based on the USAF F-111 improvement programme, modifications would involve substitution of digital flight control, navigation and weapons aiming systems for the current analogue components.

ETHIOPIA:
Rebels' success

MiG-23 'Floggers' were in action around the town of Mitsiwa during April, using cluster bombs against areas gained by rebel forces of the Eritrean People's Revolutionary Democratic Front. The bombs are alleged to have been made in Israel, implying that the USSR is reducing its support for the Marxist government. By May, government troops holding Asmara were entirely surrounded by rebels and a military airlift to the local airport was their sole source of supply.

SOUTH AFRICA:
Caravans' secret trail

An unconfirmed report has alleged that the SAAF has replaced at least some of its C4M Kudu single-engined STOL light transports by Cessna Caravan Is. Nine or more of these US-built aircraft are said to have been obtained by 'front' companies acting for the SAAF as a means of circumventing the UN arms embargo. The Caravans are alleged to have retained their civilian registrations and been assigned to Air Commando (reservist) squadrons whose members do not wear uniforms. That being the case, the Caravans are no different from the other civil machines of various makes which are flown by the SAAF's 10 reservist squadrons.

Amid the rash of RAF special schemes, this No. 63 Squadron Hawk sports markings for Chivenor's 50th birthday. Co-located No. 151 Squadron has a similar design in blue and white. Both units constitute No. 2 Tactical Weapons Unit.

Tucano T.Mk 1s are being delivered at a steady rate to replace the Jet Provost on the RAF's basic training units. This aircraft has a non-standard toucan insignia on the tail: a smaller toucan appears on all No. 7 FTS aircraft as part of the 'CF' tail badge.

North America

CANADA:
CT-142s work-up

Belated instructor training was under way at Winnipeg during the spring on the first of four DHC Dash-8 navigation trainers delivered to No. 402 (City of Winnipeg) Air Reserve Squadron. Following two transport-orientated Dash-8s – known to the Canadian Forces as CC-142s – the four CT-142s were delivered from December 1989 onwards and are being operated for the Aerospace & Navigation School. Each can accommodate four students and two instructors. The CT-142s were delayed by 18 months with avionics integration problems, but will begin training navigators early in 1991, each student receiving 33 flights during the 35-week course. The two CC-142s, temporarily deployed to the detachment of No. 412 Squadron at Lahr, West Germany, have returned to Canada and been replaced by Convair CC-109 Cosmopolitans fresh from an extensive overhaul and modification. Four Lockheed CC-130N Hercules navigation trainers of No. 249 Squadron are being de-converted back to CC-130Es and will move from Winnipeg to Trenton to augment the transport force, one source suggesting that they will become CK-130 tankers.

Hornet problems

A grounding order, followed by a return to flying with increased restrictions, was the Canadian government's reaction to the loss of four McDonnell Douglas CF-18 Hornets during April. With 13 Hornets lost in almost 170,000 flying hours, the CF attrition rate for the aircraft is 7.14 per 100,000 hours, compared with estimates of 5.6 during the first five years of operations and 3.85 thereafter, or with the USN/USMC average of 4.35. If this rate is not improved, the CF expects to be forced to disband a Hornet squadron in the mid-1990s, having been unable to order its planned attrition-replacement batch because of funding shortages. Low-level flying in excess of original plans has reduced the CF-18's fatigue-life expectancy from 20 to 12 years, prompting discussions with Australia on a joint rectification programme.

Lockheed C-130s dominate the Airlift Rodeo event in terms of numbers, although this year's top honours went to a C-141 StarLifter team. The competition is centred at Pope AFB, with airdrops at nearby Fort Bragg.

Left: Keeping track of the scores at Rodeo is no small task, with many competitions under way. Thirty-nine teams were involved, including 11 from overseas.

North America

UNITED STATES

Airlift Rodeo 1990

The 63rd Military Airlift Wing (MAW), which operates the Lockheed C-141B StarLifter at Norton AFB, California, won the Military Airlift Command (MAC) 11th Airlift Rodeo competition, held 2-8 June 1990 at Pope AFB, North Carolina. Twenty-eight US and 11 foreign teams joined in the annual event, with C-141Bs, C-130s and Transall C-160s. Second place went to an Israeli C-130 Hercules team.

Colonel Brooke P. Bailey, 63rd wing commander, said after what observers called a "beautiful" airdrop of paratroopers that the C-141B navigator was the same US Air Force lieutenant who led 20 transports into Panama during Operation Just Cause in December 1989.

Curiously, the winning C-141B wing won none of the individual events. A C-141B aircrew from the Reserve forces' 446th MAW at McChord AFB, Washington, took top honours for the aircraft type. Still, the 63rd MAW won the General William S. Moore Trophy, returning the top award to US hands after it had been won last year by the Royal Australian Air Force's No. 36 Squadron at RAAF Richmond.

Participants included Air National Guard (ANG) and Air Force Reserve (AFRes) squadrons, which usually fare better than active-duty units. This year, US Marine Corps C-130 Hercules also participated. Foreign participants included Australia, Belgium, Canada, France, West Germany, Indonesia, Israel, Japan (in observer status, with aircraft), Portugal, Thailand, and the United Kingdom – whose team of 55 was the largest, coming from RAF Lyneham headed by Wing Commander Peter Bedford.

The competition includes flying, airdrop, aircraft loading, and maintenance events. Accuracy and tactics are judged in the dropping of paratroopers and container loads at DZs (drop zones) in Fort Bragg, adjacent to Pope, with aircrews making steep descents – as they would to confound defensive fire in combat – and vying for pinpoint accuracy with drops from 500 feet, aimed at a 400-sq ft target area.

A separate competition is ERO (engine-running onload/offload), in which two trailers are loaded, then unloaded, under simulated combat conditions with engines running. Critics argue that Airlift Rodeo is only a partial test of airlift capabilities, since no night flying is performed and MAC's force of 131 Lockheed C-5A/B Galaxy airlifters does not participate. The C-5 is rarely used for airdrops in peacetime but would be expected to drop paratroops and cargo in a conflict.

Unexpected woes delay A-12 attack aircraft

Though he will admit only to being "not happy", Defense Secretary Dick Cheney is widely known to be furious that delays with the A-12 attack aircraft escaped the Pentagon's major aircraft review (MAR), conducted this spring. On 11 June, Cheney summoned the chairmen of General Dynamics and McDonnell Douglas to explain why problems with the A-12 Avenger II medium-attack aircraft – the planned A-6 Intruder replacement – escaped the review.

"I was not happy to discover that the contractors were having problems with the A-12," Cheney said at a Pentagon news conference after the meeting with Stanley Pace and John F. McDonnell. Cheney also said, however, that the A-12 has "high priority", noting that the A-6 "is getting old" and "we need the A-12 as soon as we can get it in the force."

At one time, the subsonic A-12, which makes extensive use of 'stealth' technology, was expected to fly in 1990. The schedule, which was unchanged after the MAR, had called for eight aircraft to be built in 1990. First flight and production are now set back to "beyond early 1991 to later in that year", the builders say. The two firms teamed on the project told the Navy that the A-12 schedule slide was caused by "complexity and an unanticipated delay in the tooling required for the early aircraft." As recently as May 1990, Navy visitors to the A-12 final assembly facility in Tulsa, Oklahoma, had no hint of the delay.

Of the four major US aircraft programmes – A-12, B-2, C-17 and Advanced Tactical Fighter (ATF) – the A-12 has long been considered the most essential. The price per aircraft, in the range of $80- to $96-million each, has been considered high but tolerable.

US Navy sources say the builders are having difficulty building the all-composite A-12 to weight requirements, which set a loaded weight of 60,000 lb, or slightly more than the A-6.

General Dynamics (the prime contractor) and McDonnell Douglas will have to 'swallow' $2 billion in aggregate cost overruns on the A-12 if, as expected, the US Navy refuses to provide further funding for the fixed-price development contract.

Builders of the A-12 apparently hope to gain goodwill from the Avenger nickname, since President Bush flew the Grumman torpedo-bomber with the same name during World War II.

Lockheed to end P-3 Orion production

On 17 April 1990 at Palmdale, California, Lockheed delivered the 548th and final P-3 Orion (Bureau No. 163925) to be built for the US Navy. Lockheed has also sold 85 Orions to foreign purchasers and two to the US Department of Commerce. In addition, the bulk of Japan's planned force of 100 P-3 Orions is being manufactured in Japan by Kawasaki.

Last year, Lockheed announced a corporate decision to cease production of the P-3. This was a forewarning of a 'downsizing' of the company, to use spokesman Bill Spaniel's term, subsequently announced in April 1990.

Still being completed at Palmdale are three P-3C Orions for Pakistan (Bureau Nos 164467/469) and three CP-140A Arcturus, derivatives of Canada's CP-140 Aurora, the last of which will be delivered to Canada in late 1991. South Korea has made known a strong interest in purchasing eight P-3Cs. In what appears to be a reversal, Lockheed now says that it is "actively looking" at this and other overseas customers. Though the company is proceeding to dispose of its aircraft facility at Burbank, California, the future of the Palmdale facility has not been announced.

According to Lockheed's Jim Ragsdale, the company would be able to handle a Korean requirement only if agreement were finalised in the very near future.

Ragsdale says the manufacturer has not yet decided whether production of South Korean P-3Cs, should they be ordered, would take place at Palmdale.

Kawasaki production of P-3C Orions has only reached the half-way point. Although there would be political and financial hurdles, production of P-3Cs for South Korea could be handled by Kawasaki if Lockheed were to bow out.

With regard to the A model of the well-known patrol aircraft, the last ASW (anti-submarine warfare) mission by a P-3A Orion was flown over the Atlantic on 22 March by reserve squadron VP-64 'Condors', stationed at NAS Willow Grove, Pennsylvania. The P-3A (Bureau No. 152158) made the flight from Rota, Spain, where the unit was deployed. VP-64 will now convert to the P-3B.

First flight of Special Operations MH-47E

The prototype Boeing MH-47E Chinook special-operations helicopter (88-0267) made its first flight on 1 June 1990 when test pilots Ron Mecklin and John Tulloch flew the craft from the Ridley Township, Pennsylvania, factory to Boeing's test centre at Wilmington, Delaware.

The MH-47E prototype results from a December 1987 contract to fabricate a single MH-47E from a Chinook airframe undergoing modification to CH-47C standard. Its schedule calls for completing contractor flight-testing and formal delivery to the US Army in November 1990.

The MH-47E is powered by Lycoming T-55L-714 engines and is equipped with the range of items appropriate for special operations, including air-refuelling, night vision compatibility, and terrain-following radar. Fuel capacity is double that of the CH-47D.

AH-64 Apache defended, and ordered by Israel

McDonnell Douglas, manufacturer of the AH-64 Apache battlefield helicopter, believes it has effectively countered Congressional and press criticism of the AH-64 and anticipates further production well into the 1990s. Because the US Army's LH (light helicopter) programme could be sharply curtailed or eliminated in current budget proceedings, some future version of the Apache is seen as an LH alternative.

Criticism of the AH-64 Apache includes its difficulty operating in the rain, cost of operation, maintenance problems, and jamming of its 30-mm Chain Gun cannon. The manufacturer has formed an Apache Action Team (AAT), to work on field-related problems. McDonnell Douglas acknowledges that the AH-64 has some water leakage problems, that its average operating cost is US$3,924 per hour (not $5,700 as charged), that a maintenance problem is reported every 54 minutes, and

The USAF's Flight Inspection fleet is under renewal with the delivery of six British Aerospace C-29As (based on the civil 125-800) to replace elderly T-39 Sabreliners and C-140 JetStars.

Egypt now operates the Aero L-39, thanks to a gift of 10 aircraft from Colonel Khadaffi of Libya. The aircraft are used in the basic training role, supplementing elderly Aero L-29 Delfins.

A trio of Sikorsky S-70A-1 Desert Hawks display Saudi colours. This version has been modified to cope with continuous operations in the desert, complete with uprated engines and blade protection.

One of the more unusual intercepts accomplished recently was this 'Aeroflot' Ilyushin Il-18, caught at low level over the North Sea. Its precise role is unknown, but some electronic reconnaissance function is likely.

that improvements are being sought in the performance of the cannon.

A 4 May 1990 study by the US General Accounting Office, 'Army's Apache Helicopter Has Proven Difficult to Support', concluded that AH-64 reliability problems have caused low morale and re-enlistment rates among aviation mechanics who work on the helicopter. The US Army recently asked for approval to increase by 14 the number of mechanics in an Apache battalion, currently 98.

During Operation Just Cause, the military action which ousted General Manuel Noriega in Panama, 11 Apaches flew 238 hours, including 95 at night, between 20 December 1989 and 9 January 1990. Two AH-64s experienced temporary failures: in one case, vibration from the 30-mm cannon tripped a circuit breaker and blacked out the aircraft's target acquisition and designation system. This prompted a special operations officer to say that "[The Apache] may be a little too high-tech for what we do." The aircraft completed 10 out of 10 missions with two aborts. Three Apaches were damaged in combat, with up to 23 hits, with no casualties. Seven Hellfire missiles were fired, all direct hits on targets such as General Noriega's headquarters.

Israel has become the first foreign purchaser of the AH-64 Apache, with an order for 18 aircraft to be delivered later this year. (The full purchase involves 19 Apaches,

539 Hellfires, 16 spare T700-701 engines, and other equipment for $285 million). Egypt is expected to acquire 24 Apaches in a separate purchase to be finalised this summer. (The purchase includes 24 helicopters, 429 Hellfires, 48 spare Rockwell International Hellfire launchers, and other equipment, for $488 million.)

McDonnell Douglas, which manufactures the Apache in Mesa, Arizona, is forging ahead with the Longbow Apache, an improved version with Longbow mast-mounted radar and fire-and-forget Hellfire missiles and air-to-air Stingers. In April 1990, two modified Apaches were used by the US Army to conduct early-user test and experimentation with a partial Longbow Apache configuration.

F-14A+ & S-3B maiden deployments

The USS *Dwight D. Eisenhower* (CVN-69) commenced a six-month Mediterranean cruise on 8 March when the ship left Norfolk, Virginia, with Carrier Air Wing 7/AG (CVW-7) embarked. Included within the complement of the Air Wing was the F-14A+ Tomcat and the S-3B Viking, both making their first major deployments.

Both VF-142 'Ghostriders' and VF-143

'World Famous Pukin' Dogs' were equipped with the F-14A+, operating a selection of new-production and modified aircraft all in the low-visibility 'tactical' grey colour scheme. The main improvements between the F-14A+ and its predecessor involve the fitment of General Electric F110-GE-400 powerplants instead of the Pratt & Whitney TF-30 engines, offering significantly more thrust and fuel economy and not requiring the engagement of afterburners during take-off. Other lesser improvements include advanced carrier landing equipment and a computerised fuel management system.

The S-3Bs were assigned to VS-31 'Topcats', which, although being the second squadron to convert to the type, had the honour of being the first to introduce the improved Viking to European waters. Modifications to the S-3B are considerable, as it now has the ability to launch the AGM-84A Harpoon missile, and is equipped with the Texas Instruments AN/APS-137(V)1 inverse synthetic aperture radar to enhance anti-submarine capabilities. Additional equipment changes include the fitment of a Sanders AN/OL-320/AYS acoustic processor, improved Goodyear AN/ALE-39 chaff/flare dispensing system, and an upgrade of the central air data computer to AYK-10A (V) standard.

Navy A-7s on last WestPac cruise

USS *Carl Vinson* (CVN-70) left Alameda, California, on 1 February for a six-month Western Pacific and Indian Ocean cruise with CVW-15/NL embarked, including VA-27 'Royal Maces' and VA-97 'Warhawks' flying the A-7E Corsair II on the

type's final scheduled WestPac deployment. Upon completion of the cruise the two squadrons were earmarked to commence transition to the F-18 Hornet, ending Pacific Fleet Corsair operations at NAS Lemoore, California, although VA-122 'Flying Eagles' will remain at Lemoore for the time being as the Fleet Replacement Squadron to provide crews for the last four A-7E squadrons. Atlantic Fleet A-7E squadrons VA-37 'Bulls' and VA-105 'Gunslingers' both form part of CVW-6/AE aboard USS *Forrestal* (CV-59), while VA-46 'Clansmen' and VA-72 'Bluehawks' with CVW-3/AC are assigned to USS *John F. Kennedy* (CV-67).

Independence *to replace* Midway *in Japan*

USS *Independence* (CV-62) is to replace USS *Midway* (CV-41) as the US Navy's forward-deployed carrier based at Yokosuka, Japan, when the latter returns to the USA, possibly for retirement. *Independence* has been selected primarily because she completed her Service Life Extension Program (SLEP) in August 1987, enabling her to operate in the Pacific for several years without the necessity of returning Stateside for a major overhaul.

The *Midway* has been stationed in Japan since 11 September 1973 with its Air Wing shore-based at NAS Atsugi. *Midway* has CVW-5 assigned with its complement composed of VFA-151 'Vigilantes', VFA-192 'World Famous Golden Dragons' and VFA-195 'Dambusters' all with the F-18A; VA-115 'Eagles' and VA-185 'Nighthawks' both flying the A-6E and KA-6D; VAW-115 'Liberty' with the E-2C; VAQ-136 'Gauntlets' operating the EA-6B; and HS-12 'Wyverns' flying the

SH-3H. *Independence* will embark a slightly larger Air Wing, which will include F-14s and S-3s that are not part of *Midway*'s complement.

P-3B training ends

P-3B aircrew training with the Pacific Fleet ended recently when VP-31 'Black Lightnings', the Fleet Replacement Squadron at NAS Moffett Field, California, conducted its final courses. The final pair of fleet P-3B squadrons, VP-6 'Blue Sharks' and VP-22 'Blue Geese', both stationed at NAS Barbers Point, Hawaii, commenced conversion to the P-3C during the spring and should both be operational on the version by the end of 1990. The displaced P-3Bs are being transferred to the Naval Reserve.

Last USMC A-4M transferred to Reserves

VMA-211 'Wake Island Avengers' at MCAS Yuma, Arizona, transferred its last A-4M to the Reserves on 27 February, ending the active service career of the attack version of the Skyhawk with the Corps. The last A-4M, BuNo 158428, was transferred to VMA-133 'Golden Gators' at NAS Alameda, California. The squadron commenced conversion to the AV-8B and should have become operational on the Harrier II by the autumn.

USAFE A-10 assignment changes

The 81st TFW at RAF Bentwaters, UK, commenced receiving early-production A-10As to evaluate the possibility of USAFE exchanging its Thunderbolts for elderly examples prior to any proposed arms reduction agreements with the Soviet Union. Four aircraft, serials 76-0514, 76-0522, 76-0533 and 76-0550, all formerly with the 355th TTW at Davis-Monthan AFB, Arizona, were ferried to the 81st TFW on 30 May and have subsequently been allocated one each to the wing's four squadrons (two at RAF Bentwaters and two at RAF Woodbridge).

Subsequently, a dozen A-10As of 176th TFS Wisconsin ANG from Truax Field deployed to Sculthorpe on 14 July for a two-week visit. All the participants arrived unmarked, indicating their transfer to USAFE in a major swap-around which also involves the 10th TFW at Alconbury as well as the 81st TFW. The latter wing is slated to receive 48 F-15Es at Bentwaters during fiscal year 1991, which will permit approximately 40 A-10As to return to the USA.

Negotiations are ongoing for certain types to be withdrawn from front-line NATO and Warsaw Pact service, with their scrapping being supervised by representatives from both sides. The A-10 would seem certain to be included in these negotiations, so the prior exchange of 1979, 1980, 1981 and 1982 fiscal year European-based aircraft for earlier production Thunderbolts would allow the latter to be scrapped.

B-2 test flight with all-USAF crew

The Northrop B-2A Stealth bomber was flown by an all-Air Force crew for the first time on 3 May when it was flown from Edwards AFB, California, by Lt Col Tom LeBeau and Lt Col John Small. The flight, which was the bomber's tenth, lasted seven hours and 20 minutes, reaching a speed of .76 Mach and an altitude above 35,000 ft. By mid-May the bomber had accumulated some 55 hours of flight time.

Combat Flight Inspection aircraft accepted

The first British Aerospace C-29A Combat Flight Inspection aircraft was delivered to MAC on 24 April by LTV's Sierra Research Division from its facility at Buffalo, New York. Following construction of the basic BAe 125-800 airframe at British Aerospace's Hawarden plant, the aircraft was ferried to the USA for the installation of state-of-the-art navigational aid inspection equipment.

A total of six aircraft is on order, with deliveries due for completion by September 1990. These six C-29As will replace two T-39As and four C-140A JetStars operated by the 375th AAW at Scott AFB within the 1467th FCS. The squadron has two overseas detachments at Frankfurt/Rhein-Main AB, West Germany, and Yokota AB, Japan, which for most of the time have either a Sabreliner or JetStar assigned, but will exchange these for a C-29A on loan from headquarters.

Exercise 'Elder Forest'

Exercise 'Elder Forest' was held between 23 and 27 April to evaluate the defences of the United Kingdom against sustained air attack. During the five days of the Exercise some 1,100 sorties were directed against a host of targets including the radar sites at Buchan and Boulmer, missile stations at Barkston Heath, West Raynham and Wyton, and No. 11 Group RAF interceptor stations at Leuchars, Leeming, Coningsby and Wattisham.

'Elder Forest' was billed as one of the largest air defence exercises to be staged in the United Kingdom, with participants acting as enemy 'orange' attacking forces being drawn from NATO air arms along with a number of RAF types, while the 'blue' defenders were composed of the full range of RAF interceptors. US Air Force participation was fairly extensive, with several units being deployed to Europe specifically for the Exercise, including a trio of 2nd BW B-52Gs from Barksdale AFB, Louisiana, which operated from Fairford in the maritime role. A dozen F-15A Eagles of the 122nd TFS Louisiana ANG from NAS New Orleans deployed to NS Keflavik, Iceland, to assist the RAF interceptors by patrolling the Greenland/Iceland/UK (GIUK) gap. Most of these F-15s landed at Lossiemouth at the completion of each mission before returning to Keflavik later in the day. The squadron was resident at Keflavik for two weeks to conduct its two-week active duty 'summer camp', encompassing 'Elder Forest'. Air refuelling of NATO aircraft was provided by RAF VC-10s, while US participants were fuelled by SAC KC-135 tankers operating from the European Tanker Task Force bases at Fairford and Mildenhall, along with four Air Force Reserve KC-135Es of the 314th ARS from March AFB, California, which were resident at Cottesmore.

USAFE involvement was fairly extensive, with A-10As from 81st TFW at Bentwaters/Woodbridge and F-111Fs of 48th TFW at Lakenheath being included amongst the 'orange' forces. The waves of attacking aircraft were supported by EC-130H and EF-111A electronic warfare aircraft of the 66th ECW, to mask the 'orange' forces' approach by jamming communications while 52nd TFW F-4G/F-16C defence suppression hunter/killer teams conducted anti-SAM missions. These aircraft flew from and to their home bases with the exception of the 52nd TFW, which landed at Lakenheath each day to perform a second mission during the flight back to Spangdahlem each afternoon.

On 1 June, the first Boeing Helicopters MH-47E took to the air. This major variant of the Chinook embodies numerous modifications for the Army's Special Operations role, including inflight-refuelling probe.

Vought A-7Ds from the 185th TFG, Iowa Air National Guard, took part in Exercise 'Central Enterprise 90', a USAFE exercise held in northern Europe. Guard A-7s make regular deployments to Europe to gain in-theatre practice.

With due ceremony, Lockheed handed over the last P-3 Orion to the US Navy, marking the end of a long and successful production partnership. A handful of Orions are still being completed for other customers, and with the shelving of the P-7 follow-on, the line may yet be re-opened.

Exercise 'Central Enterprise 90'

'Central Enterprise 90', hosted by Allied Air Forces Central Europe (AAFCE), was conducted between 18 and 22 June over the central region of Allied Command Europe, involving aircraft from eight NATO countries. Flying was restricted to air space over the Benelux countries, Denmark, eastern France and West Germany. Apart from USAFE aircraft, there were participants from SAC, TAC and the ANG, which deployed to Europe specifically for the exercise.

A dozen Air National Guard A-7 Corsair IIs from the 174th TFS at Sioux City MAP, Iowa, were stationed at Brustem AB, Belgium, between 1 and 27 June under 'Coronet Canyon', although it is quite likely the deployment was split between this and its sister unit, the 124th TFS, at Des Moines MAP, Iowa. The 49th TFW sent two batches of a dozen F-15As each to Gilze-Rijen AB in the Netherlands, consisting of the 7th TFS, which arrived on 12 June followed two days later by the 8th TFS as 'Coronet Bullet' and 'Coronet Shooter' respectively. The arrival of the 7th TFS Eagles was not without incident as an hydraulic fault aboard 77-0096 resulted in the landing gear collapsing upon landing, causing the pilot to eject as the aircraft slewed off the runway, eventually coming to rest on the grass.

A further 12 F-15Cs of the 60th TFS, 33rd TFW were resident at Soesterberg AB, the Netherlands, between 31 May and 25 June under 'Coronet Trigger'. The Eglin and the Holloman crews flew numerous local missions to familiarise themselves with the crowded European skies and changeable weather conditions prior to flying in the Exercise.

Five 2nd BW B-52Gs from Barksdale AFB were in temporary residence at Fairford between 12 and 25 June, participating in 'Central Enterprise' as well as a number of air shows. The 150th ARS New Jersey ANG from McGuire AFB provided four KC-135Es, which were stationed at Alconbury between 15 and 29 June to support the exercise, while at the same time performing their 'summer camp'.

Exercise 'Crested Cap'

The annual USAF Exercise 'Crested Cap', which is designed to simulate the rapid reinforcement of USAFE, took place between 30 May and 5 July, involving 24 F-16As of 68th TFS, 347th TFW based at Moody AFB, Georgia, deploying to Ramstein AB, West Germany. The concept of a wing being 'dual-based' was initiated in June 1968 when the 49th TFW, with its three squadrons of F-4Ds, was withdrawn from Spangdahlem AB, West Germany, and re-assigned to Holloman AFB, New Mexico, while retaining a commitment to USAFE when required. In order to maintain this commitment, the wing was required to return annually to Europe under Exercise 'Crested Cap', although subsequently other TAC units have been substituted, including the 4th and 347th TFWs.

Exercise 'Dragon Hammer 90'

Several US-based units flew to bases in Italy to participate in Exercise 'Dragon Hammer 90', which took place at various ranges over the northern Italian mainland and the Adriatic Sea during May. Ten RF-4Cs of 153rd TRS Mississippi ANG from Key Field, Meridian, located to Aviano AB, between 30 April and 11 May under 'Coronet Saddle'. In addition, 12 F-16Cs of 421st TFS, 388th TFW from Hill AFB, Utah, deployed to Ghedi AB from 26 April to 17 May under 'Coronet Saber', while 'Coronet Rodeo' involved eight A-10As of 355th TFS, 354th TFW from Myrtle Beach AFB, South Carolina, to Villafranca AB between 27 April and 16 May. These Stateside-based aircraft supplemented their USAFE counterparts, some of which were stationed at Aviano.

H-46 Sea Knights grounded

Following a heavy landing of a Marine Corps CH-46E Sea Knight at MCAS Twentynine Palms, California, on 4 May in which 17 Marines were injured, all 261 USMC CH/HH-46s and 81 Navy UH/HH-46s were grounded for inspection of their rear rotor assemblies.

Central America

CUBA:

'Fulcrum' flown

US monitoring agencies claimed to have detected the first test flight of a MiG-29 in Cuban airspace on 19 April, the aircraft being one of a batch shipped to the island in October 1989. The pilot for the 30-minute sortie was Russian, but training of Cuban nationals is expected to be already under way.

South America

ARGENTINA:

Pampa prospects

Hopes were raised in May for a possible major production order for Argentina's FAMA IA-63 Pampa jet trainer when President Menem signed an agreement with LTV of Dallas, under which the Texas firm will promote the Pampa as a follow-on to the Cessna T-37 and Beech T-34C Turbo Mentor. The competition – known as JPATS (Joint Primary Aircraft Training System) – also involves most of the other major trainers in the world. The significant factor at this stage, however, is that relations between the US and Argentina were formerly cool following the 1982 Falklands War. Also in May, Chincul signed a licensed production agreement with Bell for 212 and 412SP helicopters to be built in Argentina, probably leading to military orders for the types.

BRAZIL:

Naval aviation blow

Embarked aviation suffered a serious blow when a survey of the sole aircraft-carrier *Minas Gerais* revealed serious defects, making rectification uneconomical. The vessel was to have been replaced by a new carrier during the 1990s, but funding shortages will almost certainly prevent that. The only fixed-wing aircraft operated by the *Minas Gerais* were Grumman S-2E Trackers belonging to the air force. By coincidence, the first of these modified to Turbo Tracker standard was completed in May and a programme is in hand to modernise the S-2's radar, ESM and MAD systems. This will probably proceed for use of the Trackers from shore bases.

VENEZUELA:

F-5 update

A decision of 1 June awarded the contract to update some of Venezuela's fleet of Northrop F-5s to Singapore Aerospace. The FAV has 14 ex-Canadian CF-5As and three CF-5D trainers, and will take delivery later in 1990 of 12 Canadian-built NF-5s from the Netherlands (eight NF-5B trainers and four NF-5As). It is the original aircraft that are understood to be receiving the modifications.

Long since disappeared from regular service, the Convair Delta Dart still flies in USAF colours as the QF-106 target drone. These are flown from Tyndall AFB by the 475th Weapons Evaluation Group.

Trainer teams are gathering for the forthcoming US Air Force JPATS requirement. Argentina's Pampa is a contender, the manufacturer FAMA joining forces with LTV to promote the aircraft. The neat trainer made its first flight in October 1984.

An increasing number of nations has adopted the Boeing 707 as a tanker, fitting Beech refuelling pods to the wingtips. This is a Brazilian aircraft of GT 2/2, seen landing at London's Heathrow airport during regular transport operations.

BRIEFING

Northrop-McDonnell Douglas YF-23

ATF contender unveiled

On 22 June 1990 at Edwards AFB, California, the Northrop-McDonnell Douglas YF-23 demonstrator (87-800) was unveiled in a low-key ceremony. This important event not only gave a suggestion of what the US Air Force's next fighter will look like, but also highlighted the considerable departure being made with this programme from hitherto accepted fighter design.

YF-23 is Northrop-McDonnell Douglas' answer to the Advanced Tactical Fighter (ATF) requirement, a far-sighted request for a survivable fighter to replace the McDonnell Douglas F-15 Eagle in the late 1990s, and to provide air superiority well into the next century. A rival team of Lockheed, Boeing and General Dynamics is developing the YF-22 to compete for the ATF contract.

ATF requirements call for drastic improvements in many conflicting areas. To answer the threat of recently introduced Soviet types such as the MiG-29 'Fulcrum' and Su-27 'Flanker', and follow-on fighters currently under development at both bureaux, the ATF has vastly increased performance, agility and kill-power. A major feature is the ability to cruise supersonically without afterburner and with a third of its power in reserve – dubbed 'supercruise'. Range is considerably improved, while a new generation of avionics gives first-look, first-kill capability.

Reliability and maintainability are key factors of the ATF, reducing costs to allow the fighter to operate in "a more austere budget environment". Naturally, fly-away costs are balanced carefully against aircraft capability.

Finally, ATF must be survivable in the face of current and projected threats, both airborne and ground-based, hence the incorporation of advanced defensive avionics systems and low-observables ('stealth') technology.

Both ATF teams were awarded contracts for two aircraft each, designated prototype air vehicles (PAVs). One YF-22 and one YF-23 are powered by the new Pratt & Whitney advanced fighter engine, the other pair featuring the rival General Electric YF120. The flying phase of the Demonstration/Validation (Dem/Val) period is to provide a solid database with which to support a decision for the Full Scale Development contract to be awarded to one of the teams. The Air Force is keen to emphasise that this Dem/Val is not a 'fly-off' between the competing aircraft. The first YF-23 began taxi tests on 7 July at Edwards and first flew on 27 August.

As it was the first to appear, the YF-23 bears close examination for its radical departure from current service types. At first sight the aircraft bears similarities to the Northrop B-2 bomber (in the shape of its blended engine installations) and the Lockheed SR-71 (long, slender fuselage, chines and canted, slab-like fins), while at a more light-hearted level it looks a lot like the mythical Soviet 'Firefox' from the Clint Eastwood movie!

The extraordinary shape owes much to the conflicting design requirements. Creating a balanced design that is manoeuvrable, fast, long-legged *and* stealthy has been one of the key advances in warplane technology. The Commander of Air Force

Systems Command, General Ronald W. Yates, described ATF and B-2 as "not an evolution; they are a revolution."

In plan view the YF-23 has a broad fuselage that tapers into the wing. The wing itself is a cropped triangular shape, with straight wingtips. The three edges of the wing form the principal 'alignments' for other straight edges on the aircraft, conforming to 'stealth' doctrine. The large, widely-spaced fins are canted at 45°, and provide a considerable area in plan, again conforming to the wing shape. Between the fin tips the plan view exhibits the now-familiar sawtooth arrangement.

The powerplants are mounted in separate blended bodies, in the rear of the aircraft, much of which are above the wing. Air is admitted, however, under the wing, and taken by serpentine ducts that snake upwards and inwards to the compressors.

Trapezoidal panels on top of the wing and screened panels on top of the inlet are for dumping bleed air to allow a uniform airflow into the engine. Underneath each nacelle is a further bleed, and an auxiliary power unit may be mounted in the fuselage centre. While overwing intakes are better for stealth, underslung intakes are required for high angle-of-attack manoeuvring. Exhaust is ejected through large troughs above the rear edge of the wing, with a vectoring flap on the front of the trough. Both front and rear ends of the trough have radar-defeating serrations.

Control surfaces include inboard flaps and outboard ailerons on the wing trailing edge, separated by a narrow fixed section, and a large flap on the leading edge. The leading edge flaps move symmetrically, while the other surfaces move independently. There are no airbrakes as such, high drag being provided by upward deflection of the ailerons and down-

ward deflection of the leading and trailing edge flaps. The fins are pivoted at their base to provide control in all three axes.

Running from the extreme nose to the wing, the fuselage chines negate the tendency of the nose to 'slice' off during high angle-of-attack flight. These are not smooth, but form three distinct straight lines. Sitting high on the fuselage is a beautifully-crafted, scalloped canopy, giving the pilot a superb all-round view. The flat fuselage underside contains internal bays some 16 ft long for AIM-9 Sidewinder and AIM-120 AMRAAM air-to-air missiles, as well as the forward-retracting nosewheel. Fuselage doors have serrations on the leading and trailing edges to reduce reflectivity. The main gear retracts backwards to lie beside and underneath the engines. A cannon will be incorporated in service aircraft.

Underneath the computer-crafted exterior lies an equally radical aircraft. Avionics are mostly new, and all are at present classified. Using a Westinghouse-owned BAC One-Eleven flying testbed and a McDonnell Douglas-built Avionics Ground Prototype, the Northrop-McDonnell Douglas team has integrated a complete system that uses revolutionary common processors. These paperback-sized units can handle all the mission and sensor processing requirements, replacing many specialised units required by the current generation of fighters. The result is fewer 'black boxes', and therefore easier and cheaper maintenance, with greater system reliability.

Elsewhere, maintenance and operational requirements have also been reduced. Less than half the maintenance is required compared with the F-15/F-16 generation, with over twice the reliability. Turn-round times between sorties have been cut to half the current figure. New manufacturing

Designed as a survivable replacement for the F-15, the Northrop-McDonnell Douglas YF-23 was designed with Stealth as a primary requirement, hence its blended body and well-shielded intakes.

technologies and advanced materials have resulted in a dramatic reduction in procurement, stock inventory, maintenance and support requirements. Composite materials result in fewer fastenings and reduced complexity. For instance, the Northrop-McDonnell Douglas team quotes the propulsion train: the current generation F/A-18 Hornet has 37 parts, the YF-23 just three!

Northrop is the main contractor for the YF-23, with McDonnell Douglas the principal sub-contractor. As well as providing total systems integration and final assembly, Northrop is responsible for the aft fuselage, empennage, defensive avionics system and flight control. McDonnell Douglas handles the forward and central fuselage, wings, undercarriage, fuel system, armament and offensive avionics, controls and displays. The vital cockpit systems and pilot/vehicle interface are a joint responsibility. In addition to the two main companies, the YF-23 programme embraces 62 others in 31 states. Among these, the majors are General Electric, Pratt & Whitney, Martin Marietta, TRW, AT&T, Unisys and Westinghouse.

All four airframe/engine combinations are taking to the air during 1990,

Like the rival YF-22, the YF-23 features a trapezoidal wing and widely spaced twin fins. Northrop and McDonnell Douglas stole a march on their rivals early on, by taxiing the YF-23 before the YF-22 had even been rolled out.

with the teams expected to submit their Full Scale Development proposals at the end of the year. The FSD

decision is expected in September 1991. Although radar cross-section has been tested in the labs, the Air Force has expressly forbidden RCS testing of the actual prototypes during the Dem/Val phase.

Watching closely will be the US Navy, which is actively pursuing the ATF programme for its own NATF F-14 replacement plans. As such a large programme, with up to 750 air-

frames at stake for the US Air Force, it is much in the public eye, and also high on the hit-list for cost-cutting politicians. Both teams and the Air Force are maximising the cost-effectiveness of the ATF, but the current political climate both at home and overseas will ensure a rocky road for the new fighter, with procurement cuts or complete cancellation an ever-growing threat.

CASA 212ECM

Electronic Aviocar

CASA's 212 Aviocar transport first flew on 26 March 1971, and since then has achieved notable success in both military and civil fields. Around 20 air forces operate the type, the major operator being Spain itself. The basic transport has been offered in three main variants, the Series 100, 200 and 300, this last featuring increased-span wings with upturned tips.

With its good internal capacity and excellent performance, the CASA 212 has proved an admirable low-cost

platform for special missions duties. An ASW/maritime patrol model features a MAD 'sting', among other sensors, and has proved popular. At least six electronic countermeasures/electronic intelligence (ECM/Elint) versions, based on the Series 200 airframe with uprated engines, have been sold to undisclosed customers. The electronic conversion is also available for the Series 300. Two former transports of the Portuguese air force have been upgraded to this standard.

Developed from 1981 onwards, this version is readily identifiable by large

Left and below: The 360°-coverage tail and nose radomes of the Portuguese ECM Aviocar that visited Boscombe Down. Right: One of the Portuguese special duties Aviocars is seen in its hangar at BA3 Tancos.

fairings mounted on the nose and tail. On the nose is an angular black fairing with hinges on the port side to allow easy access to the antennas within. Another large black fairing is mounted on the forward portion of the fin top, the antenna held above the aircraft to provide 360° coverage. Further antennas are mounted in the tailcone. Associated equipment and operator stations are within the capacious cabin.

The equipment carried by the Aviocar undertakes automatic signal interception, classification and identification. Designed to operate in a dense electronic environment, the system can produce a detailed map locating and classifying hostile radars. Powerful jammers carried on board

can then be used to negate those radars.

The use of these aircraft by the Força Aerea Portuguesa was highlighted by a rare and welcome public appearance by a CASA 212ECM at the Battle of Britain Salute air show at A&AEE Boscombe Down in June 1990.

The FAP bought some 18 Aviocars, and these serve with four units. Esquadra 111 at Tancos trains aircrews, while Esquadra 502 and 503 at Tancos and Lajes respectively are the transport squadrons. Two of Esq 502's aircraft are the ECM version, while a small number of the ASW version are in use. Finally, four photo-survey versions serve with Esquadra 401 at Sintra.

BRIEFING

Saab JAS 39 Gripen

Swedish Superfighter

Sweden has a long history of producing its own indigenous combat aircraft. This has been a remarkable achievement for such a small nation, but a very expensive one. To the Swedes, however, who are jealous of their prized neutrality and independence, the sacrifices have been worthwhile. The Swedes, however, are not prepared to pay an excessive price for indigenous aircraft, nor are they prepared to tolerate delays or problems. The defence budget is always tight, and in order to maintain numbers, low unit price is always a major consideration.

In February 1982 the Supreme Commander of the Swedish Armed Forces proposed that the System 37 (Viggen) be replaced by a new indigenous multi-role combat aircraft, designated JAS. This new acronym stands for Jakt (Intercept), Attack, and Spaning (Reconnaissance). Cost-efficiency was to be an important factor from the very start, and this demanded that the new aircraft be relatively small (half the size of the Viggen, and 60 per cent of the price, yet with the same weapon load), and yet capable of fulfilling many different roles. For maximum combat efficiency, stand-off capability and dispersed site operation were emphasised.

In May 1980 the Swedish parliament requested an investigation into the possibilities of developing such an aircraft and, as a result, in September Saab-Scania, Volvo Flygmotor, Ericsson and FFV Aerotech created IG JAS (JAS Industrial Group). The project was of crucial importance, since the Viggen programme was drawing to a close, and the aircraft industry had no follow-on projects.

IG JAS submitted its proposal for a new fighter in June 1981, and the contract was signed on 30 June 1982, after the Swedish parliament had passed the necessary legislation. The new fighter programme was not supported by the socialist parties. The industry companies involved had to agree to take full responsibility for the aircraft, to accept a fixed-price contract for development and initial production ($6.5 billion in 1988 currency for 140 aircraft), and to guarantee perform-

The second prototype Viggen is pictured during preflight tests of its flight control system, with canard foreplanes motored fully down. The loss of the first Gripen due to an FCS software problem made such tests essential.

ance. Additionally, the defence authorities insisted that the aircraft industry reduced its dependence on military projects, with the aim of having 50 per cent civil production within 10 years.

The initial contract covered development costs and the construction of five prototypes and an initial series of 30 aircraft, with an option on a further 110 aircraft. The total Swedish JAS requirement has been estimated at between 21 and 23 squadrons, with a total of between 350 and 400 aircraft. The prototype was expected to make its maiden flight in 1987, with service entry following in 1992.

In September 1982 the name Gripen (Griffon) was chosen, and on 14 September a modified JA 37 Viggen with a new fly-by-wire control system, known as the ESS JAS, began flight trials. This aircraft's career will be extended as a result of the loss of the first prototype. Other Viggens were used to test the Gripen's electronic display system and the JAS radar.

Developing an indigenous combat aircraft is a costly and risky business, even for a large country, and in order to keep costs under control, it was quickly decided that the new aircraft should incorporate some foreign components, although dependence on other nations was to be avoided where possible, or where indigenous equipment was felt to be necessary on security grounds (eg ECM). Initially, IG JAS looked for a collaborative partner to help develop and produce

The Gripen is a very small aircraft, half the size of the Viggen and powered by a single engine. Small size, and consequent low price, was specified from the beginning of the programme.

the aircraft, but most potential partners wanted a larger, twin-engined aircraft, while smaller nations could not share the development costs.

Swedish sub-systems were avoided where similar ones had been developed abroad and were available more cheaply. Accordingly, the aircraft was powered by a development of an existing engine. Volvo Flygmotor's RM12, which ran for the first time in January 1985, was a variant of the General Electric F404-400, with increased thrust and improved bird-strike resistance. Similarly, the flight control system was purchased off-the-shelf from Lear Siegler, the APU from Microturbo, the INAS from Honeywell, the landing gear from Britain's AP Precision Hydraulics and the prototype wings from BAe.

The Gripen's full-scale mock-up was unveiled on 11 February 1986, in front of the Minister of Defence, a host of VIPs and the press, and the first prototype was ceremonially rolled out at Linkoping on 26 April 1987, the 50th anniversary of the Saab Aircraft Division. The first flight, however, was not to follow until December 1988, delayed by the need for complex flight control system tests.

The prototype was written off in a spectacular crash while landing after its seventh flight. Increasing pitch oscillations exceeded the values written into the flight control software and the pilot lost control, hitting the runway hard and cartwheeling across the airfield before coming to rest inverted. The pilot, Lars Radestrom,

Gripen No. 2 in flight. Problems, coupled with changing circumstances, have led to doubts about the aircraft's future, although the first export order, from Finland, is already a faint possibility.

The Gripen is typical of the new generation of canard delta fighters designed during the late 1980s, showing similarities in configuration to the Lavi and EAP.

survived with a broken arm.

The crash could not have come at a worse time. The Gripen programme was already running very late, with the first flight having occurred 18 months later than originally planned. Furthermore, the indigenously developed afterburner had experienced some problems, resulting in a performance shortfall. Additionally a huge loss of pilots during the 1980s led to the Viggen fleet accumulating fewer hours than had been expected, and there were pressures to keep the older aircraft in service for longer than

Small need not mean simple, nor does it infer any lack of capability. Saab's Gripen will be a formidable multi-role fighter, thanks to its sophisticated avionics and systems, and advanced aerodynamics and structure.

had been planned. A decision on development of the JAS 39B two-seater, and on the main production batch of 110 Gripens, will not be taken until 1991, to the anxiety of IG JAS, to whom the 140 aircraft total represents the programme's break-even point.

After the accident IG JAS immediately doubled the size of its software team, checking and re-writing the control laws, and increased resources were made available for simulation of the aircraft to validate the new software. The aircraft's handling characteristics were extensively examined on the ground, and by

using the USAF's variable stability in-flight simulator aircraft, a Lockheed T-33 operated under contract by Calspan. Seventy-eight flights (74½ hours) including 350 landing evaluations were flown, including 21 flights to evaluate the modifications applied to the No. 2 prototype. Before the software was modified the T-33 safety pilot in the rear seat often had to take over control to complete a safe landing. With the modified software, the control system was judged safe. This

gave a high level of confidence for the first flight of the second prototype.

Eventually, at 7.49 pm on 4 May 1990, the second Gripen prototype flew for the first time in the hands of Arne Lindholm, Saab's chief military test pilot. The flight was unfortunately cut short (to 14 minutes) by the failure of a cooler for the flight control system. This aircraft will be joined by three more prototypes during the flight test programme.

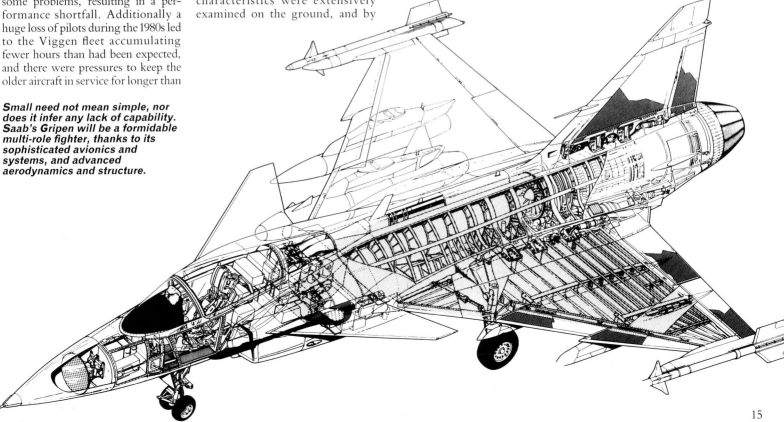

BRIEFING

Fairchild C-26A

The US Military Metro

The Fairchild Metro has long been a popular and successful civil corporate transport aircraft, and by the end of 1989 about 850 had been delivered. Military sales have been less forthcoming, however. Argentina, Belgium, the Seychelles and Thailand are the only military operators of the early Metro II. Sweden ordered the type for VIP transport duties under the designation Tp88, and the Metro III and the similar Merlin IV also serve in small numbers with Argentina, Chile, Mexico, South Africa and Thailand. All are used in the transport role, although Fairchild has offered maritime surveillance and ASW versions.

In March 1988, the USAF placed an order for six Metro IIIs, under the designation C-26A, for use in the ANGOSTA (Air National Guard Operational Support Transport Aircraft) role, for delivery between March and August 1989. The aircraft have a quick-change interior allowing the passenger seats to be replaced by a medevac or cargo interior. The USAF order was later increased to 10, and an option was taken for three further aircraft. The C-26A is now in service with the Air National Guard, recipient units being the 103rd TASS, 111th FIS, 149th TFS, 153rd TRS, 163rd TFS, 166th TFS, 169th TASS and 194th FIS.

This Fairchild C-26A Metro is operated by the Ohio ANG, and was pictured at MacDill AFB, Florida.

Sea King Mk 41 Upgrade

From SAR to ship-killing

The Marineflieger ordered 22 Westland Sea Kings for search and rescue duties, and these were delivered between 1972 and 1975. One crashed before delivery, but this was replaced. They currently serve with MFG 5 at Kiel-Holtenau. Detachments are maintained at Sylt, Borkum and Heligoland.

During the early 1980s, it was decided that the Marineflieger needed more anti-shipping capability in the Baltic. Accordingly it was decided to convert MFG 5's Sea Kings to give them an offensive capability. MBB received a contract, to convert three initial aircraft for evaluation, in March 1986, although the associated Ferranti Seaspray radar had been ordered two years previously.

The updated German Sea King can be externally identified by its offset nose radome housing a Ferranti Seaspray Mk 3 radar, and the four missile pylons.

The first three of MFG.5's aircraft were converted to anti-surface vessel attack configuration at MBB's Speyer factory between 1986 and 1988. This involved the provision of a Ferranti Seaspray Mk 3 radar in a nose radome (offset to port), a Ferranti Link II data link and the fitting of two outrigger pylons on the fuselage sides, and two additional pylons on the lower fuselage sides, under the undercarriage sponsons. These pylons allow four BAe Sea Skua ASMs to be carried. The adoption of a more offensive role infers that the aircraft will be used in

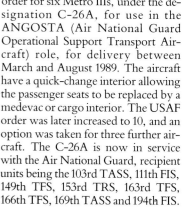

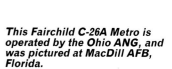

more-hostile airspace, and a number of improvements have been made to self-defence capability. An AEG/Telefunken (Litton) ALR-68 RWR and a Tracor M130 chaff/flare dispenser are fitted, and the old 'peacetime' blue and Dayglo colour scheme is to be replaced either by an overall grey scheme, or a two-tone grey camouflage, each with toned-down markings.

The whole fleet of Sea Kings was to have been in service in its new configuration by the end of 1990, but conversion of MFG 5's remaining aircraft must now be doubtful. No announcements about the programme's future have yet been made.

At least one of the three upgraded Sea Kings wears a three-tone grey camouflage. This may be the operational colour scheme intended for the new role, since the SAR aircraft wear dark grey with large Dayglo patches.

Orlando QS-55/H-19

Hind Look-Alike

Seeking to obtain drone helicopters simulating the Mil Mi-24P 'Hind-F', the most numerous version of the Soviet assault helicopter, but having a limited budget with which to do so, the US Army Missile Command in Huntsville, Alabama, latched on to a proposal from Orlando Helicopter Airways, Inc. (OHA) to modify Sikorsky H-19s (or their S-55 civilian variants) into drones. The ready availability of used H-19s and S-55s, their cheap acquisition price, and the suggested low-cost modification programme to turn them into realistic Hind Look-Alike drones with similar size, appearance, radar return, and infra-red emissions, ensured that the Army could obtain inexpensively the small number of realistic target helicopters needed for the development of surface-to-air missiles.

Located on the edge of the Sanford Municipal Airport (the former NAS Sanford which had been de-activated in July 1968) in Florida, OHA was founded in 1964. Since then, the firm has been primarily engaged in re-manufacturing, marketing and operating used Sikorsky S-55s/H-19s and S-58s/H-34s. A jointly-owned company, Guangzhou Orlando Helicopters, builds piston- and turbine-powered S-55 and S-58 derivatives in China.

To obtain a Hind Look-Alike dimensionally accurate to within four per cent and yet inexpensive enough to meet the requirements of the Army, OHA designed a new nose section, with simulated cockpits for the weapons operator in front and the pilot aft and above, and added stub wings with external store pylons. In the first two aircraft, the new nose – which was grafted forward of the engine – was built of glass fibre but the next 13 aircraft used composite structure noses. In either case, the simulated cockpits were empty (except, if desired, for the addition of mannequins to give a more realistic appearance), the Hind Look-Alike being

From head on, Orlando Helicopters' H-19 drone looks just like the Mil Mi-24/25/35 it is intended to resemble, even down to a five-bladed main rotor on all but the first two aircraft. The 'Hind' look-alike isn't a perform-alike, however.

flown by a pilot (or, in the case of the two trainers, by a trainee and an instructor pilot) in a cockpit hidden above and behind the simulated twin intakes for the absent Isotov TV3-117 turboshaft engines.

Still powered by an 800-hp Lycoming-built Wright R-1300-30 radial, the first two aircraft retained the original three-bladed rotor of the S-55/H-19. However, like subsequent drones, they were later fitted with a five-bladed main rotor designed by Ralph Alex and built by Rotaire of Fairfield, Connecticut. In all instances, the tail rotor remained the two-bladed unit of the original S-55/H-19s.

Tests were initially conducted at the Sanford Municipal Airport by Ronald H. Mander, OHA's Operations Manager and Test Pilot, with subsequent testing on behalf of the Army by Honeywell personnel at the White Sands Missile Range in New Mexico.

To simulate more realistically the operating characteristics of the Hind, the Look-Alikes were fitted, after completion of initial trials, with infra-red equipment, duplicating the exhaust of the twin-Isotov turboshaft engines of the Soviet attack helicopters, and with IR and RF jammers having capabilities similar to those in Soviet service. Two of the Hind Look-Alike helicopters have been retained as trainers, whereas the other 13 have been fitted by Sperry Defense Systems with full radio controls. Still man-rated, the 13 drones will be expended in missile trials at White Sands.

Orlando QS-55/H-19
FAA registrations and manufacturer's numbers

Registrations	Serial numbers	Registrations	Serial numbers
N188AR	OHA-55-188AR	N989AR	OHA-55-989AR
N288AR	OHA-55-288AR	N910AR	OHA-55-109AR
N388AR	OHA-55-388AR	N119AR	OHA-55-119AR
N488AR	OHA-55-488AR	N129AR	OHA-55-129AR
N588AR	OHA-55-588AR	N139AR	OHA-55-139AR
N689AR	OHA-55-689AR	N149AR	OHA-55-149AR
N789AR	OHA-55-789AR	N159AR	OHA-55-159AR
N889AR	OHA-55-889AR		

The suffix letters AR in the registrations and manufacturer's serial numbers stand for Army. The last three digits of the serial numbers indicate the manufacturing sequence and year in which the modification was completed (i.e. aircraft 1 to 5 were completed in 1988 and aircraft 6 to 15 were completed in 1989).

Above: One of the first conversions is seen during an early test flight. Dummy wings and pylons have been added, but the aircraft lacks the new nose section.

Below: A completed drone runs up on the ground. In the air, from any distance, the drone is virtually indistinguishable from the real thing.

When being flown by a live pilot, the H-19 'Hind' is flown from the original cockpit, behind the Mil Mi-24 'intakes'.

Shenyang

J-8 and J-8 II 'Finback'

Development of the Shenyang J-8 began in the early 1960s, after the split with the Soviet Union, and during the Cultural Revolution. At this time, any indigenous fighter (as opposed to a licence-built or reverse engineered copy of an existing Soviet type, taking apart a real aircraft to produce blueprints) was a very ambitious step, and the engineers at Shenyang can be forgiven for producing an aircraft which was conceptually rather stale, and which was developed from the Xian J-7 (Chinese copy of the MiG-21F).

When photographs of the new aircraft emerged in 1984, the J-8 O prototype could be seen to bear an astonishing resemblance to the Mikoyan Ye-152A 'Flipper', which was an unsuccessful twin-engined, all-weather, fighter-interceptor prototype scaled up from the MiG-21F and which took part in the June 1961 aviation day flypast at Tushino. The 'Flipper' weighed in at about 30,000lb and was powered by a pair of Tumanskii R-11F turbojets, each producing some 12,676lb st with afterburning.

The first of two prototype J-8 Os is believed to have been completed in 1968, and it made its maiden flight on 5 July 1970, in the hands of Yin Yunhuan. Production of the prototype had been severely disrupted by the violence of the 'Great Cultural Revolution', but worse was to follow. The flight test team was disbanded and many senior personnel lost their jobs, leaving a succession of junior engineers to grapple with the many problems experienced by China's first indigenous fighter.

When a US Department of Defense delegation was shown the aircraft in 1980 it was still described as a 'proto-

Below: The first prototype J-8 II on take-off. This version has a solid radar nose and re-located lateral engine intakes. The original Chinese radar was inadequate in every way.

type' for China's new air superiority fighter, suggesting a very long and troubled gestation period. At the same time, it was suggested that the aircraft's 'Tumanskii R-11' engines might be replaced by the Rolls-Royce Spey, for which China had obtained a manufacturing licence in 1975. One week later a US industry delegation was refused permission to inspect the J-8 on the basis that the factory had just closed for the installation of production tooling.

The J-8 O, and the initial production J-8 I, were dimensionally similar to the Soviet aircraft, perhaps with slightly greater wing area and perhaps with higher operating weights. Fin area is much greater. Power was provided by a pair of Wopen 7B turbojets (copies of the R-11F) rated at 13,448lb with afterburning, by comparison with the 11,243-lb Wopen 7As fitted to Chinese J-7s. Underfuselage fairings housed a pair of cannon of unknown type and calibre, and four underwing pylons could carry a range of weapons or external fuel tanks. While the Chinese-built MiG-19 (Shenyang J-6) retains the code-name 'Farmer', and the MiG-21 (Xian J-7) the code-name 'Fishbed', the J-8 was allocated a new code-name by NATO's air standards co-ordinating committee – 'Finback'.

The production J-8 I featured a new two-part canopy, a new radar, ejection seat, revised cannon installation and provision for the carriage of up to four Pili-2B 'Thunderbolt' air-to-air missiles. The first production J-8 I was lost before its first flight, destroyed by fire during ground running trials on 25 June 1980. The first J-8 I to fly was therefore the second aircraft, which made its maiden flight on 24 April 1981. Only about 50 J-8s and J-8 Is were built, and many reports suggested that the aircraft was used mainly as a test bed and research platform, for products as diverse as a new

Above: This line-up probably shows most of the original J-8 Os and J-8 Is, believed to have been used only for trials and test duties.

swept wing, the Spey engine, a 30-mm cannon system and a new semi-active radar homing missile.

An improved version, the J-8 II, with lateral engine intakes and a solid nose housing a fire-control radar, made its maiden flight on 12 June 1984, flown by Qu Xueren, only 17 months after the drawings were completed. The new aircraft had further uprated engines, in the form of the 14,815-lb st Liyang Wopen-13A II (based on the Tumanskii R-13-300), and the intakes were fitted with splitter plates and ramps similar to those found on the MiG-23 'Flogger'. Initial flight tests revealed a considerable increase in performance.

On 5 August 1987, while the J-8 II flight test programme was still at a relatively early stage, the Grumman Aerospace Corporation was awarded a $501.8-million contract under a Foreign Military Sales Programme known as Peace Pearl, sponsored by the USAF's Aeronautical Systems Division. This covered the design of an avionics upgrade for Chinese air force J-8 IIs, to allow the aircraft to fulfil a long-standing requirement for a modern interceptor to police China's northern border with the USSR.

The avionics package was to consist of a modified Westinghouse AN/APG-66 radar, fire control computer, constant wave illuminator (to allow

the use of SARH missiles like the AIM-7 Sparrow) and back-up equipment, a new HUD, and a Litton LN-39 INS. Under this contract Grumman was to instal avionics packages in two J-8 II airframes (due for delivery in March 1989, and now in storage in the USA) for flight test at Edwards AFB later in the year. Development work was to have been completed in February 1991, and delivery of 50 further shipsets was to have been completed by January 1995.

On 21 October 1988 Grumman signed an agreement with the China National Aero-Technology Import and Export Corporation covering the production of an advanced export version of the F-7 (Chinese copy of the MiG-21F) with a solid nose, lateral air intakes, a new engine (either the General Electric F404/RM-12 or the Turbo Union RB.199) and a solid nose containing a Westinghouse APG-66 radar and other US avionics. A US HUD and ejection seat were to be installed under a Northrop F-20-type canopy and windscreen.

The massacre at Tiananmen Square led to a US government ban on arms exports to China, and there was an immediate halt to work on both pro-

Two J-8 IIs were sent to Edwards AFB for flight testing of Grumman's 'Peace Pearl' modification kits.

jects. Forty Chinese nationals working at Bethpage were expelled. Twenty-five Chinese were eventually allowed to return in October 1989,

working alongside 180 Grumman employees, and development on the upgrade programme continued. This first phase of the programme was to have involved production of the modification kits, while the second phase, the initiation of which would have needed a change in US policy,

was to have included flight test and kit delivery.

In April 1990, China pulled out of the Peace Pearl project, informing the US government that it would not proceed with production of the 55 avionics upgrade kits, after some 32 months of work, and when $245-million development phase was almost complete. China's parlous economic situation and US refusal to

The demise of 'Peace Pearl' leaves the future of the J-8 II in some doubt. Some expect China to procure the MiG-29 'Fulcrum' instead of upgrading its J-8 IIs, which would not be easy without Western help.

guarantee the delivery of the upgrade packages have been blamed for the Chinese pull-out, and rumours suggest that MiG-29s may be acquired from the USSR instead.

Aero L-39 Albatros

Trainer with Teeth

Adopted as the Warsaw Pact's standard advanced trainer (except in Poland, where the indigenous I-22 and Iskra are used) the Aero L-39 Albatros has also enjoyed some export success outside Eastern Europe, and represents the jewel in the crown of the Czech aircraft industry. 2,350 had been built by 1 January 1989, and production is expected to continue at a rate of about 200 per year until at least 1994. Customers for the aircraft so far include Czechoslovakia, the Soviet Union, East Germany, Bulgaria, Romania, Cuba, Nicaragua, Vietnam, Afghanistan, Iraq, Syria, Ethiopia, Libya, Egypt, Algeria, Mozambique, Guinea-Bissau and Nigeria.

The aircraft was developed by a team led by Dipl Ing Jan Vlcek, working in close co-operation with Soviet engineers and organisations, as a replacement for the L-29 Delfin. Aero had built some 3,600 Delfins, and was understandably eager to produce a successor to the type. Two prototypes were constructed initially, the first (X-01) for static testing. The second prototype L-39 (X-02, registered OK-32) made the type's maiden flight on 4 November 1968. The aircraft performed well, and four more prototypes (X-03, X-05, X-06 and X-07) were soon flying. (X-04 was the second fatigue test airframe.) The prototypes were followed by a pre-

production batch of 10 aircraft, which introduced slightly lengthened air intake trunks, but which were otherwise similar. The first of these joined the flight test programme in 1971.

The aircraft was soon officially selected to be the Warsaw Pact's standard trainer, and production began in 1972. Service trials were conducted in Czechoslovakia and the Soviet Union in 1973, and the type entered service in 1974 as the L-39C. The aircraft encountered few problems, and quickly won a reputation for dependability, thanks partly to its excellent two-spool Ivchenko AI-25TL turbofan engine, derived from the engine of the Yak-40 'Codling' jet transport.

The next variant of the Albatros was the L-39V, which was basically the same as the L-39C but modified to single-seat configuration, with the rear cockpit occupied by target-towing equipment. X-08, the prototype, was followed by at least two production aircraft for East Germany.

OK-32, the first flying prototype L-39, made its maiden flight on 4 November 1968. The aircraft is a generation older than aircraft like the BAe Hawk.

For many air forces, rising fuel costs in the 1970s led to revised pilot training courses. The Warsaw Pact, like many Western nations, decided that initial tactical flying and weapons training could be more cheaply provided by using a low-powered trainer, rather than using ex-front-line fighter types which were in any case becoming increasingly expensive to maintain. Thus while the RAF decided that it had to replace its Hawker Hunters, the Warsaw Pact needed a replacement for the various

MiG-17s, MiG-21s and first-generation Su-7 'Fitters' being used for weapons training. The Aero L-39 Albatros, already adopted as a standard advanced trainer, was an obvious choice to fill this requirement.

The first ground-attack-capable L-39 variant was the L-39ZO (standing for Zbrojni, or armed), whose prototype (X-09) first flew on 25 August 1975. East Germany was an early customer for this variant, which has a strengthened wing with four underwing hardpoints. Other customers were Iraq, Libya and Syria, and presumably Egypt and Nicaragua, whose aircraft were donated by Colonel Khadaffi.

The L-39 demonstrator wears a smart red, white and blue colour scheme and carries the flags of some of the type's users. Those which received the aircraft second-hand, such as Nicaragua and Egypt, are not included.

L-39 prototype

Variable-incidence tailplane

L-39C basic and advanced trainer

Ivchenko AI-25 TL turbofan of 16.87 kN (3,792 lb) thrust

Lengthened intake trunks

Two optional underwing stations

L-39V single-seat target-tug

Winch in rear cockpit

KT-04 target

L-39ZO trainer with weapon capability

Strengthened wings

Inboard underwing pylons stressed for 500 kg (1,102 lb) of stores

Outboard underwing pylons stressed for 250 kg (551 lb) of stores

L-39ZA ground attack and reconnaissance platform

ASP-3 NMU-39 Z gyroscopic gunsight

Undernose gun pod housing GSh-23 23 mm twin-barrel cannon with 150 rounds in fuselage

Provision for reconnaissance pod

Underwing pylons as for L-39ZO

L-39MS/L-59 improved trainer

Uprated Lotarev/ZVL DV-2 turbofan developing 21.57 kN (4,850 lb) thrust

Pointed fin tip

Revised avionics

Fixed-incidence tailplane

Pointed nose section

Shorter-span wing of revised aerofoil section

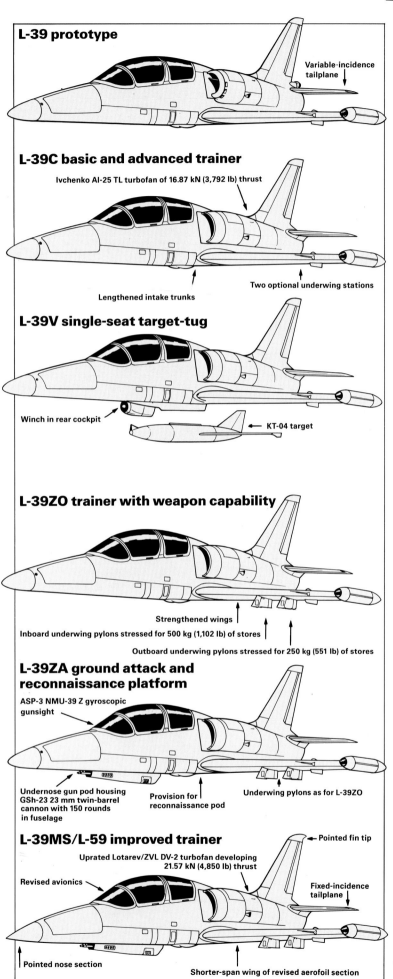

Aero L-39C Albatros

An Aero L-39ZA of the Czechoslovakian air force shows the removable undernose gun pod that distinguishes this from earlier variants. Like the attack version of the Alpha Jet, the L-39ZA is usually flown solo.

More versatile still is the L-39ZA which is a dedicated ground-attack and reconnaissance version of the L-39ZO, with provision for an underfuselage gun pod housing a single GSh-23L twin-barrel cannon. The recce pod, when fitted, contains five cameras and is fitted to the port inner pylon. The prototypes for this version were X-10 and X-11, and the first of these flew for the first time during late 1975.

A pair of Czech L-39Cs break over their home base. The L-39 is an excellent advanced pilot trainer, although visibility from the rear seat is very poor by current Western standards.

Fixed tanks
The wingtip tanks are fixed and cannot be jettisoned. They improve aerodynamic efficiency by reducing induced drag.

Neither of the armed versions packs a very heavy punch. The inboard weapons pylons can carry stores of up to 500 kg, and are 'plumbed' for the carriage of external fuel tanks, while the outboard pylons are stressed for up to 250 kg and are wired for air-to-air missiles. The aircraft cannot carry a full weapons load with full fuel and two crew, but can

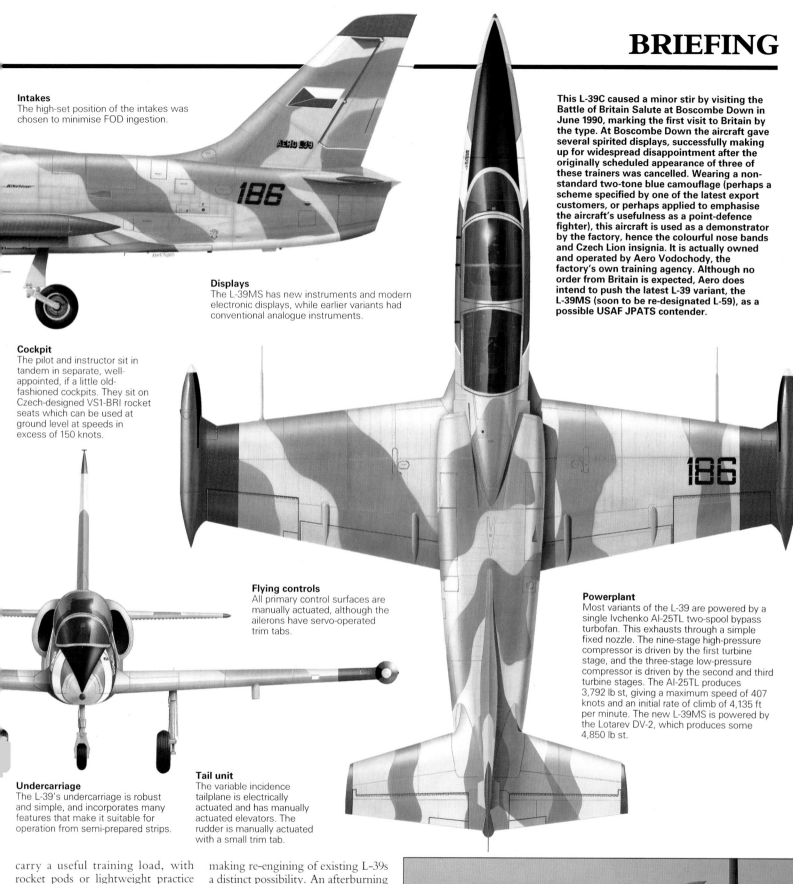

Intakes
The high-set position of the intakes was chosen to minimise FOD ingestion.

This L-39C caused a minor stir by visiting the Battle of Britain Salute at Boscombe Down in June 1990, marking the first visit to Britain by the type. At Boscombe Down the aircraft gave several spirited displays, successfully making up for widespread disappointment after the originally scheduled appearance of three of these trainers was cancelled. Wearing a non-standard two-tone blue camouflage (perhaps a scheme specified by one of the latest export customers, or perhaps applied to emphasise the aircraft's usefulness as a point-defence fighter), this aircraft is used as a demonstrator by the factory, hence the colourful nose bands and Czech Lion insignia. It is actually owned and operated by Aero Vodochody, the factory's own training agency. Although no order from Britain is expected, Aero does intend to push the latest L-39 variant, the L-39MS (soon to be re-designated L-59), as a possible USAF JPATS contender.

Displays
The L-39MS has new instruments and modern electronic displays, while earlier variants had conventional analogue instruments.

Cockpit
The pilot and instructor sit in tandem in separate, well-appointed, if a little old-fashioned cockpits. They sit on Czech-designed VS1-BRI rocket seats which can be used at ground level at speeds in excess of 150 knots.

Flying controls
All primary control surfaces are manually actuated, although the ailerons have servo-operated trim tabs.

Powerplant
Most variants of the L-39 are powered by a single Ivchenko AI-25TL two-spool bypass turbofan. This exhausts through a simple fixed nozzle. The nine-stage high-pressure compressor is driven by the first turbine stage, and the three-stage low-pressure compressor is driven by the second and third turbine stages. The AI-25TL produces 3,792 lb st, giving a maximum speed of 407 knots and an initial rate of climb of 4,135 ft per minute. The new L-39MS is powered by the Lotarev DV-2, which produces some 4,850 lb st.

Undercarriage
The L-39's undercarriage is robust and simple, and incorporates many features that make it suitable for operation from semi-prepared strips.

Tail unit
The variable incidence tailplane is electrically actuated and has manually actuated elevators. The rudder is manually actuated with a small trim tab.

---

carry a useful training load, with rocket pods or lightweight practice bombs.

The most recent Albatros variant is the L-39MS, which has been flying in prototype form since 1985. The first aircraft, X-12/OK-184, originally flew with a standard engine but from 1987 was fitted with a new power-plant jointly developed by the Soviet Lotarev engine OKB and the Czech Zavody Na Vyrobu Lozisk. Desig-nated DV-2, the new engine produces some 4,852 lb of thrust, and will fit the existing engine bay of the L-39,

making re-engining of existing L-39s a distinct possibility. An afterburning version of the engine has been de-veloped, but would not seem to have any application to the Albatros. The new variant has an improved cockpit, with upgraded avionics and a new HUD. Zero-zero ejection seats are also fitted.

One of East Germany's L-39V target tugs is pictured at Peenemünde with its KT-04 target standing ready for a mission against the MiG-23s of JFG 9.

Gathering of the
DESERT

On 2 August 1990 the world's peace was shattered as the armies of Saddam Hussein crashed across the border from Iraq into Kuwait. Within hours they were on the Saudi border, threatening the vast oil reserves that are essential to the West's economy. As a matter of urgency, the United States and United Kingdom sent vast air power reinforcements to Arabia to protect the Saudi kingdom and the Gulf states.

Just as the world was breathing a sigh of relief, Iraq's President Saddam Hussein struck. Within hours, Kuwait was militarily crushed, although valiant but futile attacks on the invaders continued for several days. Until a few months ago, the outcome would have been counterbarrages of rhetoric and recriminations in the UN whilst the victor savoured his spoils, but Saddam reckoned without the change of heart by his principal arms supplier, Moscow.

Equally unusual scenes accompanied the overture to and the aftermath of invasion, as regional and Western nations changed bedfellows faster than characters in a French bedroom farce. In fact, it had been the sudden change of relations between Iraq and Kuwait, its former (and substantial) financial backer in the 1980-88 Gulf war against Iran, that had first caused the world to doubt that Iraqi threats and troop movements during the later days of July had any great significance.

At the moment that Iraq appeared to be pulling back its forces from the border after moderating its belligerent attitude to Kuwait, there was a swift reversal. At 2 a.m. local time on 2 August 1990, the invasion began as 30,000 troops, including elite Presidential Guards, crossed the border at three points, supported by 350 T-54, T-55 and T-72 tanks. An artillery barrage on Ali Al Salin air base destroyed some of Kuwait's 20 Dassault Mirage F1CKs and four F1BK trainers on the ground, but others were able to take off after dawn and strafe the invaders before seeking refuge in Bahrain and on Saudi Arabian airfields. Troop-carrying helicopters then brought in Iraqi commandos to secure Ahmad Al Jabir, but not before an unserviceable Lockheed L-100-30 Super Hercules was deliberately set on fire to prevent it falling into their hands. At about the same time, Iraqi fighter-bombers were attacking key installations around Kuwait City, Mirage F1EQs providing close support to forces advancing on the Dasman Palace, home of the Emir. The ruler and his retinue were able to escape from the International Airport before it was overrun by an armoured column and despite one of the two parallel runways being damaged by an early-morning bombing raid.

Advance into the City was expedited by special forces brought in earlier by ship and helicopter. Other troop-carrying helicopters ferried soldiers to the uninhabited islands of Bubiyan and Warbah close to the border with Iraq and overlooking the approaches to its Umm Qasr naval base. Nearby, over Mutla, a lone KAF Mirage F1 shot down one helicopter and was preparing to attack another when it was driven off by Iraqi gunfire.

South of the capital, some of the 25 or so remaining McDonnell Douglas A-4KU Skyhawk attack aircraft were forced to operate from a road beside their air base at Ahmad Al Jabir when its runway was rendered unserviceable. As in the north, the base was overrun by helicopter-borne troops. Having transferred all its flyable aircraft to friendly nations, the KAF was unable to piece together a coherent catalogue of events, although the exiled government claimed destruction by fighters and AA guns of 12 Iraqi aeroplanes and 15 helicopters in the short but bitter conflict.

Two days after the invasion, 100,000 Iraqi troops were reported to be massing on the Saudi border. President Saddam announced that he would not invade Saudi Arabia, but that was far from convincing in view of a similar utterance regarding Kuwait a few days before. Fearing it would be next, the government in Riyadh took the only step open to it: it asked for world help in general, and American help in particular.

Against the background of a near-total trade embargo directed by the UN at Iraq, the US war machine was put into gear. President George Bush's first – and successful – aim was to dissuade Saddam's troops from crossing another border, but when the proportions of the US build-up in Saudi Arabia were realised, it became apparent that America was almost certainly bent on more long-term objectives. The options were brutally simple: destroy Saddam and his chemical weapons now, or wait five years or so until he had added nuclear weapons and long-range missiles to his armoury.

EAGLES

Left: Air defence was seen as the priority in the reinforcement of Saudi Arabia. Two squadrons of McDonnell Douglas F-15C Eagles deployed from the 1st Tactical Fighter Wing at Langley AFB, Virginia, moving in alongside Saudi Eagles at Dhahran. This F-15C takes off on a combat air patrol, flying past missile defences ringing the air base. The standard air defence load of four Sparrows and four Sidewinders is carried.

Highlighting the 'special relationship' between the US and UK, and traditional ties between the UK and Saudi Arabia, Britain was swift to add its contribution to the rapidly expanding desert air force. Twelve Tornado F.Mk 3 interceptors were hurried to Dhahran, ready to undertake combat air patrol and QRA duties with their Sidewinder and BAe Sky Flash missiles. Supporting troops accompanied the aircraft to provide defence on the ground.

Above: Tornado F.Mk 3s of Nos 5 and 29 Sqns were involved in the initial deployment to Saudi Arabia. The efforts of US, Saudi and RAF interceptors were pooled for greater efficiency, especially as only two types of aircraft were involved, both housed in open shelters to provide protection against little more than the blistering sun. Here No. 5 Squadron Tornados relax in the cool of the night with a Saudi F-15.

Gathering of the Desert Eagles

En route from Tonopah Test Range to Langley AFB, Virginia, a Lockheed F-117A tops up from a 9th SRW KC-135Q. This much publicised deployment continued to Saudi Arabia, where 20 of the aircraft settled in as a prime weapon for precision attacks against strategic targets.

US mobilisation

Throughout August 1990, the United States poured thousands of troops and tons of weapons and equipment into the Middle East as a deterrent against an Iraqi invasion of Saudi Arabia. At the request of King Fahd, US President George Bush ordered a massive airlift of defensive forces, under the codename Operation Desert Shield, to strategic locations in Saudi Arabia, Egypt, Oman and Turkey and subsequently to Bahrain and the UAE.

After the invasion of Kuwait on 2 August, Secretary of State James Baker visited several Gulf states and had meetings with NATO allies in Europe to discuss what the US/UN response should be. He flew aboard an 89th MAW Boeing VC-137B.

Within a short time the Pentagon had assembled an enormous force in the Middle East, using experience gained conducting exercises in the region, such as Bright Star, in which elements of the Rapid Deployment Force (RDF) had been re-assigned to the Gulf states and Egypt to counter just such an emergency. Under the control of Tactical Air Command's 9th Air Force with headquarters at Shaw AFB, South Carolina, the RDF was established as part of the US Central Command Air Forces (USCENTAF), which is itself the air component of US Central Command (USCENCOM) with headquarters at MacDill AFB, Florida. The 9th Air Force is responsible for the majority of East Coast TAC flying wings, and its commander is also the CinC of USCENTAF. SAC moved a number of Boeing B-52s to forward locations, and it is quite likely that additional bombers were placed on a higher state of readiness at their home bases.

Tactical Air Command

Several Tactical Air Command units were given orders to prepare for relocation to the Middle East, taking with them sufficient aircraft and spare parts to sustain flight operations for an indefinite period.

Air defence was selected as the greatest priority, and the 1st TFW at Langley AFB, Virginia, quickly despatched 46 McDonnell Douglas F-15Cs of the 27th and 71st TFS to Dhahran AB, Saudi Arabia. The flights are believed to have taken place on 7 August with the Eagles flying non-stop from Langley AFB, a distance of 6,500 miles which took most of the aircraft 14 hours and involved seven mid-air refuellings. Some 1st TFW Eagles were in the air for 17 hours as aircraft were required to keep clear of Libyan and Jordanian airspace. Once established at Dhahran, the 1st TFW pilots wasted no time in joining the Saudi Tornados and Eagles in performing a round-the-clock air defence patrol of the Iraq/Kuwait border. It is reported that a number of these F-15s were subsequently transferred to the Royal Saudi Air Force.

The 363rd TFW at Shaw AFB, South Carolina, despatched 44 General Dynamics F-16Cs from the 17th and 33rd TFS to Sharjah in the United Arab Emirates. The deployment commenced on 8 August, which is probably the date when the F-16s actually left Shaw AFB for the Gulf. At least 16 Lockheed C-5 Galaxy flights were employed to transport maintenance and support personnel to the Middle East. Shaw AFB also provided the 507th Tactical Air Control Wing together with its deployable radars, communications equipment and ground-based forward air controllers, and TAC's 9th Air Force relocated from Shaw AFB to Riyadh to take command of the defensive Air Force units. The 9th AF wings that remained in the USA were reassigned directly to Headquarters TAC at Langley AFB.

F-117s taxi off the Langley runway at the end of the first leg of their Gulf deployment flight. In addition to the squadron sent to Saudi Arabia, it is believed that another squadron was earlier flown to Turkey. The use of the F-117 is as much for propaganda as for its military potential.

Three hundred personnel were flown to Doha International Airport, Qatar, on 31 August to prepare for the arrival of 24 F-16Cs from the 401st TFW at Torrejon AB, Spain.

The 4th TFW at Seymour Johnson AFB, North Carolina, sent 22 McDonnell Douglas F-15E Eagles of the 336th TFS to Thumrait AB, Oman. The aircraft are believed to have left the USA on 9 August. They were equipped with Martin Marietta LANTIRN (Low-Altitude Navigation and Targeting Infra-Red for Night) AAQ-3 navigation pods, which provide a wide-view forward-looking infra-red capability for visual piloting and terrain-following. They were not equipped with targeting pods, however.

An unspecified number of Fairchild A-10As from the 354th TFW at Myrtle Beach AFB, South Carolina, were flown to the region, possibly from either the 353rd or 355th TFS. The date when the deployment commenced and the exact number of aircraft involved have not been released. Television footage of the A-10s performing training flights has shown the aircraft at Al Jubayl which, although not completed, can nevertheless operate the type.

Five Boeing E-3 Sentries from the 552nd AW&CW at Tinker AFB, Oklahoma, were sent to Riyadh AB to conduct airborne early warning patrols of the Gulf region alongside the five E-3s of the Royal Saudi Air Force. TAC E-3s are no strangers to the Middle East, as a detachment known as 'Elf One' was stationed at Riyadh until 18 Squadron, RSAF, became operational in its own right during 1989. Since arrival in the Middle East the E-3s have conducted a 24-hours-a-day airborne alert throughout the crisis.

The 35th TFW at George AFB, California, sent a squadron of McDonnell Douglas F-4G 'Wild Weasels' to Saudi Arabia. An unknown number of aircraft were flown from the USA to the Middle East on 16 August.

A squadron of 22 Lockheed F-117A stealth fighters was flown out on 21 August. The 22 aircraft, belonging to the 37th TFW, left their home base at Tonopah Test Range, Nevada, shortly after 7 a.m. on Sunday 19 August for the 4½-hour flight to Langley AFB, Virginia, where they remained overnight before 20 continued their journey to the Gulf. They received air refuelling

across the USA from a dozen Boeing KC-135Q tankers from the 9th SRW at Beale AFB, California, which continued their journey to Riyadh via RAF Mildenhall. Reports suggest that the F-117s were then air-refuelled across the Atlantic by McDonnell Douglas KC-10As. Not surprisingly, the exact location of the F-117s remains unknown at present, although one of the bases in the southern part of Saudi Arabia, such as Taif, would seem a logical choice.

According to *Stars and Stripes*, the unofficial news publication for the US armed forces, this deployment was the second involving F-117s to the region, as 22 Night Hawks were reported to have flown to Turkey. The newspaper stated that the deployment to Turkey took place during the first half of July, well in advance of the crisis, although US press reporters aboard the tankers

Above: A fully-armed F-15C of the 27th Tactical Fighter Squadron, 1st TFW, rests in its revetment at Dhahran. The combination of F-15s and Tornado F.Mk 3s provides an excellent defence against any Iraqi intruders, both types equipped with long-range radars and operating under the control of Boeing E-3 Sentries.

Left: Supporting the fighter deployments have been numerous supply sorties by transport aircraft to build up the stocks of air-to-air missiles (AIM-9M Sidewinders illustrated). Ground and aircrew alike had to learn to cope with the blistering desert heat on arrival in Saudi Arabia, a problem compounded by the omnipresent fear of a chemical attack and the requirement to wear and carry NBC/CBR protection.

Below: Dhahran is in the centre of the main oil-producing region of Saudi Arabia, and so was a natural choice for the main interceptor base. The need for a successful policing of the borders with Iraq and Kuwait is heightened by the fact that most of the defending aircraft are housed in the open, and consequently are vulnerable to Iraqi air attack.

Gathering of the Desert Eagles

on 19 August were given no indication of any previous transatlantic flight by F-117s.

A number of Air National Guard McDonnell Douglas RF-4Cs of 106th TRS from Birmingham MAP, Alabama, were flown to Saudi Arabia early in the crisis to provide tactical reconnaissance of Iraqi forces' positions on the Iraqi/Kuwaiti border. The squadron was later mobilised by order of the President, along with many other ANG and AFRes airlift and refuelling units.

Military Airlift Command

From the moment Operation Desert Shield started, MAC was stretched to the limit, with Lockheed C-130 Hercules, C-141 StarLifters and C-5 Galaxies flying hundreds of missions each week between the USA and bases in the Middle East. The delivery of troops of the 82nd Airborne Division from Fort Bragg, North Carolina, together with their equipment and the airlift of support personnel and supplies for the RDF fighters, required a great many MAC flights during the first few days of the Operation. To this end, C-5s and C-141Bs flew direct from the USA to bases including Dhahran, Riyadh and Thumrait, with air refuelling provided by KC-135s and KC-10s strategically placed at forward operating bases in Europe and the Azores. The bulk of the urgent airlift seems to have been carried by the two intercontinental types, leaving MAC C-130 Hercules to conduct resupply flights back home.

However, the C-130 was not entirely omitted from support of the build-up of US forces in the Middle East. A C-5 arrived at RAF Mildenhall on 8 August containing 20 C-130 flight crews from the 317th TAW at Pope AFB, North Carolina, who were being forward-located to await the delivery of Hercules. Sixteen 317th TAW C-130Es arrived at Mildenhall on 10 August, and were all flown to Cairo West Airport, Egypt, by the forward-located aircrew following a short re-

Left: A highly important air asset moved to Saudi Arabia during mid-August was a squadron of F-4G 'Wild Weasel' defence suppression aircraft from the 35th TFW at George AFB, California. One is seen here refuelling from a 380th BW KC-135Q off the coast of Massachusetts on 17 August. Carried under the wing pylons are a pair of AGM-88 HARM missiles, which home in on and destroy hostile SAM radars. Given the number of SAMs possessed by Iraq, such aircraft would be a vital asset during any operations over Iraqi territory.

Below: A massive airlift accompanied the tactical aircraft as they deployed to the Gulf, and continued unabated to keep the troops supplied. Heavily involved was the Lockheed C-5 Galaxy fleet, able to transport most outsize items and other materiel in bulk. One of these giants crashed at Ramstein taking off on a Gulf supply flight, marking the first casualties of the US involvement.

As front-line units were called away to support Desert Shield, Air National Guard and Air Force Reserve personnel increased their operations to cover the shortfall in other theatres and to augment the main airlift effort. These Texas Guardsmen board C-130s bound for MAC bases, where they will assist in cargo-handling.

fuelling stopover. A second batch of 16 arrived at Mildenhall two days later and were ferried to Cairo West by the aircrew who had flown the first 16 to Mildenhall.

During early August the scheduled relay swap-over of aircraft with the Bravo Squadron at Mildenhall had just commenced with 16 C-130Es from the 314th TAW at Little Rock AFB, Arkansas, replacing a similar number of C-130Hs from the 463rd TAW at Dyess AFB, Texas. As a tentative measure the departure home of the latter was halted until the situation became sufficiently clear and the incoming C-130Es were all in place. The drain on resources was such that only 12 aircraft were available from the 314th TAW, and the nominal strength of the Bravo Squadron was maintained by the Air Force Reserve (AFRes), who sent four C-130Es from the 96th TAS at Minneapolis St Paul IAP, Minnesota.

A further 16 AFRes C-130Hs were forward-located to RAF Alconbury on 19 August to be available should the need arise for inter-theatre airlift. These aircraft were drawn from five different units, consisting of 700th TAS from Dobbins AFB, Georgia; 357th TAS from Maxwell AFB, Alabama; 758th TAS from Greater Pittsburgh IAP, Pennsylvania; 64th TAS from Chicago-O'Hare IAP, Illinois; and 95th TAS from Mitchell Field, Milwaukee, Wisconsin.

Air National Guard and Air Force Reserve C-5 and C-141 units were included in the airlift, flying alongside their front-line counterparts, while personnel from AFRes (Associate) squadrons manned MAC aircraft to fulfil their requirements.

Eight special operations aircraft were included in the build-up of forces, with four 8th SOS Lockheed MC-130Es from Hurlburt Field, Florida, together with two 9th SOS HC-130Ps plus two HC-130Ns from Eglin AFB, Florida, all deploying to RAF Woodbridge in the UK on 12 August, where they remained for approximately a week making preparations for their deployment. The four HC-130s eventually left for Cairo West while the MC-130Es departed for Riyadh, where they were joined by four 1st SOW MH-53Js airlifted from Hurlburt Field.

A considerable volume of heavy equipment and thousands of troops were transported to the Middle East by Military Sealift Command using chartered ships, but the requirement for airlift was nevertheless far in excess of that which MAC could provide. The Command therefore resorted to the Civilian Reserve Air Fleet (CRAF) and for the first time in its 38-year history the CRAF has been ferrying thousands of troops. Television news reports from the Gulf showed wide-body jets from World Airways, United Airlines and United Parcels Service on the ramp at Dhahran. In addition, Southern Air Transport stationed three Boeing 707-369Cs at Mildenhall to conduct a regular freight service between the USA (including Pope AFB) and Dhahran. Some

Above: Also seen at Incirlik were several F-16Cs from the 401st Tactical Fighter Wing, based at Torrejon in Spain. This was the only known deployment to Turkey with direct involvement with Desert Shield (a squadron of F-117s also being reported), the others being standard USAFE detachments for weapons training. Further F-16s were deployed from Spain to Qatar, and from Shaw AFB, South Carolina, to Sharjah in the UAE.

Below: Europe provided a natural staging post for supply flights between the United States and the Middle East. This was the scene at Rhein-Main AB (Frankfurt) on 22 August as Lockheed C-141B StarLifters loaded passengers and cargo en route to the Gulf. The MAC fleet was stretched to the limit, its aircraft still needed to supply US forces in other areas of the globe.

Gathering of the Desert Eagles

of these aircraft were frequently positioned on the 'hot ramp' at Mildenhall, indicating they were transporting ordnance.

To co-ordinate the vast number of MAC aircraft arriving at bases in the Middle East, airlift control elements were relocated from their home bases and pre-positioned at Dhahran (438th MAW), Thumrait (437th MAW), Al Dhafra (435th TAW) and Riyadh (presumably the 436th MAW). These units provided the aerial port facilities and equipment to unload and regenerate the aircraft as quickly as possible, as reports from the region have spoken of limited ramp space with aircraft queueing to park.

The airlift suffered its first major accident on 29 August when AFRes/433rd MAW C-5A 68-0228, carrying medical supplies, food and maintenance equipment to the Gulf, crashed shortly after take-off from Ramstein AB, West Germany, on a flight to Rhein Main AB, killing 13 of the 17 Reservist personnel aboard. The C-5 had just become airborne when it lost height and struck the ground, breaking up upon impact. The accident happened at around 20 minutes before 1 a.m. local time.

Onboard scene on a 552nd Airborne Warning and Control Wing Boeing E-3 Sentry during a routine patrol over Saudi Arabia. Controllers report several dummy runs and feints by Iraqi aircraft, which fly at speed towards the border before turning back. These screens display the Saudi coastline and Kuwaiti border.

Air National Guard

Type	Wing/ Group	Squadron	Base/State
C-5A	105th MAG	137th MAS	Stewart ANGB, New York
C-130A	164th TAG	155th TAS	Memphis IAP, Tennessee
C-130B	179th TAG	164th TAS	Mansfield Airport, Ohio
C-130E	143rd TCAG	143rd-TAS	Quonset Point Airport, Rhode Island
	167th TAG	167th TAS	Martinsburgh Airport, West Virginia
C-130H	118th TAW	105thTAS	Nashville Metro Airport, Tennessee
	136th TAW	181st TAS	NAS Dallas, Texas
	130th TAG	130th TAS	Kanawha Airport, West Virginia
	139th TAG	180th TAS	Rosecrans Memorial Airport, Missouri
	166th TAG	142nd TAS	Wilmington Airport, Delaware

Type	Wing/ Group	Squadron	Base/State
KC-135E	126th ARW	108th ARS	Chicago-O'Hare IAP, Illinois
	128th ARG	126th ARS	Mitchell Field, Milwaukee, Wisconsin
	134th ARG	151st ARS	Knoxville Airport, Tennessee
	151st ARG	191st ARS	Salt Lake City IAP, Utah
	157th ARG	133rd ARS	Pease AFB, New Hampshire
	160th ARG	145th ARS	Rickenbacker ANGB, Ohio
	161st ARG	197th ARS	Phoenix Sky Harbor IAP, Arizona
	170th ARG	150th ARS	McGuire AFB, New Jersey
	190th ARG	117th ARS	Forbes Field, Kansas
C-141B	172nd MAG	183rd MAS	Jackson Airport, Mississippi
RF-4C	117th TRW	106th TRS	Birmingham MAP, Alabama

Air Force Reserve

Type	Wing/ Group	Squadron	Base
C-5A	439th MAW	337th MAS	Westover AFB, Massachusetts
C-130H	908th TAG	357th TAS	Maxwell AFB, Alabama
C-141B	459th MAW	756th MAS	Andrews AFB, Maryland

In addition the 732nd MAS (Associate) at McGuire AFB, New Jersey was mobilised to fly front-line C-141Bs.

Operating from Riyadh, the E-3 Sentry force flies continuous coverage of the war zone, monitoring Iraqi air activity and directing fighters to meet any potential threats. The USAF aircraft are integrated with the Royal Saudi Air Force's own E-3s, the latter being fitted with fuel-efficient F108 turbofans.

Strategic Air Command

SAC was as busy as MAC, although it was the tanker fleet rather than the bomber force that was most heavily committed. A large number of KC-135s and KC-10s were flown from bases in the USA to forward locations such as Lajes AB, Azores, along with Moron and Zaragoza ABs in Spain, while tankers were flying from NAS Sigonella, Sicily, on occasions.

The extensive flightline at Lajes must have supported a large number of aircraft, as routine flights scheduled to transit the base were redirected elsewhere, including Keflavik in Iceland. SAC personnel from Europe and the USA were sent to these bases to bolster the resident staff, who would have been unable to cope with such a huge number of additional traffic.

Likewise, additional SAC ground personnel were detached to bases in the Middle East to handle the vast number of tankers supporting the fighter aircraft, with the 306th SW at Mildenhall providing staff at Dhahran and Riyadh. Although SAC tankers were visitors to most of the bases in the Middle East where US personnel were located, the main facilities were at Riyadh and Jeddah, which handled the bulk of the traffic. KC-135E and R models were the two types approved for regular operations in the Gulf as the increased thrust of their JT3D and F108-CF-100 powerplants respectively were more capable in the desert heat than the J57 turbojets of the KC-135A and Q versions. However, the latter two types were frequent visitors at Gulf bases.

Air Force Reserve and Air National Guard units as well as regular SAC units were involved, including the 126th ARS from Mitchell Field, Wisconsin, operating from Moron, while the 117th ARS from Forbes Field, Kansas, was at Jeddah, both flying the KC-135E. In addition,

Left: A pair of Boeing RC-135V strategic reconnaissance aircraft are seen at RAF Mildenhall, a regular staging post for these electronic specialists on their way to the Mediterranean and Middle East. RC-135s are operating from Athens-Hellenikon in Greece and Riyadh in Saudi Arabia to monitor Iraqi communications, radars and any other form of electronic intelligence that can be gleaned. Further SAC reconnaissance assets include Cyprus-based Lockheed U-2Rs.

Above: Large numbers of sorties have been flown by SAC's tanker fleet, from both sides of the Atlantic as well as in the Middle East. This 305th ARW KC-135R is typical of the many involved in refuelling deploying aircraft from bases in England. Only the KC-135E and KC-135R models have been used in Arabia, the earlier KC-135As and Qs having less powerful engines.

Above: Renowned as the bombers of Tripoli during the 1986 raid on Libya, the 48th TFW again provided F-111F aircraft for Desert Shield. Sent to an undisclosed base in Saudi Arabia, the aircraft were armed with GBU-15 TV-guided bombs and 2,000-lb laser-guided weapons.

Left: Owing to the enormous strain placed on the MAC fleet, civil carriers have been called in to make up the shortfall. In addition to trooping flights from the US, military cargo has been carried. Southern Air Transport provided three 707s for Mildenhall-Arabia transport duties.

approximately 15 ANG KC-135Es had flown to Alconbury by 16 August, performing missions to various locations including Moron and Jeddah before relocating to Mildenhall. Units included 116th ARS Fairchild AFB, Washington, 117th ARS Forbes Field, Kansas, 145th ARS Rickenbacker ANGB, Ohio, 151st ARS from Knoxville Apt, Tennessee, 168th ARS Eielson AFB, Alaska and 191st ARS Salt Lake City IAP, Utah.

AFRes tanker units were in the process of conducting their two-week summer camp at Mildenhall when the invasion of Kuwait took place with two KC-135Es from the 72nd ARS at Grissom AFB, Indiana. Likewise, these aircraft were called upon to perform missions to a variety of locations.

Some idea of the scope of SAC tanker operations can be gauged from events at Mildenhall. On 8 August the commander of the 306th SW

was notified that all routine tanker missions were cancelled until further notice, as the aircraft would be required to participate in the night refuelling of fighter and MAC aircraft deploying non-stop to the Middle East. Missions of eight to 10 hours were flown that evening and subsequent evenings for the remainder of the week, with the number of aircraft in residence increasing from 14 to 20 by 11 August. These were composed of an almost equal split between turbojet and turbofan examples. Throughout the following week the base continued to operate mostly night missions with approximately 20 aircraft in residence at any one time until 18/19 August, when the ANG examples from Alconbury began to arrive and the KC-135R versions deployed to the Gulf.

However, the number of tankers rose to more than 40 on 20 August with the appearance of the dozen 9th SRW KC-135Qs mentioned earlier,

although this quantity was not on the ground at any given time as KC-135s were arriving and departing at all hours of the day and night. This situation continued, with many new aircraft arriving daily carrying cargo and passengers destined for the Middle East, and it appears that many of these flights were in place of MAC aircraft. More than 60 different KC-135s visited or were in residence at Mildenhall between 17 and 26 August, and the month's total comfortably exceeded 100 different aircraft!

KC-10As were also much in evidence, although very few were visitors to Mildenhall as these conducted the dual role of air refuelling combined with airlift of cargo in their spacious holds. RC-135s of the 55th SRW operating from Athens and Riyadh were heavily involved in gathering intelligence, while the U-2R stationed at Akrotiri no doubt flew numerous sorties. A

Operation Desert Shield represents the biggest deployment of US air power since Vietnam, calling on virtually every airlift and tanker unit within the air force. In addition to AFRes aircraft, the Reserve has supplied aircrew for active-duty aircraft under the Associate programme. As ever, the workhorse of the airlift has been the C-141B StarLifter, available in large numbers and carrying a useful load non-stop from the United States.

pair of 9th SRW U-2Rs were reported to have transitted through Alconbury during August, including 80-1070, fitted with C-Span satellite communications antennas. It is presumed that these were destined for the Middle East.

As mentioned earlier, SAC moved a small number of B-52s to forward locations, including some 42nd BW aircraft from Loring AFB, Maine, to Diego Garcia in the Indian Ocean. The exact number of aircraft involved is unknown, although four B-52Gs were flown to Diego Garcia during the first week of Desert Shield. Additional B-52Gs from 42nd BW and 93rd BW at Castle AFB, California, were sent to Diego Garcia, with 26 aircraft forward-based by the third week in August. The Saudi government approved the basing of B-52s on its soil, and six 42nd BW aircraft had flown to an unspecified location by 27 August.

United States Air Forces in Europe

The majority of units participating in Desert Shield were from the USA, although some 401st TFW F-16Cs from Torrejon AB in Spain were reported to have flown to Incirlik AB to provide additional defence against a surprise Iraqi attack against Turkey. During early August General Dynamics F-111Es of the 77th TFS from Upper Heyford were in residence at Incirlik AB, while F-111Fs of the 493rd TFS from Lakenheath were detached to Zaragoza AB, Spain. Both detach-

ments were routine NATO commitments to conduct weapons delivery training on nearby ranges, and were unconnected with the Iraqi invasion.

Shortly after 7 a.m. on 25 August, 20 48th TFW F-111Fs departed Lakenheath together with four air spares, which returned later in the day, for an undisclosed location in Saudi Arabia. Although composed mostly of 492nd and 493rd TFS aircraft, there were a handful of 494th and 495th TFS examples. Each F-111F was carrying four 2,000-lb GBU-15 TV-guided bombs, but with the fuses removed to avoid disaster in the event of an accident. Several aircraft were fitted with underwing chaff/flare dispenser pods and at least two had AIM-9 Sidewinder missiles. In addition, most had the AN/ALQ-131 ECM pod beneath the rear fuselage.

Support for the flight to the Gulf was provided by a dozen tankers, which departed Mildenhall at the same time as the F-111s were leaving Lakenheath. These were mostly Air National Guard KC-135Es, which arrived in the UK nine days earlier, and all returned to Mildenhall later in the day.

A second batch of 20 F-111Fs left Lakenheath early on 2 September. They were armed with 2,000-lb GBU-15 and 2,000-lb 'Pave Spike' laser bombs, except for the last pair of each of the three waves, which had long-range underwing tanks and Sidewinder missiles only.

US Navy

USS *Independence* (CV-62) was the first aircraft-carrier to arrive in the region when she sailed into the Gulf of Oman on 8 August along with her task force, to take up her position to blockade the Indian Ocean. On the same day, the USS *Dwight D. Eisenhower* (CV-69) task force transitted the Suez Canal and sailed into the Red Sea to blockade shipping heading for the Jordanian port of Aqaba if necessary. USS *Saratoga* (CV-60) sailed from the USA on 7 August to the Mediterranean, followed eight days later by the USS *John F. Kennedy*, which left Norfolk, Virginia, on 15 August. Between them these four carriers could muster some 300 aircraft and helicopters with formidable striking power.

Details of the complements of the four carriers are as follows.

USS *Independence* with CVW-14/NK embarked:
   VF-21 and VF-154 with Grumman F-14As
   VA-196 with Grumman A-6E/KA-6Ss
   VAQ-139 with Grumman EA-6Bs
   VAW-113 flying the Grumman E-2C
   VS-37 with the Lockheed S-3A
   HS-8 flying the Sikorsky SH-3H
   Grumman C-2A from VRC-50 for COD
USS *Eisenhower* with CVW-7/AG embarked:
   VF-142 and VF-143 flying the Grumman F-14A+
   VFA-131 and VFA-136 flying the McDonnell Douglas F-18A
   VA-34 with the Grumman A-6E/KA-6D
   VAW-121 with Grumman E-2Cs
   VAQ-140 flying the Grumman EA-6B

Above: *Vought A-7Es deployed on board USS* **John F. Kennedy** *for its Gulf cruise, one of the units being VA-46 'Clansmen'. Two of the other three carriers have McDonnell Douglas F-18 Hornets in the light attack role, while* Independence *has extra A-6s.*

Left: *Each of the four Gulf carriers has a pair of Grumman F-14A Tomcat squadrons on board, although the units on board* Eisenhower *have F-14A+ aircraft with uprated engines. Tasked with protecting the carrier battle group and its attack aircraft, the F-14s can also undertake tactical reconnaissance duties. Although primarily carried for light attack tasks, the F-18 Hornets can also augment the air defence force. This F-14A is from VF-32 on board* **John F. Kennedy,** *seen during training flights just prior to leaving Norfolk for the Gulf.*

VS-31 with the Lockheed S-3B
HS-5 flying the Sikorsky SH-3H

USS *Saratoga* with CVW-17/AA embarked:
   VF-74 and VF-103 both flying the Grumman
      F-14A
   VFA-81 and VFA-83 both operating the
      McDonnell Douglas F-18A
   VA-35 with the Grumman A-6E/KA-6D
   VAQ-132 with Grumman EA-6Bs
   VAW-125 flying the Grumman E-2C
   VS-30 with the Lockheed S-3A
   HS-3 with the Sikorsky SH-3H

The composition of *John F. Kennedy* was not confirmed at the time, although it was believed to include VF-14 and VF-32 with the F-14A, VA-75 with the A-6E/KA-6D, VAQ-130 flying the EA-6B, VS-22 with S-3Bs, plus possibly VAW-126 with the E-2C, and HS-7 flying SH-3Hs. Two A-7E light attack squadrons complete the Air Wing

Lockheed P-3C Orions were stationed on the island of Masirah off the coast of Oman, along with EP-3Es presumably detached from VQ-2 at NAS Rota, Spain. In addition, P-3s from the USA are stationed at Diego Garcia to conduct routine patrols over the Indian Ocean, and could therefore extend their area of operation towards the Gulf.

US Marine Corps

The bulk of the ground forces being sent to the Gulf are 45,000 US Marines composed of 16,000 men of the 1st Marine Expeditionary Brigade (MEB) from Hawaii and the 7th MEB from Twentynine Palms, California, who will join with the 4th MEB from North Carolina. These forces were expected to meet up with their equipment at the port of Al Jubayl, which is on the east coast of Saudi Arabia, at the end of August. Apart from an assortment of tanks and assault vehicles, the Marine Corps will be supported by a variety of aircraft and helicopters including AV-8Bs, F-18A/Cs, A-6Es, EA-6Bs, CH-53Ds and AH-1Ws.

Several assault carriers had either arrived in the region or were sailing to the Gulf including the USS *Inchon* (LPH-12) with the 26th Marine Expeditionary Unit, while the USS *Guam* (LPH-9), USS *Iwo Jima* (LPH-2) and USS *Nassau* (LHA-4) were also participating. These four ships normally have a mixed complement of CH-46Es, CH-53s and AH-1s, although some carry the AV-8B as well.

The sharp end of the carrier air wing is the Grumman A-6E Intruder, which can carry huge warloads and deliver them in all weathers. Four squadrons are available to **US Navy** *commanders in the Gulf, one flying from each of the carriers. This aircraft is from VA-75.*

Right: A flock of Sikorsky UH-60 Black Hawks lifts off from a desert air base in Saudi Arabia, some toting empty ESSS (External Stores Support System) pylons that can accommodate weapons such as Hellfire anti-tank missiles and rockets. Army helicopters became increasingly important as ground units spread out into the desert to take up defensive positions near the border, the rotary-wing assets providing rapid transport of men and supplies between the outlying posts and the main supply base.

Below: After an initial airlift of Army helicopters and troops of the 82nd Airborne Division, a further build-up of Army forces went by sea. Here Bell AH-1F Cobras await shipment to the Gulf at the port of Savannah, Georgia. Both AH-1s and AH-64s were moved to the theatre to blunt any Iraqi armoured thrust into Saudi Arabia.

No details of the units involved nor quantities of aircraft were available at the time of writing, although elements of the 2nd Marine Aircraft Wing with headquarters at MCAS Cherry Point, North Carolina, would seem to be likely candidates. Three of the four AV-8B units from MCAS Cherry Point, consisting of VMA-231, -331 and -542, were believed to be amongst those deploying. No doubt F-18As of the six squadrons that constitute MAG-31 located at MCAS Beaufort, South Carolina, were among the Hornet units. At least one squadron of AH-1W gunships from MCAS New River, North Carolina, were airlifted to Dhahran. USMC KC-130s of all three stateside front-line units, as well as the two Marine Corps Reserve squadrons, were heavily involved transporting support equipment and personnel to locations in Saudi Arabia and Bahrain.

US Army

The 82nd Airborne Division sent its 1st Brigade and part of the 2nd Brigade by air to Dhahran, composed of several thousand men. Amongst other units sent to the Gulf were two brigades of the 24th Infantry Division (Mechanised) and the 11th Air Defense Artillery Brigade from Fort Bliss, Texas, armed with Patriot and Stinger anti-aircraft missiles.

Helicopters airlifted to the region included 14 Sikorsky UH-60A Black Hawks of 2nd Brigade and 15 McDonnell Douglas AH-64A Apaches of 1st Brigade to Dhahran to support the 82nd Airborne Division, while at least four Bell OH-58A and four OH-58D Kiowa scouts were also at Dhahran, along with a number of Boeing-Vertol CH-47 Chinooks. Additional helicopters and personnel from units stationed with the US Army in Europe were being readied for transfer to the Gulf during late August, including examples of the AH-64A .

An Army OH-58D crashed in Saudi Arabia 20 miles north-west of Dhahran on 20 August during a night training sortie. The crew of two were uninjured.

At the time of going to press, the Pentagon had announced that the strength of forces in the Gulf had reached the predetermined stage known as 'Threshold A', which was the level at which an Iraqi attack could be repelled. The next stage, known as 'Threshold B', had yet to be reached, this being the level at which US forces could launch an offensive operation. However, the combination of sanctions and diplomatic negotiations by the UN were still being sought to avoid a confrontation.

Call-up of reservists

In response to the crisis in Kuwait and the relocation of vast numbers of front-line forces to the Gulf, President Bush authorised the mobilisation of military Reserve and National Guard forces on 23 August, including a number of flying units. Although details are still to be finalised, those units that have been notified are listed separately, some of which have personnel who have volunteered, while others have been called to active duty.

It is likely that some of these squadrons will be reassigned to operational Air Force installations to replace the front-line units that have been sent overseas, but this is not entirely the case, as the 106th TRS at Birmingham MAP, Alabama, has flown its RF-4Cs to the Gulf to conduct tactical reconnaissance for the Commander, US Central Command. Likewise, the C-5 and C-141 units have flown numerous resupply missions to bases in the Middle East. At least two KC-135E squadrons were flying routine air-refuelling sorties from bases in Saudi Arabia.

It is quite likely that other reservists will be mobilised, particularly fighter squadrons such as those operating the A-10 and F-16. However, this is dependent upon more front-line squadrons being sent to the Gulf.

British and other deployments

Though by far the largest, the American military presence in the Gulf was not the only boost for the threatened states. Moderate Arab and other Islamic countries offered nominal support on the ground, and several Western states despatched naval vessels to enforce the mandatory UN blockade. With its close historic and current trade links with the region, the United Kingdom was well poised to make a significant contribution, its determination perhaps further strengthened by both the equally long-term solidarity with the USA and the outrage felt when Saddam seized Western women and children as a human shield for his military bases and arms plants.

First commitment

Throughout the first full week of August, preparations were made to despatch RAF aircraft under Operation Granby to bolster air defences in several states. A first, public commitment was announced by Defence Secretary Tom King on 9 August in the form of a dozen each of Jaguars and

Tornado F.Mk 3s, plus Rapier SAMs. Almost on the scene already were the 11 Panavia Tornado F.Mk 3 long-range interceptors, of No. 29 Squadron from RAF Coningsby, which were at Akrotiri, Cyprus, on their annual Armament Practice Camp. As negotiations continued on basing in the Middle East, a further 11 aircraft from co-resident No. 5 Squadron were sent out over the weekend of 11-12 August to expand the force. Six of the new arrivals, plus a similar number from No. 29 proceeded straight to Dhahran, where they took up residence alongside the similarly-equipped No. 29 Squadron of the Royal Saudi Air Force. The remaining 10 stayed on Cyprus, reinforced by six McDonnell Douglas Phantom FGR.Mk 2s of Nos 19 and 92 Squadrons detached from Wildenrath, West Germany.

Taking up QRA duties, the Phantoms allowed the remaining Tornados to return to Coningsby. Also present were the BAe Rapier close-range SAMs of No. 20 Squadron, RAF Regiment, from Honington. They had also flown out by Lockheed C-130K Hercules on 11-12 August, but onward movement to Dhahran to protect the Tornado force was cancelled when it appeared that there were sufficient US-operated Raytheon MIM-104 Patriots and Saudi Thomson-CSF/MATRA SA10 Shahines (Crotales) to accomplish the task. Patriot has an anti-ballistic missile

capability, the usefulness of which became significant on 21 August when it was revealed that Iraqi SS-1 'Scuds' had been moved to Kuwait, placing Dhahran within reach of their possibly chemical warheads.

In Saudi Arabia, the RAF build-up was being controlled by Air Vice-Marshal 'Sandy' Wilson, the Air Commander British Forces Arabian Peninsula (normally commander of No. 1 Group, Strike Command), who was assigned his personal No. 32 Squadron BAe 125 executive jet to liaise with the expanding British presence. The mixed Tornado detachment gained the title of No. 5 (Composite) Squadron, Dhahran, under the squadron's 'boss', Wing Commander Euan Black, but with Leeming station commander and experienced Tornado hand Group Captain Rick Peacock-Edwards in overall control of the air defence. Close co-operation was immediately initiated with the Saudis, whose No. 29 Squadron under Colonel Yahya Zahrani took turns with the RAF and USAF McDonnell Douglas F-15 Eagles to mount round-the-clock standing patrols.

The RAF Tornado detachment included personnel from Nos 5, 11 and 29 Squadrons. No. 11, based at Leeming, was destined to play a wider role when the decision was made to move modified Tornado F.Mk 3s to the Gulf, the transfer

Dhahran's ramp groans under the mass of helicopters assembled on 26 August, while in the distance part of the Saudi Hawk force is gathered. Among the helos are some examples of the deadly AH-64A Apache, positioned in Arabia to take on Saddam's tanks.

taking place on 29 August to replace the original aircraft. Behind-the-scenes activity in the UK had included weekend flying by many RAF squadrons, including BAe Harrier GR.Mk 5s, and trials of a Tornado chaff/flare dispenser system by BAe's Warton plant and the Tornado F.Mk 3 Operational Evaluation Unit at Coningsby. Pilots brushed up their air fighting skills against BAC Canberras and 'aggressor' BAe Hawks from the two Tactical Weapons Units at Brawdy and Chivenor. As during the Falklands war, France provided a Mirage for the RAF to practise against – not a IIIE this time, but an F1B two-seat trainer from the 12e Escadre de Chasse at Cambrai, with characteristics identical to those flown by Iraq. This operated from Leeming immediately before departure of the second wave.

Tornados made extensive use of the new BAe-operated air combat manoeuvring facility in the North Sea and received AIM-9M Sidewinders to replace their normal AIM-9Ls. Latest model BAe Sky Flash 90 semi-active radar-homing AAMs were carried under the fuselage.

Below: Flight Lieutenant Alex Muskett of No. 54 Squadron was one of the pilots sent to Thumrait with No. 6 (Composite) Squadron. The unit was formed from all of Coltishall's squadrons.

Above: Four of the Jaguars sent to Oman from Coltishall carried centreline reconnaissance pods, as seen here. All the aircraft carried Phimat chaff dispensers on the starboard outboard pylon and an AN/ALQ-101V ECM pod on the port outer. Tracor AN/ALE-40 flare dispensers were 'scabbed on' under the engine nacelles. Most of the aircraft sent to the Middle East were repainted the night before in an overall desert sand colour scheme, with a slight pink tint that led to the adoption of the nickname 'Pink Panthers'.

Gathering of the Desert Eagles

Above: The original Tornado F.Mk 3s sent out to Dhahran from RAF Coningsby as No. 5 (Composite) Squadron were replaced by No. 11 (Composite) Squadron, with pilots from the Leeming Wing and newer aircraft drawn from the squadrons at Leuchars. These incorporated various modifications, including Tracor TACDS (Threat Adaptive Countermeasures Dispenser System) under the engine nacelles.

Right: Tornado GR.Mk 1s are resprayed for service in the Gulf with No. 14 (Composite) Squadron. Aircrew and aircraft for this unit came from German and UK-based units.

Above: Although No. 11 (Composite) Squadron's F.Mk 3s carried long-range fuel tanks underwing when they were ferried out, in theatre they carried a Phimat chaff dispenser under the port wing and a Marconi Sky Shadow ECM pod to starboard. The aircraft were drawn from Nos 43 and 111 Squadrons, and as such were equipped with the latest standard of Foxhunter radar.

Below: The Tornado F.Mk 3s of No. 11 (Composite) Squadron carried no unit markings and left for the Gulf in two batches of six, with each batch taking two air-spares as far as Akrotiri, Cyprus. The first batch, led by Wing Commander David Hamilton, left Leeming on 29 August 1990, the second batch following on 16 September.

Surprise was evidenced in some quarters when the first attack aircraft despatched by the RAF proved to be SEPECAT Jaguar GR.Mk 1s, rather than Tornado GR.Mk 1s. Given the limited aim at the time of stopping Iraqi armour should it invade Saudi Arabia, the Jaguar was the right aircraft. By 10 August, the Coltishall wing had removed squadron markings from 18 aircraft, comprising 12 of No. 6 Squadron and six from tactical reconnaissance-tasked No. 41. Overnight, 10 were repainted in a pink-tinged overall desert camouflage. Led by Wing Commander Jerry Connolly (commanding No. 6 Squadron), nine of the pink aircraft and three in European green and grey departed Coltishall on 11 August, refuelled by VC10 and Victor tankers on their way to Thumrait, in Oman. Four of the group were fitted with a linescan and visual spectrum recce pod on the centreline, some of the pilots and ground staff coming from co-located Nos 41 and 54 Squadrons. On 18 August, Bahrain extended a welcome to the Jaguar force, which thenceforward planned to make regular detachments to the island.

On departure, Jaguar self-defence equipment comprised a Westinghouse AN/ALQ-101(V)-10 jamming pod on the port outer wing pylon and a Philips-MATRA Phimat chaff pod to starboard. Under an earlier modification programme, two Tracor AN/ALE-40 flare dispensers had been scabbed to the rear undersides of the engine nacelles. In theatre, some of the aircraft were expected to change ALQ-101 for an AIM-9 Sidewinder for mutual defence. Ordnance issued was the standard 1,000-lb (454-kg) bomb with parachute-retarding tail and the Hunting Improved BL755 cluster bomb.

Enforcement of the naval blockade on oil tankers carrying Iraqi oil was partly assisted by the RAF's BAe Nimrod MR.Mk 2s of the Kinloss Wing. With detachment commander, Wing Commander Andrew Neil aboard, the first Nimrod left for Seeb, on the north-east coast of Oman, on 12 August, followed soon afterwards by a second aircraft. Persistent reports of a third Nimrod in the area suggested that a shadowy R.Mk 1 intelligence-gathering variant of No. 51 Squadron was also plying its trade in the Gulf. Having spent much of their service careers seek-

Above: The Handley Page Victor K.Mk 2s of No. 55 Squadron have been extensively used in support of British forces being deployed to the Middle East as part of Operation Granby.

Powerplants
The RAF's Jaguars are now powered by a pair of Rolls-Royce Turboméca Adour Mk 104 turbofans, each rated at 8,040 lb st with afterburning. These lack the power of the 9,270-lb Mk 811s fitted to some export aircraft, including half of Oman's own Jaguars.

Chaff dispenser
A Matra Phimat chaff/flare dispenser is carried under the starboard wing, loaded with chaff cartridges.

Night operations
It is not known whether the Jaguar Force still includes pilots qualified and practised in the use of night vision goggles, but even without NVGs the aircraft has relatively good night all-weather capability.

Avionics
The simplicity of the Jaguar's avionics should not be overstated. Although the aircraft doesn't have an attack or terrain-following radar, its Ferranti FIN 1064 INS is extremely accurate and 'user-friendly' and allows a high degree of bombing accuracy, especially when used in conjunction with the Laser Rangefinder and Marked Target Seeker.

Flare dispensers
A pair of Tracor AN/ALE-40(V) chaff/flare dispensers are fitted below the engine nacelles. These are loaded with IR decoy flares to deal with enemy heat-seeking missiles.

Self defence
For self-defence the Jaguar relies mainly on tactics, flying at ultra low level to avoid detection by enemy radar. It also has two 30-mm Aden cannon in the nose, and can carry AIM-9L Sidewinder AAMs on the outer pylons.

Cluster bombs
The most likely weapon for the RAF's Jaguars participating in Operation Granby would be the Hunting BL755 cluster bomb, an excellent weapon against soft and armoured targets.

SEPECAT Jaguar GR.Mk 1A

The Jaguar was a natural choice for the RAF's contribution to Operation Granby, since the Coltishall Wing is already assigned to NATO as a regional reinforcement and for support of the AMF in Norway. Operations outside NATO's Central Front are routine, and the aircraft is ideally suited to operation from primitive semi-prepared airstrips by virtue of its rugged, energy-absorbing undercarriage. The RAF's Jaguar Force is experienced at flying at very low level in a desert environment, having participated in 'Red Flag' exercises and having made a number of deployments to the region. One pilot stated that the desert pink camouflage scheme was developed for a deployment to Jordan. Finally, there is skilled manpower and equipment readily available in Oman for Jaguar servicing, since the Sultan of Oman's Air Force operates two Jaguar squadrons at Masirah.

Role
Once the RAF's primary interdictor and tactical strike aircraft, the Jaguar has now lost its nuclear commitment and is used for interdiction and BAI (Battlefield Air Interdiction) tasks, including tank-killing.

Radar warning receiver
An RWR is carried, with forward and rear hemisphere antennas on the fin.

Bombload
The Jaguar can carry up to eight 1,000-lb bombs, with one on each outboard pylon, and with two on the centreline and on each inboard pylon. Normally, however, at least one external fuel tank will be carried (or a recce pod as shown here) and the outboard pylons will be occupied by AAMs, ECM pods or chaff/flare dispensers.

XX970

Left: France's initial airborne contribution to the International Forces in the region consisted mainly of Armée de Terre helicopters embarked on the carrier Clemenceau. These included Pumas, Gazelles and Dauphins. France also provided a pair of maritime reconnaissance Atlantiques.

ing out Soviet warships in the Atlantic, the crew of one of the Nimrods must have been more than surprised on 26 August to be called by a Russian warship captain requesting help with investigating a possible blockade-runner. RAF and *Voyenno Morskoy Flot* conducted an impromptu joint operation to establish the vessel's innocence.

As tension built, UK Defence Secretary Tom King on 23 August promised reinforcements, resulting in deployment of the first strike/attack versions of the Tornado to join the 1,700 British military personnel already in the Gulf. In line with the policy of showing solidarity with all the Gulf states, the dozen Tornado GR.Mk 1s despatched on 26 August were installed at Bahrain.

Drawn from RAF Germany, the aircraft were to the highest modification standard and powered by Mk 103 versions of the RB.199 turbofan delivering a little more power in the searing heat of the Middle East than the Mk 101s of UK-based GR.Mk 1s. Air crews for the detachment were provided in equal shares by RAFG and the Marham Wing (Nos 27 and 617 Squadrons), but were led by Wing Commander Vaughan Morris of No. 14 Squadron from Brüggen, one of the units specialising in dropping the Hunting JP233 anti-airfield weapon. Most groundcrew were also from No. 14 Squadron.

In support were the unsung heroes: the transports and tankers. No. 101 Squadron, with Brize Norton-based VC10 K.Mk 2s and 3s, was assisted by the Victor K.Mk 2s of Marham's No. 55 Squadron, while No. 10 Squadron and its VC10s, with No. 216 flying Lockheed TriStars, looked after some of the troop movements. Two VC10s accompanied the Jaguars to Thumrait and remained there on detachment, one crew flying a punishing 19-hour shift during the initial stages of deployment. Equipment (and personnel who drew short straws) went by Hercules of the Lyneham Transport Wing, the 100th Gulf-bound sortie of which was launched on 17 August.

Not all left from Lyneham; one Hercules collected a highly secret cargo from Boscombe Down on 12 August amid unprecedented security measures. Proximity to the Chemical Warfare Establishment at Porton Down was one speculative explanation. The civil fleet was also busy, and in the first few days after the invasion of Kuwait, two Boeing 707s left Manston packed with Tornado spares for BAe aircraft serving the RSAF.

At sea, the Royal Navy's Westland Lynx HAS.Mk 3 anti-submarine helicopters flew from the stern platforms of destroyer HMS *York*, and frigates HMS *Battleaxe* and HMS *Jupiter*, just as they had done during years of the Armilla Patrol in the Gulf. As a precaution against attack by Iraqi Mirage F1EQ-5s fitted with Aérospatiale AM39 Exocet anti-ship missiles, the Lynx carried a podded Whittaker AN/ALE-167(V) 'Yellow Veil' jamming pod on the port outer torpedo pylon.

Later arrivals included the tanker RFA *Olna* with two No. 825 Squadron Westland Sea King HAS.Mk 5s, replenishment ship RFA *Fort Grange* with two Sea King HC.Mk 4 transport helicopters and the Lynx-equipped survey ship, HMS *Herald*. Two Netherlands navy SH-14B Lynxes were aboard HrMs *Peter Floris*, which sailed for the Gulf in late August.

The French contribution was the carrier *Clemenceau*, which discarded its air defence and attack aircraft before departing Toulon on 13 August, and arrived at Djibouti with a primary armament of army Aérospatiale SA 342M Gazelle helicopters armed with Aérospatiale HOT anti-tank missiles and subsequently joined by a flight of Aérospatiale Puma assault helicopters.

On 15 September, France announced it would send a large force to Saudi Arabia. Air assets accompanying the ground troops included 48 helicopters and 30 tactical aircraft, the latter consisting of Mirage F1s, Mirage 2000s and Jaguars.

Above: A crew from No. 14 (Composite) Squadron pictured at RAF Brüggen before their departure for Bahrain. These aircraft gave the multi-national force in the area a formidable all-weather precision attack capability, particularly useful against Iraqi airfields.

Below: Saudi Arabia's Tornado IDS squadrons vacated Dhahran to make way for US and RAF interceptors, but the Hawk trainers remained, conducting normal advanced training sorties at the crowded base.

Military airfields involved in Operation Desert Shield and Granby

US, British and other international forces have deployed to the Gulf in unprecedented numbers, crowding into airfields in every friendly neighbouring country. A map of this type can only give a partial indication of the extent of the build-up of air power in the area, since it does not show the aircraft-carriers steaming in the Red Sea, the Persian Gulf and the Gulf of Oman, nor does it show Diego Garcia in the Indian Ocean, reportedly home to large numbers of B-52 bombers, or the various bases in Europe being used by transport aircraft committed to the airlift. In the event of hostilities, allied air commanders would face major targeting problems. The main bases used by the Iraqi air force are well known, but there are a plethora of other airfields which are occasionally used, or which could be used, by Iraqi fighters and fighter-bombers.

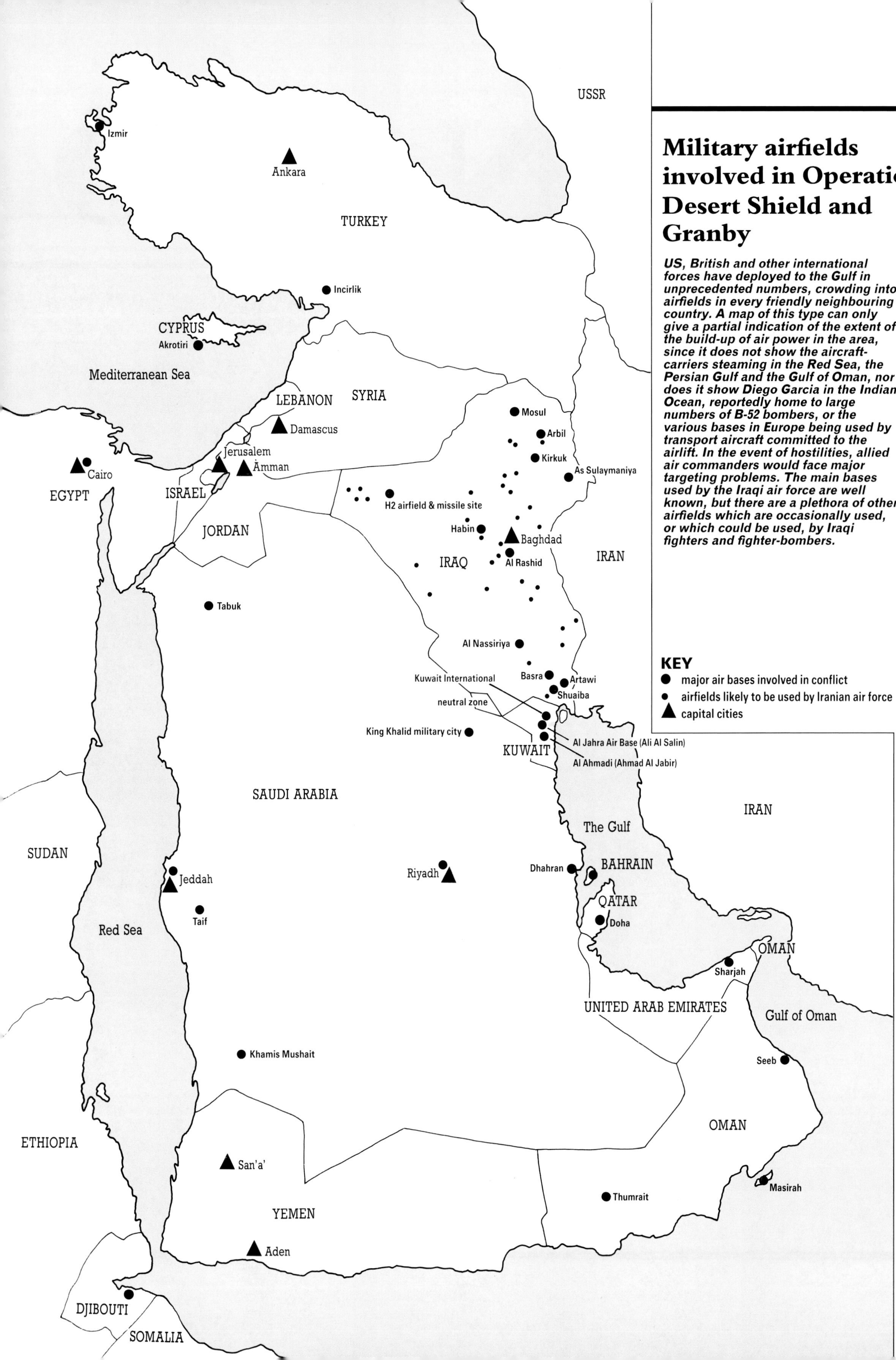

KEY

● major air bases involved in conflict

• airfields likely to be used by Iranian air force

▲ capital cities

Izmir

Ankara

TURKEY

Incirlik

CYPRUS

Akrotiri

Mediterranean Sea

LEBANON   SYRIA

Damascus

Jerusalem

Amman

Cairo

EGYPT

ISRAEL

JORDAN

Mosul

Arbil

Kirkuk

As Sulaymaniya

H2 airfield & missile site

Habin

Baghdad

IRAQ

Al Rashid

IRAN

Tabuk

Al Nassiriya

Kuwait International

Basra

Artawi

Shuaiba

neutral zone

King Khalid military city

KUWAIT

Al Jahra Air Base (Ali Al Salin)

Al Ahmadi (Ahmad Al Jabir)

SAUDI ARABIA

IRAN

The Gulf

Dhahran   BAHRAIN

Riyadh

QATAR

SUDAN

Jeddah

Doha

Taif

OMAN

Red Sea

Sharjah

UNITED ARAB EMIRATES

Gulf of Oman

Khamis Mushait

Seeb

OMAN

ETHIOPIA

San'a'

Masirah

Thumrait

YEMEN

DJIBOUTI

Aden

SOMALIA

Panavia TORNADO

Tornado has confounded the cynics who predicted that an aircraft designed to fulfil all roles would be master of none. Today it is the undisputed king among low-level, all-weather interdictors and strike aircraft, renowned for its ability to hit pinpoint targets with unerring accuracy. As a long-range bomber destroyer, the widely misunderstood Tornado F.Mk 3 is also becoming a great success, despite early radar problems.

Tornado in its element. Seemingly skimming the ground, a Tornado IDS practises the low-level terrain-following flight that enables it to operate in all weathers while evading most of an enemy's ground-based radar defences.

Available in other colours. Light grey medium-level camouflage denotes the ADV (Air Defence Variant) of Tornado. Emphasising the adaptability of Panavia's basic design, the ADV has a stretched fuselage, different radar and avionics, plus provision for eight air-to-air missiles in its specialist role of long-range, all-weather air defence of the United Kingdom and (illustrated) Saudi Arabia.

Panavia Tornado

Ground features to each side are but a blur as the Tornado races across the landscape at a mere 200ft, automatically adjusting its height to the undulating terrain and pulling up to avoid obstacles as insubstantial as high-tension wires. In wartime this is the safest place to be, but the trade-off is that incredibly accurate navigation is required to ensure a first-pass strike on the target. And if enemy fighters or SAMs do get a lock-on, it is highly desirable to have a comprehensive suite of warning and deception equipment to evade their unwelcome attentions.

Guarding the home base is another variant of the same aircraft, its radar capable of tracking and engaging several intruders at once, striking them down with missiles launched beyond visual range. Day, night, fair weather or foul, the Tornado is equally capable of performing the disparate roles of attacker or defender, its sophisticated avionics packed inside a fuselage shorter than that of an F-4 Phantom.

Conceived as a strike/attack aircraft for NATO, the Tornado now serves with distinction three of the Alliance's members and has achieved moderate export success. West Germany, Italy and the United Kingdom employ the aircraft as a major component of their air forces, having just completed the initial round of re-equipment envisaged at the start of the production programme. Unquestionably, the Tornado projected a lagging European combat aircraft design industry to the forefront of world military aviation, demonstrating with alacrity what could be achieved by enthusiastic service of a common objective. The path to that objective was far from smooth, and at times it appeared in danger of petering out altogether.

Even when the aircraft was up and running, some found it difficult to credit the remarkable compactness of a design incorporating the extremely accurate navigation equipment necessary to undertake an ultra-low penetration mission and then deposit a bomb with pinpoint accuracy at the first pass.

Such missions were, surely, what giant, strategic bombers attempted to achieve. Speaking in October 1984, US Under-Secretary of Defense, Richard DeLauer, put the American view: "I just don't think it's a good plane. The Tornado is the worst goddam thing for survivability there is."

Days later, when the results of that year's Strategic Air Command bombing competition were released, it became embarrassingly clear that RAF Tornados had thrashed mighty SAC by winning two of the three main trophies, and running-up for the other. Twelve months later, the Brits came back and achieved the same results with increased scores. In the interim (February 1985), the survivability accusation was addressed during a 'Green Flag' electronic warfare trial. Despite being permitted to descend to 'only' 100ft (30m) – higher than their pilots would have liked – RAF Tornados entirely avoided SAM 'kills' and only suffered a few hits by simulated ZSU-23/4 anti-aircraft cannon.

Left: Fitted with radar and cannon, P.06 (XX948, the third UK aircraft) flies through the Welsh mountainscape on an early test sortie to give an impression of operational usage. With its rear cockpit occupied by instrumentation, the aircraft undertook many of the early armament trials and is here seen with an underwing load of two 1500-litre tanks and two Marconi Sky Shadow ECM pods.

Genesis

What was initially known as the Multi-Role Combat Aircraft (MRCA) had its genesis in a January 1968 meeting of the air force chiefs of staff of Belgium, West Germany, Italy and the Netherlands with the aim of securing a replacement for the Lockheed F-104G Starfighter. They commissioned a Joint Working Group which began work on 3 March with Canada as an additional member, and the UK joined in July. The six governments agreed on 17 July 1968 to launch the conceptual phase of an MRCA programme, which lasted to 30 April 1969.

Canada was also a large-scale Starfighter user, leaving the UK as odd-man-out in the sextet. In this instance, the RAF's need resulted from a catalogue of disasters through the mid-part of the 1960s. There had been the NATO fiasco of the VTOL strike aircraft (NBMR-3) which led to cancellation of the Hawker P.1154; the axeing of the BAC TSR-2; and France's abandonment of a joint variable-geometry strike aircraft once it had got what it wanted by way of design leadership of the SEPECAT Jaguar programme.

Arguably, Britain was clutching at straws when it joined MRCA, but West Germany had also suffered disappointment when a similar venture with Republic in the USA collapsed during 1967 due to lack of American interest. By October 1968, MRCA requirements had been defined, although only with the cost-increasing compromise of having both single- and two-seat versions. Nevertheless, at this stage Belgium and Canada withdrew, leaving BAC (now in BAe), MBB, Fiat (now Aeritalia) and Fokker to refine the design and estimate the manufacturing requirements and work-sharing.

This done, the four companies formed Panavia Aircraft GmbH in Munich, West Germany, on 26 March 1969. Central to the eventual success of the MRCA, the four customers also established a single body to transmit their requirements to Panavia. This was NAMMA (NATO MRCA

Italy's first contribution to the prototype programme was P.05 (MMX586), which flew at Turin on 5 December 1975 with Pietro Trevisan in the front seat and monitoring equipment to the rear. P.05 was the last Tornado to wear red and white company colours, but it suffered a heavy landing in January 1976 and did not fly again for 18 months.

Management Agency, formed on 15 December 1968 as the Interim Management Organisation) and it occupied the same address at 26 Arabellastrasse. The common language was English, but the advantage thus gained by BAC representatives was offset by the adoption of metric units throughout for design.

Equally important in keeping the MRCA on cost and on target was the adoption of Memoranda of Understanding (MoUs), which described the goals to be achieved at regular intervals in the programme. As each phase was completed, NAMMA's member governments would sign the next MoU – a valuable means of preventing unilateral tinkering with the programme for domestic political ends.

Above: The German contribution. Lined up at the Manching flight-test centre are five of the six prototype and pre-series aircraft built by MBB. P.01 now wears the new serial number 9804, while P.04 (9805) displays its later, naval colour scheme. It was the first aircraft with the full avionics system, but was lost in an accident in April 1980. At the rear, P.11 (9801) and P.13 (9802) are to pre-series standard.

Above right: Refuelling trials were conducted with the Tornado as both receiver and tanker. Both the German navy and Italian air force required the latter capability, and between them ordered 73 Sargent Fletcher SFC 28-300 'buddy' refuelling pods for fitment on the centreline. The pod holds 1136 litres, but two 1500-litre tanks can be installed beneath the fuselage in its place. Two tanks and two Sky Shadow pods are under the wings.

Unfortunately, this did not prevent the Netherlands from leaving in July 1969, although thereafter the MRCA's development phase ran remarkably smoothly. After workshares were re-allocated on the departure of Fokker, the position was 42.5 per cent each for West Germany and the UK, and 15 per cent for Italy. As far as possible, there was to be no transfer of cash across borders, so the procurement of equipment items was equally proportioned.

By far the most important of these 'extras' were the two engines which would propel the MRCA at speeds above Mach 2. The Rolls-Royce RB.199 was selected in September 1969 against competition from Pratt & Whitney's TF30, and the international firm of Turbo Union Ltd was formed to undertake manufacture. Rolls and the West German MTU took 40 per cent each, and Fiat's engine division was the re-

maining partner. Likewise in the case of avionics, Avionics Systems Engineering GmbH was the single voice of the companies responsible for that equally vital component of a modern combat aircraft.

With skilled labour representing a significant proportion of aircraft costs, it was decided to open assembly lines in each member country, but to save on production jigging and other duplication by single-sourcing all components. Consequently, Britain built the aircraft's nose and tail; West Germany made all fuselage centre-sections; and Italy, all wings – basically, the parts that each had been responsible for designing. Normally high standards in aircraft engineering had to be raised still further in view of the dispersed manufacturing effort, with proof of this achievement being reflected in a diminution of the production test pilot's job satisfaction. Where once each aeroplane coming off an assembly line had its own individual foibles to be corrected before delivery, rigorous quality control ensures that every new Tornado flies almost exactly like the last, without need for trimming.

Seven roles

In their challenging specification, member air forces required the MRCA to be capable of performing seven basic roles, even though some of the operators would not require all of the options. These were:
1 Interdiction (i.e. deep penetration of enemy airspace)
2 Counter-air attacks (against enemy airfields)
3 Battlefield air interdiction
4 Close air support
5 Reconnaissance
6 Maritime strike/attack
7 Point interception

Although some new weapons *were* developed for the MRCA, the aircraft had to be compatible with a broad spectrum of existing ordnance used by the three prospective operators. In this connection, the air forces of West Germany and Italy – and, as far as practicable, the West German navy – have generally pooled their efforts, whereas the RAF has adopted some different weapons and protection aids. The development effort required of Panavia was considerable as a result of having to clear numerous items for carriage and release, but the outcome was that the aircraft has an unusually diverse armoury. Furthermore, this was done in the days before the digital databus made systems integration the comparatively simple job it is today.

Like its close parallels in the interdiction role, the General Dynamics F-111 and Sukhoi Su-24 'Fencer', the aircraft has variable-geometry wings. In the period during which all three were designed, VG was the optimum means of gaining the performance required, although if on the drawing board today the MRCA would almost certainly have fixed wings and more advanced aerodynamics to compensate.

is simply designated Tornado Nose Radar. In fact, this comprises two units: Ground Mapping Radar (GMR) for navigation and Terrain-Following Radar (TFR) to fly the aircraft over any obstruction detected ahead.

In the often forgotten areas of servicing and maintenance, the MRCA was intended to break new ground. The aircraft's surface is covered with 350 removable or hinged panels for ease of access, and most routine servicing can be accomplished by men standing on the ground. The status of vital systems and displays is shown on two boards under hinged panels which are monitored by ground crew as the aircraft is readied for flight. Many components are line-replaceable units, and it is thus an easy matter to remove a defective item of electrical equipment and insert a replacement without having to abort the sortie. The design goal was 0.5 of a fault per flying hour, and although the aircraft began by recording two faults per hour, the position has improved considerably during the first decade of service to one per hour.

Development of the MRCA was covered by an MoU of 22 July 1970 calling for, amongst other things, nine flying air-

Below left: An impressive picture of P.06 (XX948 – note instrumentation in the rear cockpit) firing its IWKA-Mauser 27-mm cannon in flight. The aircraft was the first to test the weapons in the air at both rates of fire (1,000 or 1,700 rounds per minute). Each of the two internally-mounted cannon weighs 102 kg (225 lb) and projects shells at an initial rate of 1030 m/sec (3,380 ft/sec) – or, more understandably, 3,700 km (2,304 miles) per hour, equivalent to Mach 3. Seven types of ammunition may be carried, according to the mission: practice (ball), high explosive (HE), HE incendiary, armour-piercing (AP), AP incendiary, AP HE, and AP HE incendiary.

Below: P.03's weapon trials, as seen from this unusual angle, included the MBB Kormoran anti-ship missile required by the West German navy and later ordered by Italy. Note that at maximum sweep, the wing pylons are fully normal to the airflow – unlike the General Dynamics F-111, on which only the inboard weapons are slewed to match wing movements.

With wings forward, the aircraft has good low-speed handling, allowing it to take off from short and/or damaged runways. Landing is simplified by one of the first reverse-thrust systems on a military jet aircraft. Panavia also incorporated the first fly-by-wire control system conceived for a production combat aircraft, but was beaten into squadron service by the General Dynamics F-16, which had a shorter development phase.

Difficult target

The comparatively small dimensions of the MRCA have already been mentioned; these make the aircraft a more difficult target to sight and hit. Furthermore, because size equals cost in combat aircraft design, Panavia was displaying attention to economy, not lack of foresight, by hanging extra fuel tanks and defensive aids beneath the wings. Unlike the F-111, all four wing pylons remain parallel to the fuselage as the wings are swept. A high wing loading is employed to reduce gust response and so give the best possible crew comfort during fast flying in the bumpy air close to the ground. At 500 ft (152 m) and Mach 0.9, the average crew of a Phantom will begin to suffer loss of efficiency after 1 hour 7 minutes of buffeting, whereas Panavia can offer 2 hours 55 minutes before the same stage is reached. Add to this a remarkably spacious, comfortable and quiet cockpit, and it can be seen how crew efficiency contributes to the Tornado's enviable record of precision in attack.

Terrain-following radar which allows the aircraft to fly at 200 ft (61 m) in complete darkness is the one critical component not developed in Europe. Texas Instruments, which was responsible for a family of similar equipment for the F-111 series, was contracted in October 1971 to produce what

Panavia Tornado

Liberally covered with datum marks, P.09 (MMX587) was used in Italy for weapon trials at Decimomannu following its first flight on 5 February 1977. Armament on this sortie includes AIM-9 Sidewinder AAMs on the inboard side of the inner wing pylons and eight 1,000-lb (454-kg) bombs below. What appears to be a Sky Shadow outboard is, in fact, a camera pod to film weapon releases from the wing and underfuselage positions.

Right: Release trials of a Kormoran anti-ship missile. The Mk 1 version initially used by Italy and the West German navy was first employed by the latter's Lockheed Starfighters. With a range of some 37 km (23 miles), the 'fire and forget' Kormoran 1 is programmed just before launch with the target's position, as determined by the Tornado's radar. An inertial navigation system takes the missile to the area of the target, where an active radar seeker takes over for positive acquisition and homing. The final run-in is made at wave-top height. Kormoran 2 has a smaller, solid-state seeker-head.

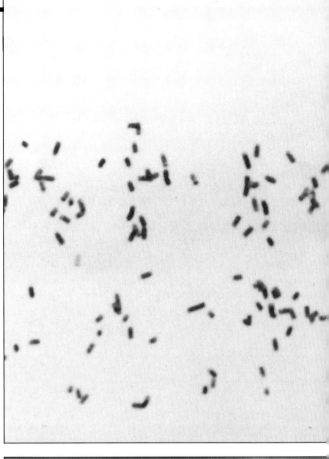

craft and a static test airframe. There was to be no single-seat aircraft, previously designated Panavia 100, as Italy had been convinced of the merits of the two-place Panavia 200 in spite of its tradition of pilot-only fighters. This was a sound move, for the sophistication being built into the aircraft demanded two men to operate it efficiently.

West German reduction

West Germany proposed the largest fleet, numbering 700 aircraft for its air force and navy, followed by Britain with 385 and Italy's 100. When it became apparent that some Starfighters would need replacement before the MRCA was available, the West Germans bought Phantoms instead, and the MRCA target dropped first to 420, then 324. By March 1973, when an MoU for six pre-series aircraft was signed, the programme had been mapped out in its final form: 805 production aircraft, plus four refurbished pre-series machines to satisfy the military requirement for 809.

Of 16 pre-production aircraft, P.01, 04, 07, 11, 13 and 16 were to be completed in West Germany; P.02, 03, 06, 08, 12 and 15 in the UK; and P.05, 09 and 14 in Italy, leaving P.10 as the static airframe in the test rig at Warton, UK. Rolled out at Manching on 8 April 1974, P.01/D-9591 first became airborne on 14 August, piloted by BAC's Paul Millet and with the West German Nils Meister in the back seat. In the following month, the MRCA was given the title of Tornado, under which name P.02/XX946 executed a maiden flight from Warton on 31 October. Four more Tornados flew in 1975, two in 1976, three in 1977, two in 1978 and two in 1979 to complete the trials batches.

These aircraft became increasingly more complex, starting with little more than a flying shell and progressing to the full production standard. P.01 concerned itself with handling and performance, while P.02's duties included flying with external stores. P.03/XX947 was the first with dual control, and P.04/D-9592 brought in full avionics. P.05/MMX586 flew on 5 December 1975 with its rear cockpit full of instruments, but a heavy landing during the following month put it out of the programme for 2½ years. The only aerodynamic changes seen on these early aircraft reflected the search for a more aerodynamic tailfin root fairing, the aircraft being in all other respects almost right from the start. A near-definitive fairing was applied to P.06/XX948, the duties of which included trials of the Mauser 27-mm cannon developed specifically for internal fitment on each side of the forward fuselage of production aircraft.

P.07/9806 majored in autopilot and terrain-following trials; P.08/XX950 was a second dual-control machine; and P.09/MMX587 was dedicated to weapons development. Two of the nine (P.08 and 04) were lost in accidents, the first of which did not occur until June 1979, when Tornados had accumulated 2,750 hours. In contrast to their predecessors, P.11 to P.16 were generally assigned to the military test centres of their respective countries, undertaking trials which would lead to squadron service. The first production-standard wing was fitted to P.14, and P.16 had the definitive forward fuselage design.

Production batches

Moves towards quantity manufacture gathered momentum in July 1976 when Batch 1 was authorised in the form of 23 RAF and 17 West German Tornados. Throughout Europe, 500 firms of various sizes began issuing components to the three production centres while major sections of aircraft were delivered by road from their sole sources. At Warton, the initial production Tornado, ZA319, flew on 10 July,

Above and top: MW-1, developed by MBB and Diehl, is used against airfields or concentrations of armoured vehicles with weapons ejected laterally from 224 apertures. Different strengths of charge ensure an even spread, while a mixture of up to five types of weapon is arranged according to the type of target. Bomblets are STABO for runway cratering; KB44 against tanks and armour; the MIFF passive mine; MUSA fragmentation charge; and MUSPA passive fragmenting mine.

Panavia Tornado

Above: Release trials of JP233 began at medium level, the operational method being a fast run at 200 ft (61 m), ejecting at one of two rates according to whether the aircraft is flying along or across the runway.

Right: In place of an MW-1, the RAF Tornado IDS carries two Hunting JP233 pods of 2335 kg (5,148 lb) each. Optimised for airfield attack only, a JP233 pod contains 30 SG357 26-kg (57-lb) concrete-cratering bombs and 215 HB876 2.5-kg (5½-lb) area-denial mines.

Far right: No. 27 Squadron RAF was the first combat unit in any air force to receive the Tornado. Flying with full 67-degree sweep, this pair is pictured shortly after delivery – as evidenced by carriage of two Sky Shadow pods and no BOZ-107 chaff/flare dispenser. Other early shortages included ammunition for the internal cannon.

with the first West German, 4301, following at Manching just seven days later. Italy did not plan to introduce the aircraft until slightly later than its partners, so its first Tornado was the 42nd interdictor, flown at Turin on 25 September 1981. RAF aircraft were designated Tornado GR.Mk 1 to indicate ground-attack and reconnaissance, and the other air forces merely used the name Tornado, although to Panavia the aircraft was the IDS (Interdictor/Strike) variant.

Batch 2, signed in May 1977, covered 110 (later amended to 113) aircraft; Batch 3, in June 1979, 164; Batch 4, in August 1981, 162 (including the RAF's first interceptors); Batch 5, in August 1982, 171; and Batch 6, January 1984, 155 to complete the initial requirement for 805. On 10 June 1986, Batch 7 was agreed for a further 124 Tornados, including exports, follow-on purchases and attrition replacements, while an eighth

production lot is under consideration, containing perhaps nearly 100 more aircraft if all options are exercised. If not, completion of Batch 7 in 1992 will mark the end of this highly successful venture.

Unlike many arms procurement programmes, the Tornado IDS deserves great credit for holding down costs. A politically-inspired 'cost scandal' blew up in West Germany during 1981, but Panavia was able to demonstrate that the price of the aircraft had increased by only 17.8 per cent, much of that because NAMMA had asked for refinements such as ECM to be added after the price was fixed. As further proof of prudent management, the 40 Batch 1 aircraft were delivered at a cost 7 per cent *less* than the maximum specified in the contract five years earlier.

Engine problems

There were more legitimate grumbles which, being technical, failed to interest the press and politicians. The RB.199 Mk 101 reheated turbofans consistently failed to achieve their overhaul targets and caused higher-than-anticipated aircraft unavailability and additional work for the engineers. Though officially claimed to be dry rated at over 40.0 kN (8,992 lb st), the engines were (and still are) limited to 38.7 kN (8,700 lb st) on combat squadrons – equivalent to 66.0 kN (14,837 lb st) with afterburning – and de-rated to only 37.0 kN (8,318 lb st) at the tri-national training unit, RAF Cottesmore. This last figure provides a cooler environment for the turbine discs and allows them to achieve a 400-hour life – short of the 600 planned, but an improvement on the early days, when blade replacement at 200 hours was not uncommon.

Beginning at Batch 4 (the 318th IDS and 761st engine) the change was made to RB.199 Mk 103s rated at 40.5 kN (9,104 lb st) dry and 71.5 kN (16,073 lb st) afterburning. With a new oil system possessing negative g provisions, reduced oil consumption and a number of mechanical features to im-

Panavia Tornado

prove reliability and maintainability, the Mk 103 has become the baseline RAF engine, in that 100 kits were purchased to convert earlier powerplants and allow RAF Germany to be thus equipped throughout. Again for reasons of service life conservation, the Mk 103 is down-rated to 38.5kN (8,655lb st) dry.

Undercarriages were another minor source of trouble in the early days and there were the inevitable problems with getting spares through the system. Several squadrons resorted to the policy of having a 'Christmas tree' from which parts were removed to keep other aircraft flying, but the supply situation rapidly improved after 1986. Overhaul intervals extended as experience accumulated, the 'major' or depot-level interval increasing from 900 to 1,200 to 1,600 hours, with 2,000 applicable to those aircraft which have undergone a Structural Improvements Programme (SIP). On October 1984, West German 4304 completed the first 900-hour major servicing (at Erding), the work lasting 10 months and including the addition of 150 modifications introduced since the aircraft had entered service. By 1989, all West German aircraft had received SIP modifications, and those of the RAF and Italian air force were well advanced. The SIP is a comprehensive rectification of shortcomings identified in the early stages of service which involves – in Britain's case – 3,355 RAF man-hours over 76 days, plus a similar contribution by British Aerospace.

For reasons previously explained, the Tornado IDS mounts most of its weaponry and defensive equipment externally on pylons. Three beneath the fuselage normally carry the offensive armament, but may also be fitted with fuel tanks (centreline or the two 'shoulder' positions – but not three at once). In the strike role, one nuclear weapon is fitted on the centreline: US-owned B61s in the case of West Germany and Italy; WE177s of up to 500 kilotons for the RAF. Eight 1,000-lb (454-kg) bombs can be fitted under the fuselage, although a more normal load would be four fitted with retarding systems for low-level delivery. The additional size of Paveway laser-guided weapons limits the total to three, each weighing 1,210lb (549kg).

Close air support

RAF Tornado GR.Mk 1s and West German navy aircraft may also carry Hunting Improved BL755 cluster bombs for close air support, although the aircraft is generally regarded as too valuable for such high-risk missions in the centre of a battlefield. More usual for the RAF would be an anti-airfield attack with a pair of giant Hunting JP233 pods under the fuselage. Weighing 5,148lb (2334kg), each pod contains 30 SG357 runway-cratering bomblets and 215 HB876 area-denial mines to disrupt repair parties. JP233 weapons are ejected from their container as the aircraft flies at about 575mph (927km/h) at 200ft (61m), two pre-set rates of

Two Turbo Union RB.199 reheated turbofans at full power launch a Tornado IDS for a night mission. To extend its overhaul life, the initial Mk 101 variant of the RB.199 is down-rated to 66.0 kN (14,837 lb st). Turbine discs are overhauled every 400 hours – twice the original rate, but still short of target.

spread accommodating passes down or across the runway. The empty pods are automatically dropped from the aircraft a few moments later. Flown under a Tornado (ZA354) for the first time on 23 February 1982, JP233 was issued to the RAF in April 1985.

In West Germany and Italy, the MBB MW-1 submunitions pannier performs the same role as JP233. MW-1/HZG-2 (for Hauptzielgruppe 2 – Main Target Group 2) is filled with bomblets optimised for airfield attack: StaBo cratering weapons, plus fragmentation, anti-vehicle and fragmentation munitions. However, MW-1/HZG-1 substitutes KB44 anti-armour weapons for StaBo and becomes a battlefield weapon. First tested on 19 June 1984 at Erprobungsstelle 91, Meppen, MW-1 completed its trials four months later. An initial 344 MW-1s were ordered on 31 August 1984, the first HZG-1s arriving with 31 Wing on 22 November. HZG-2 became operational in 1987. Italy

No. 617 Squadron bomber dispersal, 1980s style. From the outset, all operational RAF squadrons have flown daily from hardened aircraft shelters.

Tornado IDS weapons are mounted below the fuselage on up to three stores carrier rails. Six 1,000-lb (454-kg) bombs are seen here after release during a sharp pull-up (note wingtip vortices). Maximum load is eight, but four is more normal.

No. 14 Squadron RAF, based at Brüggen, West Germany, celebrated its 75th anniversary on 3 February 1990 and marked four Tornado GR.Mk 1s specially for the occasion. The squadron converted to Tornados from Jaguars in 1985 and is dedicated to NATO's 2nd Allied Tactical Air Force alongside seven other RAF Tornado units on the European continent.

⊙RAF UNIT GOOSE BAY⊙

ordered 100 MW-1s in October 1984, all but 10 of them HZG-2s. The two continental air forces also have obtained the Hughes Maverick precision–guided missile in the form of 'Scene Magnification' AGM-65Bs for West Germany, and 'Imaging Infra-Red' AGM-65Ds for both.

There is collaboration by the West German navy and the IAF's anti-shipping attack squadron, both having obtained MBB Kormoran 'fire and forget' missiles. West Germany's Marineflieger adapted Mk 1s taken from Starfighters and is now receiving Mk 2s, usual aircraft load being two. Against coastal landings, the West German navy plans to fit its Tornados with three BL755s, or five for short-range missions with external fuel tanks discarded. Stocks of 1,000-lb (454-kg) Mk 83 and 500-lb (227-kg) Mk 82 bombs are also held, the former available in retarded form as well as 'slick'.

For the future, both countries are looking at stand-off sub-munitions dispensers to reduce aircraft vulnerability, Italy having already begun trials in 1987 of the CASMU Skyshark system to complement its MW-1s. Initially a glide weapon carrying 1,642 lb (745 kg) over a range of 3.7-7.5 miles (6-12 km), it is intended to add power at a later stage, doubling its reach. The NATO programme for unified development of such weapons collapsed in disagreement during 1989, although it is clear that this is only a temporary setback and an alternative programme will emerge. How this leaves the RAF's Air Staff Requirement 1238 for an interim BL755 replacement is uncertain. Both original contenders have been replaced by newer challengers, and it is unlikely that a development contract can be placed before mid-1991. Also to be obtained on a longer time-scale is a stand-off nuclear weapon to replace WE177 in the RAF, as required by SR(A) 1244. A joint venture with France on a weapon to be known as ASLP was mooted, then dropped in favour of the American Boeing AGM-131 SRAM-T, but regained credibility by the end of 1989.

Defensive stores

With the exception of 330-gal (1500-litre) fuel tanks, underwing stores are of a defensive nature. All three NATO Tornado operators fit AIM-9L Sidewinders to the inside edge of the inboard pylons and will add an anti-radar weapon to the opposite side. This will be a Texas Instruments AGM-88A HARM on the Continent, and BAe ALARM on RAF aircraft.

The first HARM launch (after six dummy drops) was con-

Above: Following a mid-air collision between a German Alpha Jet and an RAF Tornado, enhanced visibility trials were conducted early in 1989 on a few RAF Germany aircraft. Nos 14 (illustrated), XV and 17 tested red fins, and Nos 2, IX and 31 tried white. Results were poor, so the aircraft reverted to standard.

Top left: Getting in close to a No. 14 Squadron (RAF) Tornado GR.Mk 1. The unit badge is applied to the forward fuselage, displacing the national roundel to the side of the air intake trunks. Note also the crash rescue instructions in both German and English – a common feature of RAF Germany aircraft.

Centre left: Evading USAF F-15 Eagle interceptors is but one task facing crews deployed to Nellis AFB for the realistic 'Red Flag' exercises. The Tornado has established a formidable reputation for itself.

Bottom left: With the exception of the winter months, RAF (here No. 14 Squadron) and West German Tornados are permanently resident at Goose Bay, Canada, for low-level flying practice. Aircraft from several units are pooled.

Panavia Tornado

ducted from P.13/9802 on 26 March 1987, and a further eight firings of unguided rounds took place before the following September to clear the weapon for release throughout the flight envelope. On 18 October 1989 MFG 2 aircraft 4529 flew at WTD 61 for the first time using ADA software to interlink with HARM, and then spent the first four months of 1990 at China Lake, California, conducting three firing trials to clear HARM for use.

ALARM made its first Tornado flight on 13 February 1985 when the unrepresentative total of nine dummy rounds began aerodynamic tests. Captive trials began in January 1986, but rocket motor faults delayed the first guided trial firing from a Tornado (at China Lake, California), until November 1988. Service acceptance tests are due to begin at the same location in 1990, conducted by the specially-formed No. 32 Joint Trials Unit. Outboard are an electronic jamming pod and a chaff and flare dispenser, the latter in all cases a Philips BOZ-100 series (BOZ-107 to starboard in the RAF, BOZ-101 to port in West Germany and BOZ-102 similarly in Italy). A Marconi Sky Shadow listens for and jams enemy

radars to protect RAF Tornados, while the West Germans and Italians rely on an AEG Cerberus II, which is being replaced by Cerberus Mk III and eventually Mk IV.

No fewer than three Tornado variants are tasked with reconnaissance of slightly different types. First of these to become operational, in 1988, were some German navy and Italian Tornados fitted with an 838-lb (380-kg) centreline pod developed jointly by MBB and Aeritalia and containing two Zeiss visual spectrum cameras and a Texas Instruments RS-710 infra-red linescan for all-weather photography.

The RAF, on the other hand, has a totally internal system which replaces the two Mauser cannon and warrants the amended designation of GR.Mk 1A. Beneath the forward fuselage is a small fairing protecting a semicircular window for Vinten 4000 horizon-to-horizon linescan. As this provides a distorted picture of objects close to the horizon, those areas are covered by side-facing infra-red looking through windows just ahead of the engine air intakes. Six video recorders complete the package.

This, Western Europe's first tactical reconnaissance aircraft not to carry traditional film, is entirely reliant on video

Left: The Trinational Tornado Training Establishment at RAF Cottesmore epitomises the international nature of the MRCA programme. Operating from an English base, still in the early Luftwaffe camouflage, this aircraft could be carrying an Italian instructor and a Marineflieger student. The code group 'G-38' denotes a German dual-control aircraft, as 'single-stick' IDS versions have numbers above 50.

Below: At high speed in full operational fit, a Luftwaffe IDS shows the standard 'lizard' overall camouflage adopted from 1983 onwards and the self-protection aids on outboard wing pylons: BOZ-101 chaff/flare dispenser port and AEG Cerberus jamming pod to starboard. Beneath is the MW-1 munitions ejector, which can be used for missions against airfields and concentrations of armoured vehicles. Alternative weapons include precision-guided missiles and US-supplied nuclear bombs – which may soon be withdrawn.

Right: West German navy test aircraft 9860 conducted early carriage trials of dummy Texas Instruments AGM-88A HARM high-speed anti-radiation missiles, including a non-standard load of four, with drop-tanks removed. Outboard wing pods are Cerberus IV jammers. The Luftwaffe has also ordered HARM.

Lower right: The first squadron of MFG 2 fits its Tornados with an MBB-Aeritalia reconnaissance pod, carried on the centreline pylon. This contains two Zeiss visual spectrum cameras, plus a Texas Instruments RS-710 infra-red linescan for use at night or in bad weather.

Tornado IDS – German Naval Aviation

Marinefliegergeschwader 2, based at Eggebeck, is part of a NATO force tasked with closing the Baltic approaches to hostile shipping. An operational weapons fit might include two MBB Kormoran anti-ship missiles beneath the fuselage and a pair of TI AGM-88A HARM anti-radiation weapons on the inboard wing pylons. The latter each support a Bodensee-built AIM-9L Sidewinder self-defence AAM on their inboard edges. A Philips BOZ-101 chaff/flare dispenser occupies the port outer position and an AEG Cerberus II jamming pod is on the opposite side. A Sargent Fletcher refuelling probe fits flush with the starboard side of the cockpit for tanking from a 'buddy' Tornado.

HARM

The sixth batch of Tornados incorporates a number of avionics upgrades, including a MIL-1553B databus, upgraded RWR equipment, active ECM, and provision for the Texas Instruments AGM-88A HARM anti-radar guided missile. HARM is used by MFG 2's second Staffel as an anti-ship weapon, in conjunction with the dedicated Kormoran. HARM has a range of up to 25 km, and its 66-kg HE fragmentation warhead is extremely powerful.

BOZ-100

The BOZ-100 chaff/flare dispenser is used by most German Tornados, including those operated by the two Marineflieger wings. RAF aircraft use the BOZ-107.

tape to record its information. During interpretation, up to 11 frames at a time can be held in a solid-state store that allows them to be magnified to reveal detail. The RAF contract covered 30 Mk 1As, comprising 16 conversions and 14 from new, Batch 7, production in 1989-90. The prototype, ZA401, first flew on 11 July 1985 and re-deliveries began on 3 April 1987, but development of the equipment was delayed, and by January 1990 only eight aircraft of 20 built had received it.

ECR version

Luftwaffe requirements for a dedicated reconnaissance aircraft have been met by the Tornado ECR – known in West Germany as the EKA (Elektronische Kampfführung und Aufklärung). Following approval by the West German parliament in May 1986, this version was ordered in the following month to the extent of 35 aircraft additional to the original requirement.

Improvements featured in Batch 6 Tornados, such as an MIL STD 1553B digital databus and 128K computer, are included in the ECR, but the most notable difference from previous aircraft is the incorporation of equipment for both reconnaissance and defence suppression ('Wild Weasel')

Radome
The radome is the responsibility of AEG-Telefunken, assisted by Aeritalia and BAe. It hinges to starboard to provide access to the antennas of the ground-mapping and terrain-following radars. A slice of the forward fuselage immediately aft of the radome also hinges to starboard to give access to the forward avionics bay and to the rear parts of the radar black boxes.

Inflight refuelling probe
The Tornado IDS can be fitted with a neat 'bolt-on' semi-retractable refuelling probe. This lies along the starboard side of the front cockpit when not in use. German navy Tornados use this in conjunction with a centreline buddy refuelling store.

Ejection seat
The crew sit in tandem on Martin Baker Mk 10A zero-zero ejection seats under the single-piece Kopperschmidt/AIT canopy, which is hinged at the rear and opens upward. In the event of an ejection, MDC buried in the canopy detonates to shatter the Perspex into tiny fragments.

Underwing pylons
The Tornado IDS has two pairs of underwing pylons, both of which swivel to remain aligned with the direction of flight when the wings sweep. The inboard pylons are plumbed for the carriage of jettisonable auxiliary fuel tanks, or can be wired to carry Kormoran missiles. A stub pylon carries an AIM-9 Sidewinder launch rail inboard.

Cerberus
Cerberus, named after the three-headed watchdog of Hades in Greek mythology, is a highly effective ECM jamming pod manufactured in two versions by AEG. The Elettronica EL/73 ECM pod is an alternative to Cerberus.

Outer wings
The variable-geometry outer wing panels are Italian-built, with Aeritalia having prime responsibility for final assembly and production, assisted by sub-contractors Aermacchi, Piaggio, SIAI-Marchetti, Saca and Aeronavali Venezia. Microtecnica of Italy is responsible for the wing sweep system.

Tailerons
The low-set all-moving horizontal tail surfaces move differentially to provide roll control, or in unison to provide pitch control. The wing spoilers are also used for roll control when the wings are not fully swept.

Above: P.16, the last pre-series aircraft, was re-worked in West Germany as the prototype Tornado ECR (Electronic Combat and Reconnaissance), taking to the air once more in a part-primer paint scheme on 18 August 1988. A second aircraft, 9878 (intended to have been production machine 4575), joined the programme two months later. West Germany is receiving 35.

Right: Initiating a fast climb from damp air close to the Adriatic Sea, an early Italian production Tornado of 6° Stormo is seen here in 'clean' configuration at 67 degrees of sweep. In addition to being a combat unit, 6 Wing also converted the two other squadrons that fly the aircraft in southern Europe. Italy received 99 production aircraft and may buy 16 more ECRs.

Above: Two Tornado IDS of No. 7 Squadron, RSAF, test the effectiveness of their desert camouflage against typical Saudi Arabian terrain. Aircraft 701 and dual-control 704 were among 18 originally laid down for the RAF and diverted to form the first RSAF Tornado squadron. After crew training, an initial batch of four aircraft was ferried from Warton to Dhahran on 26/27 March 1986.

Left: Even without the nose-code, the yellow lightning flash is sufficient to identify the 36° Stormo of the Aeronautica Militare Italiana, based at Gioia del Colle with one squadron of Tornados (156° Gruppo) and one of Starfighters (12° Gruppo). A small, white 'HS' logo at the base of the fin recalls Helmut Seidl, after whom the wing is named, whilst the 156th Squadron's wildcat badge appears on the engine air intake trunks. Second of Italy's three Tornado units, the 156th includes anti-shipping attack amongst its duties, for which its aircraft may be armed with MBB Kormoran 'fire and forget' missiles. Inflight refuelling probes and 'buddy' pods are available to extend the anti-ship mission range, while the first of a planned four Boeing KC-707 tankers completed conversion in 1990.

missions. In wingroot leading edges are the antennas for an emitter locator system to pinpoint the position of ground-based radar stations, while under the wings are at least two Texas Instruments AGM-88A HARM anti-radar missiles. Like the RAF's GR.Mk 1A, the ECR replaces cannon with an internal infra-red linescan reconnaissance unit, but it also has forward-looking infra-red in an undernose pod, an ODIN digital data link and advanced cockpit displays.

Flight testing

A prototype ECR, converted from pre-production Tornado P.16/9803, initially flew at Manching on 18 August 1988 and was joined by a second aircraft off the assembly line two months later. First of the 35 ordered in Batch 7 was 4623, which flew on 26 October 1989, powered by Mk 105 versions of RB.199 powerplants, delivering an extra 10 per cent of power. Mk 105 began flight testing in May 1987 and features

a type 62B fan with increased pressure ratio and single crystal intermediate and HP turbine blades. There is also a digital engine control unit for improved fuel economy, as fitted to Batch 6 aircraft still with Mk 103s. The prime armament, HARM, was test-launched by naval aircraft 4529 in a four-month programme at China Lake, California, between January and April 1990.

Britain's answer to the defence suppression requirement is to fit BAe ALARM anti-radar missiles to a designated 'path-finder' squadron, No. IX. Although all RAF Tornado GR.Mk 1s will eventually have the ability to carry a pair of ALARMs, the first 18 such capable aircraft began to arrive at the squadron's base in West Germany during 1989. They can fit up to nine ALARMs if Sidewinders and external tanks are relinquished. No. IX is also to receive a dozen Ferranti TIALD (Thermal Imaging Airborne Laser Designator) pods ordered in 1988 to satisfy Air Staff Requirement 1015. As a re-

Panavia Tornado

Right: Simplicity of maintenance was a vital aspect of the MRCA specification, with the result that the Tornado has been designed for ease of access and speed of fault diagnosis. The double-hinged IDS nose reveals components of the Texas Instruments radar – the principal non-European component – and its line-replacable units. Personnel are holding the ground-mapping radar antenna, but the smaller terrain-following unit is partly obscured by the airman on the right.

Right: The UK chose BĀe's ALARM anti-radar missile, which has been delayed until late 1990 by rocket motor problems. A typical 'Wild Weasel' weapons fit includes seven ALARMs, at the expense of two self-defence AIM-9Ls. All Tornado GR.Mk 4s will carry an ALARM on the outside edge of each inboard wing pylon opposite the AIM-9.

Below: No. 20 is one of two RAF squadrons armed, in part, with 1,380-lb (626-kg) Paveway laser-guided bombs, designation for which may come from Buccaneers detached from Lossiemouth to Laarbruch, West Germany. The Tornado cannot designate for its own bombs.

sult, the RAF Tornado force will no longer be dependent on ground sources or other types of aircraft to provide target designation for laser-guided bombs.

One further, 'non-existent' variant of Tornado remains to be mentioned: the so-called trainer. Although all the Tornado's original customers required dual-control aircraft to assist with converting new pilots, none was prepared to forego operational capability. The result was a hybrid aircraft in which the navigator's controls in the rear cockpit were rearranged to accommodate a control column and basic set of flying instruments for an instructor pilot. The instruments replace one of the two multi-function display screens, thus slightly reducing the navigator's efficiency, and the latter also has the hand-grip controller for video symbology moved from the centre of the cockpit to the right side. Naturally, foot pedals are added, as are throttles operated by the left hand. No special designation is given to the two-stick Tornado, except that Panavia uses production line numbers with a 'T' prefix – for example, BT050.

Colour scheme

RAF Tornado IDS aircraft wear a standard disruptive camouflage of dark green and dark sea grey overall, with low-visibility red and blue roundels and fin flashes. The disruptive camouflage extends to the undersides to give maximum protection even when manoeuvring hard at very low level. Aircraft based in RAF Germany wear bilingual rescue markings. A handful of Tornado GR.Mk 1s and GR.Mk 1As sent from RAF Germany to Bahrain following Iraq's invasion of Kuwait had a coat of desert pink applied overall, leaving only the radome unpainted. These wear toned-down pale blue and pink roundels.

Tail unit

This cantilever all-metal structure consists of a single, broad-chord sweptback twin-spar tailfin, with very low-set all-moving tailerons. The entire unit is the responsibility of BAe. The tailerons, like the rudder, are actuated by electrically controlled tandem hydraulic jacks, and operate in unison for pitch control, or differentially for roll control. The tailerons are augmented by differential deployment of the upper wing spoilers when the wings are not fully swept. Carbon fibre composite tailerons have been built and test-flown.

Wing glove box

Within this box, which is integral with the wing centre section, lie the pivot points for the outer wing panels. These are Teflon-plated bearings, with a titanium pivot pin. The wing root mates with this through titanium alloy attachment members. A so-called 'round rib' made from titanium alloy transmits normal aerodynamic forces to the wing box. The sweep actuators are hydraulically driven, and are of the ballscrew type. In the event of a wing sweep failure the aircraft can land safely with the wings in any position. Microtecnica (Italy) is the prime subcontractor for the wing sweep mechanism.

Powerplants

The Tornado IDS is powered by a pair of Turbo-Union R.B.199-34R Mk 101 (or Mk 103s from the 761st aircraft in May 1983) bypass turbofans mounted side by side in the rear fuselage. These produce more than 9,000 lb st in dry power, and more than 16,000 lb st with afterburner. The Mk 103 engine produces some 5 per cent more thrust than the Mk 101, and 100 modification kits have been ordered by the RAF to convert the engines of some early GR.Mk 1s to Mk 103 standard. These engines are particularly impressive performers at low level, but are less well suited to high speed at high altitude. Large doors in the underside of the rear fuselage allow easy access to the engines, simplifying servicing and engine changes. Each engine is fitted with an integral thrust reverser. These consist of large steel plates which swing down behind the jet pipes, deflecting the jet wash upwards and forwards. This gives remarkable deceleration, and unlike a brake chute does not need to be re-packed between sorties.

High lift devices

The entire trailing edge of each outer wing panel (apart from a small section at the tip) consists of a fixed-vane, double-slotted Fowler-type flap in four sections, with a Microtecnica actuation system. Three-section slats occupy the full span of the leading edge of each outer wing panel, with Krueger flaps on the fixed portion of the inner wing.

Tornado weapons

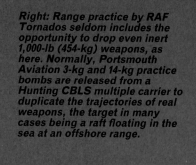

German-development Tornado 9802 launches an AGM-88 HARM anti-radiation missile during trials at China Lake. The HARM is carried by Luftwaffe, Marineflieger and AMI aircraft.

Right: Range practice by RAF Tornados seldom includes the opportunity to drop even inert 1,000-lb (454-kg) weapons, as here. Normally, Portsmouth Aviation 3-kg and 14-kg practice bombs are released from a Hunting CBLS multiple carrier to duplicate the trajectories of real weapons, the target in many cases being a raft floating in the sea at an offshore range.

Despite agreeing on a common specification for the MRCA, the three partner nations were unable to force the same policy upon weapons procurement, with the result that the Tornado IDS has been adapted to carry a remarkably broad range of armament. Key to a successful mission is, however, a highly accurate navigation system, permitting the aircraft to strike on target and on time with formidable precision. Minute adjustments on the run-in can be made by RAF Tornados, which are fitted with a laser rangefinder and marked target seeker.

In addition to the two internal 27-mm cannon on all but reconnaissance aircraft, standard weaponry includes the ubiquitous 1,000-lb (454-kg) bomb, which is usually parachute-retarded because of the low dropping height; this prevents 'skipping' and ensures a vertical fall. The CPU-23 Paveway laser-guidance system can be applied to 'slick' bombs for pinpoint accuracy, but the extra length and width reduces the under-fuselage load to just three. Only with forthcoming delivery of TIALD pods to one RAF squadron will the Tornado acquire self-designation capability. All three NATO countries have some nuclear-armed Tornados. West Germany and Italy have access

to US-owned B61 bombs, and the UK fits the WE177B weapon, but the last-mentioned, at least, is seeking stand-off capability.

Perhaps wastefully, the UK and West Germany developed their own underfuselage weapon dispensers. The RAF's JP233 is used only for anti-airfield attacks, whereas the German MW-1 (also bought by Italy) may be adapted for both this and anti-armour missions. Britain's Hunting Improved BL755 cluster bomb is the prime weapon used by the RAF against armoured vehicles. A stand-off replacement was commissioned, but abandoned in 1990, pending development of a European powered bomblet dispenser system.

Two anti-radiation missiles have been adopted: BAe ALARM in the UK and Texas Instruments AGM-88A HARM in West Germany and Italy. As a 'Wild Weasel', Tornado will be armed primarily with these weapons, but they may also be carried for self-protection, augmenting the two AIM-9L Sidewinder AAMs. Hughes AGM-65 Maverick precision missile is a West German/Italian option, while the RAF similarly plans to use the BAe Sea Eagle anti-ship missile when Tornados replace maritime strike/attack Buccaneers in the late 1990s.

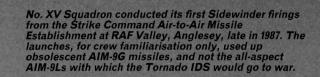

No. XV Squadron conducted its first Sidewinder firings from the Strike Command Air-to-Air Missile Establishment at RAF Valley, Anglesey, late in 1987. The launches, for crew familiarisation only, used up obsolescent AIM-9G missiles, and not the all-aspect AIM-9Ls with which the Tornado IDS would go to war.

Left: Providing protection against missiles is a 325-kg (717-lb) Philips BOZ pod: BOZ-101 for West Germany, -102 for Italy and -107 for the RAF. The 14 large holes eject flares to lure heat-seekers, while chaff needles are sown from the slot immediately behind the finned band to disrupt radar-homing weapons.

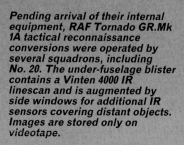

Pending arrival of their internal equipment, RAF Tornado GR.Mk 1A tactical reconnaissance conversions were operated by several squadrons, including No. 20. The under-fuselage blister contains a Vinten 4000 IR linescan and is augmented by side windows for additional IR sensors covering distant objects. Images are stored only on videotape.

Panavia Tornado GR.Mk 1A

No. 13 Squadron is the latest RAF unit to re-equip with the Tornado IDS. The unit's last existence was as a Canberra photo reconnaissance squadron, and it disbanded on 1 January 1982. Appropriately enough, No. 13 Squadron's number plate was chosen for the second Tornado recce unit when it formed at RAF Honington at the beginning of 1990. From the start, the Tornado has always been intended as a replacement for the Canberra and Jaguar in the tactical photographic reconnaissance role, although the re-equipment of tactical strike and interception squadrons was the first priority. A special sub-variant of the basic Tornado IDS has been developed by BAe to meet the RAF's reconnaissance needs in the 1990s and beyond, under the designation Tornado GR.Mk 1A. The new aircraft retains virtually full air-to-ground capability, albeit without the twin 27-mm Mauser cannon of the GR.Mk 1, which were deleted to make room for the reconnaissance equipment.

GR.Mk 1A development

A Tornado IDS, ZA402, served as the prototype GR.Mk 1A, and was converted at Warton during 1986. Fifteen more GR.Mk 1s were converted to GR.Mk 1A standard, one (ZA401) remaining at Warton for trials, and the rest being despatched to RAF Germany. These 14 aircraft received structural modifications only and initially lacked the side windows for the SLIR, although they did have the distinctive undernose fairing aft of the laser rangefinder. They were effectively strike Tornados without cannon, and were distributed through a number of RAF Germany squadrons, awaiting the fitting of their reconnaissance kit at No. 431 MU at RAF Brüggen. They were later allocated to No. II (AC) Squadron, a former Jaguar reconnaissance unit, which reformed on 1 January 1989 (reportedly one year later than had originally been planned). Initially No. II Squadron's Tornados lacked side windows, and there have been reports that the squadron was not able to start reconnaissance training until late in 1989. No. 13 Squadron has received new-build GR.Mk 1As.

Fuselage

The fuselage is an all-metal semi-monocoque structure built mainly in aluminium alloy in three main sections. The front fuselage, including both cockpits, and the rear fuselage, including engine installation, are the responsibility of BAe, while the centre fuselage, including the intakes and wing pivot mechanism, is the responsibility of MBB. The fuselage accounts for a considerable proportion of the total fuel capacity, housing multi-cell Uniroyal self-sealing integral tanks. These incorporate press-in fuel sampling and water drain plugs. Refuelling is from a single-point NATO connector. Pilot and navigator (known, perhaps more accurately, as a WSO in Germany and Italy) sit in tandem in separate cockpits, on Martin Baker Mk 10A zero-zero seats under the single piece Kopperschmidt/AIT canopy.

Engine intakes

Tornado's two-dimensional horizontal double-wedge intakes have hydraulically actuated variable inlet ramps. These are controlled by a fully automatic digital control system, which maintains them at the optimum setting for best engine performance under all flight conditions. The intakes incorporate a de-icing system made by AEG-Telefunken.

Head Up Display

The pilot's electronic Head Up Display (HUD) and weapons aiming computer was developed by Smiths Industries/Teldix/OMI and incorporates a Davall camera. It provides a multi-purpose display for a variety of weapon-aiming, delivery and navigation profiles.

Windscreen

The steeply-raked windscreen was built by Lucas Aerospace and comprises a flat centre panel with two curved side panels. All are armoured to meet the RAF's formidable birdstrike requirements. The entire windscreen incorporates Sierracote electrical conductive heating, which is effective for both demisting and anti-icing. In front of the windscreen, rain dispersal ducts bleed hot pressurised air from the air conditioning system, which keeps the screen free of rain, ice or snow. The entire windscreen hinges forward to allow easy access to the Head Up Display and to the back of the pilot's instrument panel.

No. 13 Squadron history

No. 13 Squadron has a long and distinguished reconnaissance tradition. Formed at Gosport on 10 January 1915, No. 13 served in the bomber role during the World War I, then switched to Army co-operation duties when it reformed in 1924. During the World War II the squadron flew Westland Lysanders before converting to Bristol Blenheims in the intruder role. These were replaced by Martin Baltimores and then Douglas Bostons. In 1946 No. 13 Squadron reformed at Ein Shemer, Palestine, as a Mosquito photographic reconnaissance unit. The squadron moved around the Middle and Near East for the next 32 years, receiving Meteor PR.Mk 10s in December 1951 and Canberra PR.Mk 7s in 1956. The squadron returned to RAF Wyton in October 1978, and finally disbanded on 1 January 1982. Exactly eight years later, on 1 January 1990, the squadron officially reformed at RAF Honington, having received its first aircraft by mid-October 1989. On 10 January 1990, No. 13 Squadron's 75th birthday, it held its reformation parade in one of Honington's hangars.

Aerial

A small blade antenna under the nose serves the Marconi Avionics AD2770 TACAN, which gives range and bearing from any TACAN ground station or suitably equipped aircraft.

Underfuselage pylons

Long weapons pylons are fitted to the 'shoulders' of the lower fuselage. These can carry a wide range of stores, including JP233 airfield denial dispenser weapons, Kormoran or Sea Eagle anti-shipping missiles or up to four 1,000-lb bombs or CBUs. They are plumbed for the carriage of fuel tanks and would also be the most likely location for nuclear weapons. No. 13 Squadron has a secondary attack role, with the most likely weapon being the BL755 cluster bomb.

Reconnaissance equipment

Interestingly, the Tornado GR.Mk 1A carries no conventional optical cameras, relying instead on advanced electro-optical sensors, which promise better all-weather performance and simpler interpretation, since they eliminate the need for time-consuming and costly wet film processing and print-making. The primary sensors carried by the new aircraft are a BAe sideways-looking infra-red (SLIR) system and a BAe Linescan 4000 infra-red surveillance system, the sensors together giving the option of full cross-track horizon-to-horizon coverage. Images gathered are processed and recorded on video film and can be replayed in flight, with the navigator able to designate areas of interest for magnification. In future, images could be transmitted to a ground station in real time, over a secure digital data link. New interpretation techniques and equipment have been developed for the new equipment, and the old style RICs (Reconnaissance Interpretation Centres), with their rapid film processing equipment, have been withdrawn from the front line, except with the Harriers of No. 1417 Flight in Belize, and the Jaguars of Coltishall-based No. 41 Squadron. The Canberras of No. 1 PRU are the only other users of optical cameras in the reconnaissance role in the RAF.

Laser rangefinder

Use of a laser is an excellent method of determining target distance, and also allows a properly-equipped aircraft to 'home' onto reflected energy from a target designated by friendly ground forces, a helicopter-borne FAC, or a designator-equipped aircraft. A Ferranti Laser Rangefinder and Marked Target Seeker is housed in an undernose fairing offset to starboard under the forward fuselage. This equipment suffered from early problems, and for a short time some aircraft were flying with empty fairings. It is understood that LRMTS deliveries are now satisfactory.

Radar

Underneath the radar-transparent AEG-Telefunken radome lies the Texas Instruments multi-mode, forward-looking terrain-following and ground-mapping radar. This is effectively not one but two radars, with two separate antennas mounted one above the other. The larger upper antenna serves the ground mapping/attack radar, while the smaller antenna below serves the terrain-following function. The most important purposes of the ground-mapping radar are to identify the IP and to update the inertial navigation system by identifying and locating radar offsets on the IP-to-target run. These can normally be fixed using the radar for only a very short time, giving enemy radar warning receivers less chance of picking up the incoming bomber. The terrain-following radar scans about the aircraft centreline, 'nodding' above and below the aircraft flightpath and generating an imaginary ski-toe shape ahead of the aircraft. When terrain 'penetrates' this shape an automatic pull-up command is given by the TFR computer. The ski-toe shape, superimposed on a cross-sectional view of the terrain ahead, is displayed on the pilot's E-scope, allowing him to continuously monitor the TFR equipment. The equipment allows fully automatic, 'hands-off' terrain-following flight at very low altitudes.

Tornado ADV

This cutaway drawing depicts one of the three Tornado ADV prototypes, with Foxhunter radar fitted (they initially flew with ballast), a test camera in the fin, camera pods under the outer wings, and F.Mk 2 style 330-Imp gal tanks and single Sidewinder pylons. The aircraft is also fitted with RB.199 Mk 103 engines, with short reheat pipes.

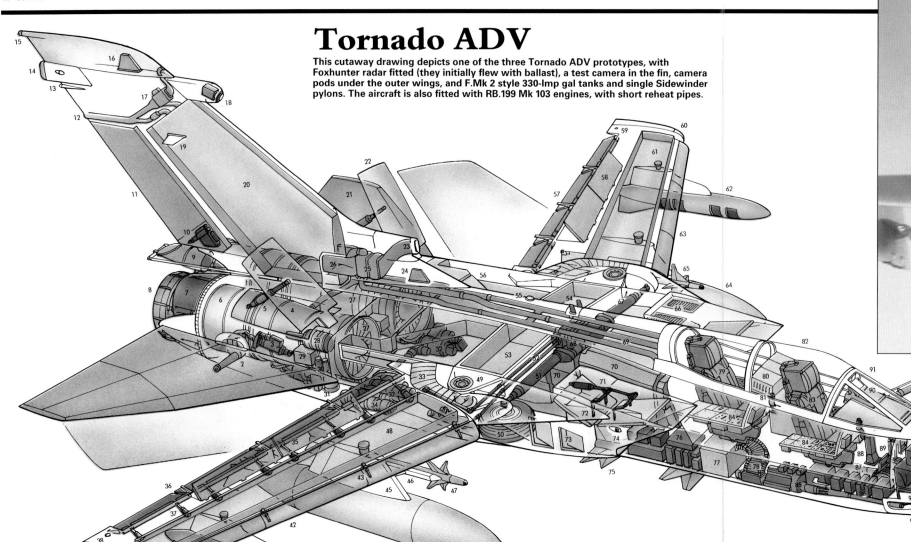

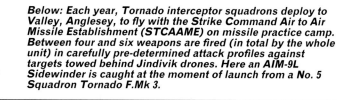

The Tornado F.Mk 3 is powered by a pair of Turbo-Union RB.199-34R Mk 104 turbofans. These are essentially similar to the engines that power the Tornado IDS, but have extended afterburner nozzles which increase thrust and reduce drag. Like the bomber version, the Tornado ADV is extremely fast at low level, where an indicated airspeed of 800 knots is possible. Unfortunately, many aircrew feel that the Tornado ADV remains underpowered at altitude, where burner is frequently needed for adequate manoeuvrability.

Below: Each year, Tornado interceptor squadrons deploy to Valley, Anglesey, to fly with the Strike Command Air to Air Missile Establishment (STCAAME) on missile practice camp. Between four and six weapons are fired (in total by the whole unit) in carefully pre-determined attack profiles against targets towed behind Jindivik drones. Here an AIM-9L Sidewinder is caught at the moment of launch from a No. 5 Squadron Tornado F.Mk 3.

1 Starboard all-moving tailplane	27 Turbo Union RB.199 Mk 103 afterburning turbofan engine	51 Wing sweep actuating screw jack	76 Weapons system avionics equipment
2 Tailplane pivot point	28 Hydraulic reservoir	52 Flap and slat drive shafts	77 Ammunition magazine
3 Tailplane hydraulic actuator	29 Tailplane automatic flight control system equipment	53 Wing pivot box integral fuel tank	78 Ammunition feed chute
4 Starboard airbrake	30 Hydraulic filters	54 UHF homing aerials	79 Tactical Navigator's Martin-Baker Mk 10 'zero-zero' ejection seat
5 Airbrake hydraulic jack	31 Engine fuel system equipment	55 Anti-collision light	80 Tactical Navigator's instrument console
6 Engine afterburner duct	32 Engine-driven auxiliary equipment gearbox, port and starboard	56 Rear fuselage fuel tanks	81 Radar hand controller
7 Thrust reverser bucket door	33 Wing glove flexible sealing plates	57 Port double-slotted flap	82 Cockpit canopy cover, upward hingeing
8 Variable area afterburner nozzle	34 Auxiliary power unit (APU)	58 Spoiler panels	83 Pilot's Martin-Baker Mk 10 ejection seat
9 Spin recovery parachute	35 Starboard spoiler panels	59 Formation light	84 Side console panels
10 Rudder hydraulic actuator	36 Double-slotted flap	60 Obstruction strobe light	85 Mauser M. 27 cannon
11 Rudder	37 Flap screw jacks and drive shaft	61 Port wing integral fuel tank	86 Avionics equipment racks
12 Fuel vent	38 Formation light, above and below	62 Recording camera pod	87 Nose undercarriage, stowed position
13 Tail obstruction light	39 Wing tip obstruction strobe light	63 Port leading-edge slats	88 Control column
14 Rear passive ECM antenna fairing	40 Recording camera pod	64 Port external fuel tank	89 Rudder pedals
15 Tail radar warning antenna	41 Outboard swivelling pylon	65 AIM-9 Sidewinder air-to-air missile	90 Pilot's head-up display
16 VHF aerial	42 Leading-edge slat	66 Intake by-pass air bleed louvres	91 Windscreen panel hinged for instrument access
17 Fuel jettison valves	43 Slat drive shaft and screw jack	67 Port wing screw jack	92 Retractable flight-refuelling probe
18 Recording camera	44 330-Imp gal external fuel tank	68 Wing sweep system, flap and slat drive motor and gearboxes	93 Nose avionics equipment racks
19 ILS glideslope and localiser aerial	45 Inboard swivelling pylon	69 Air system ducting	94 Cannon muzzle aperture
20 Fin fuel tank	46 Pylon-mounted missile launch rail	70 Forward fuselage fuel tanks	95 Lower IFF aerial
21 Port all-moving tailplane	47 AIM-9 Sidewinder air-to-air missile	71 Intake ramp hydraulic actuator and linkage	96 Foxhunter radar equipment package
22 Port airbrake	48 Wing integral fuel tank	72 Variable area intake ramp doors	97 Upper IFF aerial
23 Heat exchanger air intake	49 Wing pivot bearing	73 Intake suction relief doors	98 Cassegrain radar antenna
24 HF aerial	50 Mainwheel, stowed position	74 Starboard navigation light	99 Radome
25 Primary heat exchanger		75 BAe Sky Flash air-to-air missile (4) in semi-recessed housing	100 Pitot head
26 Heat exchanger exhaust duct			

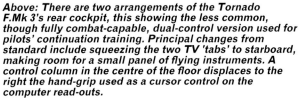

Above: There are two arrangements of the Tornado F.Mk 3's rear cockpit, this showing the less common, though fully combat-capable, dual-control version used for pilots' continuation training. Principal changes from standard include squeezing the two TV 'tabs' to starboard, making room for a small panel of flying instruments. A control column in the centre of the floor displaces to the right the hand-grip used as a cursor control on the computer read-outs.

British interceptor

Although interception capability was included in the list of requirements for the MRCA, no air force contemplates using the Tornado IDS for limited point defence. Only the UK elected to develop an Air Defence Variant (ADV) optimised for air combat – and even then, 'combat' was to be in its most impersonal form. Whereas NATO air forces on the Continent have consistently required fast, agile interceptors to deal with the threat of opposing fighters over a central European battlefield, island Britain has needed to plan for a different air battle. The prime danger was seen as coming from long-range Soviet bombers launching cruise missiles, the answer to which would be a long-range interceptor able to track and engage multiple targets in all weathers. Though given a gun, the new aircraft was envisaged as shooting down intruders with air-to-air missiles (AAMs) while they were still out of visual range.

In the days of the V-Bomber deterrent, the now-disbanded Fighter Command had concentrated its fighters and radars along the East Coast to provide point defence of the crucial strategic air bases. With deterrence a submarine responsibility after 1969, and in the knowledge that 40 per cent of NATO's air power would concentrate in the UK during a European conflict, the RAF Strike Command adopted a new policy of all-round, far-reaching air defence. For this, it needed 'long-legged' interceptors, tankers to take the fighters even further, AEW aircraft to watch the Iceland-Faroes-UK gap and ground radars on the western coast. The central component was to be the Tornado ADV.

During 1976 it was announced that 165 of the 385 Tornados required by the RAF would be of the ADV version, having 80 per cent airframe commonality with the IDS. One of the main changes was a 4 ft 5½ in (1.36 m) longer fuselage,

partly resulting from a more pointed radome, but mainly due to an extra bay added forward of the wings. With its new length, the aircraft could accommodate four BAe Sky Flash radar-guided AAMs under the fuselage (the front pair semi-recessed). Two, and later four, AIM-9L Sidewinders were to be attached to the sides of the inboard wing pylons, although the outer hardpoints were not used.

Three prototype Tornado ADVs were retrospectively added to Batch 1, of which the first (ZA254) flew at Warton on 27 October 1979, piloted by David Eagles, and with Roy Kenward in the back seat. Fitted with dummy Sky Flashes from the outset, the aircraft made a favourable impression by exceeding Mach 1 on its maiden sortie and achieving 8¼ flying hours within a week, including an airborne refuelling and a night landing. Early tests showed that supersonic acceleration was better than the IDS because of the fuselage's improved fineness ratio, but that the more forward centre of gravity demanded extra elevator angle at lift-off.

ZA267 joined the programme on 18 July 1989, introducing a main computer and associated cockpit TV displays into the trials programme. Assigned to weapons development, '267 was a dual-control Tornado. Finally, on 18 November 1980, ZA283 took to the air in an overall light grey air defence colour scheme and with a radome, although its radar trials did not begin until June 1981.

Assisted by earlier trials of IDS Tornados, ZA254 had by mid-1980 been able to demonstrate an IAS of 800 knots (1480 km/h) at 2,000 ft (610 m). This was of significance, in that most other modern combat aircraft are restricted by structural considerations to 700-750 knots (1297-1390 km/h) at such heights, so giving the ADV a useful margin of speed over its quarry. Early in 1982, the same aircraft demonstrated a further important aspect of its specification (ASR 395) when it convincingly flew a simulated CAP sortie involving a 2 hour 20 minute loiter at a distance of 375 miles (604 km) from base. The feat was achieved with a pair of 330-gal (1500-litre) tanks as used on the IDS, and not the 495-gal (2250-litre) drop-tanks with which the definitive interceptor Tornado is fitted. West German and Italian Tornados are unable to emulate the feat for two reasons: RAF IDS and ADV aircraft have an extra fuel tank inside the fin holding 121 Imp gal (551 litres), and the additional fuselage length of the ADV

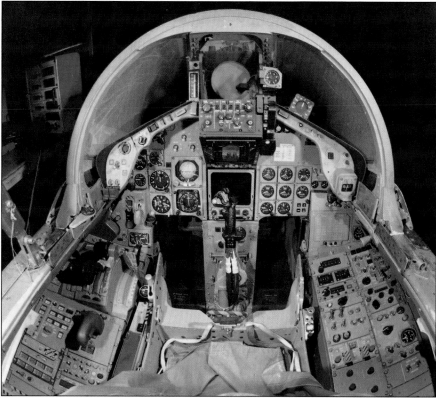

Above: The Tornado ADV's instrumentation was some of the last to be designed before the change to 'glass cockpit' technology, using multi-function TV screens. A HUD displays all vital flight and target engagement parameters, while the head-down screen can repeat radar and navigation displays from the rear cockpit. Controls on the left side-panel include throttles, flanked by wing sweep selector and flap/slat lever.

enables it to be fitted with an internal tank holding 165 Imp gal (750 litres). Internal capacity of the West German and Italian aircraft is 1,340 gallons (6092 litres).

Turbofan engines are fuel-efficient at low level, but the trade-off is that at medium heights and above their thrust output is reduced in comparison with a turbojet. The ADV is therefore at a disadvantage to many potential opponents when pursuing at anything other than minimal heights. Similarly, if forced into air combat – for which it was not designed – the aircraft would be outclassed by opponents optimised for such a role. Off the coast of Iceland, such a possibility seemed remote until the advent of the Sukhoi Su-27 'Flanker', which combines long-range bomber-escort capability with agility and power.

Realising that the aircraft might have to 'mix it' with highly capable opponents, the RAF commissioned a twin-dome combat simulator which became operational at the main ADV base of Coningsby on 4 December 1987. For the future, BAe has developed a new control column grip containing all the switches necessary for close combat and GEC is designing, as a private venture, a modification to optimise the radar for that regime.

Fighter Tornados have the same wing sweep range of between 25 and 67 degrees as their bomber compatriots, except

that later production aircraft introduced automatic sweep selection to suit flight conditions – this facility to be retrofitted in the software of earlier machines. Because of the more-forward centre of gravity, the 'nibs' (inboard, non-moving leading edges) of the wings have their sweep increased from 60 to 67 degrees. Additionally, they include the forward antennas for a Marconi radar warning receiver, the rear component of which is mounted on the tailfin trailing edge. In contrast to the 'clip-on' refuelling probe on the starboard side of the IDS's forward fuselage, the ADV has a fully-retractable unit on the port.

Radar problems

There were differences, too, between early-production fighter Tornados. An initial 18 aircraft, designated F.Mk 2, were from Batch 4 and fitted with RB.199 Mk 103 engines. The first of these, ZD900, flew on 5 March 1984 and the aircraft were used for trials and training until the later F.Mk 3 became available. They were then placed in storage. First flight of a Mk 3 was made on 20 November 1985 by ZE154, externally recognisable by having a straight continuation of the rudder's trailing edge down to the engine jetpipes, instead of the cutaway fairing of the IDS. Engines themselves are 14 in (36 cm) longer to accommodate an extra afterburner section, so that this, the Mk 104, delivers 2kN (450lb) more thrust despite being slightly more fuel-efficient than the Mk 103.

Other changes include a second Ferranti FIN1010 inertial navigation system for increased accuracy, as the ADV does not have the same opportunity for confirmatory radar fixes as its companion IDS. A Spin Prevention and Incidence Limitation System allows 'carefree handling' when manoeuvring at high angles of incidence, while an Automatic Manoeuvre Device System reduces buffet by deploying flaps and/or slats according to wing sweep, speed and attitude. F.Mk 2s were never flown with tanks by the RAF and their Sidewinder capacity was limited to two. It is intended that the Mk 2s will eventually be brought to F.Mk 2A standard by incorporating all the Mk 3's features except the uprated engines. In both versions, there is a single Mauser 27-mm cannon in the starboard side of the forward fuselage.

Delays in development and production of the GEC Avionics (Marconi) AI.Mk 24 Foxhunter pulse-Doppler radar resulted in the Tornado ADV gaining IOC much later than planned. Following trials in a Canberra and Buccaneer, Foxhunter first became airborne in a Tornado on 17 June 1981, almost a year after the target date. The third prototype, ZA283, was the test aircraft and by March 1983 was on to its third version of the radar, known as 'B' Series. Production F.Mk 2s were due to begin rolling off the line with Foxhunter that year, although it was not until July 1983 that the first of 20 pre-production radars was received. As a result, Tornado deliveries to the RAF began on 5 November 1984 with lead ballast in their noses, and not until mid-1985 did aircraft begin leaving Warton in a complete state.

Acceptance of Foxhunter did not imply complete RAF satisfaction with the equipment. Early radars were delivered below specification, partly as a result of the RAF demanding greater capability after the development contract had been agreed. No tail-chase programming was initially requested, and this had to be added later. Principal shortcomings were large sidelobes increasing vulnerability to jamming and substandard multi-target tracking capability – the specification apparently calling for 20 aircraft to be tracked while continuing to scan. A three-year programme of improvement was initiated with the intention of having all Tornado ADV radars up to the required standard by the early 1990s.

The original allocation of radars was Foxhunter Type W (70 built) in 62 Block 8-10 aircraft and Type Z (80 built) in 80 from Blocks 11-12. The final 76 sets (comprising 50 for 46 RAF aircraft and 26 for 24 Saudis) have been fitted in Block 13-15 aircraft from early 1989 onwards. Type Z radars meet the original ASR 395 specification before the RAF asked for additional capabilities, so to obtain this minimal performance, all but 26 Ws have been upgraded to Zs, beginning in 1988. Type Z includes improved range and tracking, whilst the new Stage 1 standard, though having better cooling, relies mainly on revised software to give improved ECCM and close-combat capability. Manufacture of Stage 1 radars began in September 1988, and their software is also being installed in 124 Type Zs (including those modified from Type W). Finally, modification kits will be delivered in 1991 to upgrade Type Z Foxhunters to Stage 2, with the addition of a new processor giving automatic target acquisition and tracking and discrimination between head-on targets by analysis of the radar signature of their first and second stage compressor blades.

JTIDS installation

Similarly delayed is the installation of JTIDS (Joint Tactical Information Distribution System) to provide the crew of an aircraft with up-to-the-minute information on the air battle and allow them to relay information on weapon states and targets located back to their tactical HQ. After being held back on the production line for 10 months, the second F.Mk 3, ZE155, flew on 16 October 1986 with a JTIDS terminal installed and spent part of the next year at Yuma, Arizona, on trials. No further aircraft have been modified and a proposed introduction date has not been announced as the result of programme delays.

Bottom: Slightly modified from its original condition of the previous year, ADV prototype ZA254 was demonstrated in public for the first time at the 1980 Farnborough air show. Shortly before its debut, the aircraft had proved its stability at low level by flying at an indicated airspeed of 800 knots (921 mph/1483 km/h).

Below: No. 23 Squadron formed as Leeming's second Tornado unit in 1988, led by Wing Commander Neil Taylor. Operational since 1 August 1989, No. 23 is one of five units assigned to protection of the northern half of the UK Air Defence Region. Long-range interception sorties are regularly supported by VC10 tankers of No. 101 Squadron, based at Brize Norton.

Panavia Tornado

Cannon
The Tornado F.Mk 3 and ADV are armed with a single 27-mm IWKA-Mauser 27-mm revolver cannon in the starboard lower fuselage. The capacity of the magazine is unknown. The second cannon of the IDS is not fitted, the space saved being used to house avionics items rendered 'homeless' by the built-in fully retractable refuelling probe.

Long-range armament
For beyond visual-range engagements, the Tornado ADV relies on the BAe Dynamics Sky Flash semi-active radar homing missile. Four of these are carried in tandem semi-recessed pairs under the fuselage. Frazer Nash ejector release units allow them to be fired over the entire flight envelope. Sky Flash is to be replaced eventually by the new AIM-120 AMRAAM, a fire-and-forget missile employing inertial and active radar guidance.

Radar
The Tornado ADV is equipped with a GEC Avionics AI-24 Foxhunter airborne intercept radar. Early problems with this radar have now been mostly solved, although RAF aircraft presently have a variety of radar standards. The radar operates in the I-band using a pulse-Doppler technique known as frequency modulated interrupted continuous wave. The advanced cassegrain antenna gives good performance even in a high-clutter or jamming environment, and the hydraulic servos that drive it give precise and stable beam pointing even under heavy g.

Auto wing sweep
The Tornado ADV is fitted with automatic wing sweep, with four pre-programmed settings. 25 is fully forward, used for speeds of up to Mach 0.73; 45° is for speeds of up to Mach 0.88; 58° is set at speeds of up to Mach 0.95, and 67° (fully aft) is used for higher speeds.

ROYAL SAUDI AIR FORCE

القوات الجوية الملكية السعودية

Wing Commander David Hamilton leads No. 11 Squadron from the front of his Tornado F.Mk 3, decorated with a black tailfin and the appropriate code letters 'DH'. His aircraft was the first Tornado ADV to receive non-standard markings, late in 1988. No. 11 is based at Leeming maintains a commitment to maritime air defence off the shores of Britain.

Mid-life update

The NATO Tornado operators are now looking towards a mid-life update (MLU) of their IDS aircraft. West Germany and Italy are still defining the new equipment required, but the RAF has already launched its programme, signing the contract on 16 March 1989. Britain had plans to order 26 more IDS Tornados in Batch 8, these being the first to the new GR.Mk 4 standard, but the order was abandoned in June 1990. From 1992 onwards it is planned to upgrade 165 early- and mid-production GR.Mk 1s to Mk 4, each aircraft taking 10 months, but with 20 at a time receiving attention. The first 70 are to be modified by BAe at Warton, followed by 15 more in a joint BAe/RAF project at operating bases and the final 80 by a contractor to be selected by tender. Batch 7 aircraft are not included.

In order that terrain-following radar need not be used (so eliminating tell-tale emissions which can alert the defence) the Mk 4 will have a GEC SPARTAN terrain-referenced/terrain-following navigation system in conjunction with pilot's night vision goggles and a forward-looking GEC TICM II infra-red sensor in an underfuselage pod on the opposite side of the nosewheel to the existing Marconi LRMTS (Laser Ranger and Marked Target Seeker). With TF radar redundant, it has been proposed that the original ground mapping radar should also be removed and replaced by Ferranti Blue Vixen (as in the Sea Harrier FRS.Mk 2) as it has broader capabilities, including compatibility with Sea Eagle anti-ship missiles.

Ferranti is to provide a new wide-angle HUD for the GR.Mk 4 and Smiths Industries has been contracted to supply a multi-purpose screen for a head-down display. This will be the first such aid for the pilot, whose instrumentation is just one generation behind the 'glass cockpits' of recent combat aircraft. There is to be a new ECM suite which will almost certainly be the Marconi ZEUS installed in the Harrier GR.Mk 5/7. Other changes slated for the MLU are Mk 103B versions of the RB.199 engine for a 12 per cent operating cost reduction, digital powered flying controls, 592-gal (2691-litre) underwing fuel tanks, provision for AIM-132 ASRAAM missiles in place of Sidewinder and the proposed new stand-off nuclear weapon.

The future is also likely to see RAF Tornados equipped with BAe Sea Eagle, this weapon having been earmarked for use in the 1980s before the RAF decided to run on two squadrons of Buccaneers and divert the Tornados thereby saved to duties on the Central Front. With a reduction in prospect for RAF Germany and the Buccaneer's service life coming to an end late in the 1990s, Britain could then become the operator of a maritime Tornado Wing with duties parallel to those of the West German navy.

Tornado ADV

The Royal Saudi Air Force was the first export customer to receive both the IDS and ADV Tornado versions. The latter wear RAF-style grey medium-level camouflage, 2250-litre (495-Imp gal) drop-tanks and are armed with AIM-9L Sidewinder and BAe Sky Flash AAMs. In order to expedite deliveries, 24 F.Mk 3s were diverted on the production line to the RSAF, 2907 having been laid down as ZE885. Following flight-testing, 2907 was delivered to Dhahran on 20 September 1988 to join the newly-formed No. 29 Squadron, RSAF, whose badge it wears on the fin. Saudi ADVs were the first to be fitted on the production line with Stage 1 versions of AI.Mk 24 Foxhunter radar, having the target-tracking performance called for by the RAF in its revised specification.

The definitive F.Mk 3 Tornado differs in several respects from the limited-production Mk 2, most notably in having a 14-inch (36-cm) extension to the jetpipes for an extra afterburner section, adding 2 kN (450 lb) more thrust per engine. Additionally, Sidewinder complement is increased from two to four, but there are other internal changes, such as a second Ferranti FIN 1010 inertial navigation system to compensate for the inability of the aircraft to take accurate ground fixes, like the GR.Mk 1. Performance up to but not beyond the limits of safety is guaranteed by a Spin Prevention and Incidence Limitation System linked to the fly-by-wire computer.

Radar warning receiver
Whereas the Tornado IDS is fitted with a fin-tip mounted Elettronica ARI 8284 radar warning receiver, the ADV enjoys the more sophisticated Marconi Space and Defence Systems Hermes modular radar homing and warning receiver. Antennas for this are mounted on the fin and at the wingtips, and threats are displayed aurally and on CRTs in both cockpits. Threats are analysed and classified and displayed in alpha-numeric form, with accurate range and bearing information. This can be compared with AI radar tracks, allowing the crew to classify and allocate priorities to the threats. The RHWR can operate passively, or can 'burn through' enemy jamming.

External fuel tanks
Whereas the Tornado F.Mk 2 used the small 330-gal fuel tanks used by the Tornado IDS (seen here), the F.Mk 3 and export ADVs can carry much larger tanks underwing. These contain 495 Imp gal each and are fitted with distinctive symmetrical cruciform fins. For long-range ferry flights, a pair of the smaller tanks can be carried under the fuselage, although this renders the underfuselage missile launchers unusable. The outboard pylons carried by the Tornado IDS are not fitted to the ADV, so extra ECM pods cannot be carried. Because of its stretched forward fuselage, the Tornado ADV already has considerably greater internal fuel capacity than the Tornado IDS.

Short-range missiles
The Tornado ADV has twin launch rails under each wing for the AIM-9 Sidewinder missile, compared to the single rails of the IDS. These are carried on stub pylons mounted on both sides of the underwing pylon. Saudi Arabian Tornado ADVs use the Ford/Raytheon AIM-9L version of the Sidewinder, whereas RAF F.Mk 3s would now use AIM-9Ms in wartime, and took these missiles with them when they deployed to Dhahran in August 1990. Both variants of the missile have an excellent all-aspect capability, and the AIM-9 has notched up an impressive combat record.

Colour scheme
The Saudi Tornado ADVs wear an air defence grey colour scheme very similar to that of the RAF's Tornado F.Mk 3, with small Saudi roundels in four positions (forward fuselage, above port wing, below starboard) and with the Saudi flag on the tailfin. No. 29 Squadron also has a small squadron badge on the lower part of the fin. The serial number and the legend 'Royal Saudi Air Force' are repeated in Arabic, 'RSAF' is painted above the starboard wing and below the port. The grey colour scheme has proved as effective over the Saudi desert as it has over the North Sea, much to the delight of the Saudi aircrew.

Export prospects

In spite of firm and genuine interest expressed by several air arms, only the Royal Saudi Air Force has taken delivery of export Tornados. The fact that Saudi Arabia is one of the world's wealthiest countries is perhaps a clue to the reasons why more have not bought this unquestionably effective combat aircraft. During the late 1980s, the fly-away cost of a Tornado was some £22 million, to which a purchaser would have to add up to an equal amount in spares, training, support and weapons. After long deliberations, Saudi Arabia signed the 'Al Yamamah I' ('Bird of Peace') defence agreement with the UK in September 1985, its provisions including 30 Pilatus PC-9 turboprop trainers, 30 BAe Hawk advanced trainers, 48 IDS and 24 ADV Tornados and a pair of BAe Jetstreams fitted out as navigator trainers with either IDS or ADV avionics. The Tornados were to come from Batch 7, but in order to expedite deliveries, the RAF gave up 18 of its last GR.Mk 1s from Batch 5 and 24 F.Mk 3s from Batch 6.

Weapons ordered by the RSAF included Sky Flash and AIM-9L Sidewinders for the interceptors and JP233 anti-runway dispensers, Sea Eagle anti-ship missiles and ALARM ARMs to equip the IDS variants. Some of the latter will be equivalent to the GR.Mk 1A reconnaissance version. In July 1988, 'Al Yamamah II' was provisionally agreed as covering a further 12 IDS and 36 ADV aircraft, but was cancelled in July 1990. It was, however, Oman which opened the export sales book with an August 1985 order for eight ADVs, deliveries of which were to have begun in 1988. For financial reasons, this was put back to 1992, and then abandoned altogether by early 1989, when the SOAF began looking at cheaper alternatives such as BAe Hawk 200s.

Jordan was another Middle-Eastern nation that withdrew from a Tornado purchase at the last moment. Intent to obtain eight IDS versions and place a further 12 on option was revealed in March 1988 and firmed up with a signature during the following September. Unfortunately for Panavia, Jordan was in a poor financial state and was forced in March 1989 to cancel its order 'until more favourable circumstances prevail'. Meanwhile, Malaysia was making erratic progress towards an order after reaching preliminary agreement in September 1988 on a package of UK defence equipment including 12 Tornados. Talks were discontinued early in 1989 when Malaysia protested against restricted landing rights in the UK for its airliners, but resumed shortly afterwards. The RMAF wished to include four ECR-type aircraft in its order, these probably to have been based on the RAF's GR.Mk 1A with the addition of a Marconi emitter-locator system. By May 1990, the cost and complexity of the proposed sale had resulted in its virtual abandonment and a similar switch of interest to armed Hawks.

Less firm prospects – in that no written expression of interest has been received – include Turkey, South Korea and Thailand. Turkey's requirement for 40 Tornados goes back to 1985 when the prospect emerged that regular West German military aid funds could be used in buying the aircraft. Each Panavia member company is responsible for following up sales prospects in its own sphere of influence, so just as Saudi Tornados were built in the UK, any for Turkey would come from the Manching line. As yet, however, none has

prototype, ZA283, flew demonstration sorties with outboard underwing pylons activated to give it the same capacity as the IDS, but this stretched multi-multi-role Tornado appears to have lapsed.

Perhaps the most difficult order to secure will be USAF's 'Follow-On Wild Weasel', involving 150 aircraft. An agreement of 16 December 1988 appointed Rockwell as US agent for a version of the Tornado ECR modified to American requirements. The accord provides for the North American division of Rockwell to have design leadership in integration of advanced emitter-locator systems, such as AN/ALQ-99, with the Tornado airframe, and for final assembly of completed aircraft at Palmdale. However, FOWW is still in the 'concept exploration' stage and it is uncertain whether funds will be allocated to the programme – doubly so that a foreign aircraft will be chosen. Ironically, the costly sophistication built into the Tornado to equip it to do combat on the Central Front will militate against export orders now that the European threat has diminished.

materialised. In South Korea, the unusual scene has emerged of BAe competing with MBB to sell almost the same type of aircraft, for the RoKAF needs the unusually high number of 40 electronic combat/reconnaissance aircraft within its possible purchase of 50 Tornados. West Germany is offering 'genuine' ECR versions against the UK's modified GR.Mk 1A as proposed for Malaysia, and no decision is expected from here until 1991.

Japanese collaboration

In Thailand, all three Panavia firms are seeking to sell 12 IDS and four ECR (or similar) Tornados. Britain and Italy appear to have the better chances of success, as the RTAF also requires a light-attack aircraft in the same package, giving an opening for the BAe Hawk 200 or Aeritalia/Aermacchi AMX. Japan at one time appeared to be a Tornado prospect before selecting a modified version of the F-16 Fighting Falcon to meet its 130-aircraft FS-X requirement. By early 1987, BAe was promoting a 'Tornado J' to be jointly developed with the Japanese aircraft industry, combining long-range maritime attack using the large Mitsubishi ASM-1 anti-ship missile with interception capability. This developed from the earlier 'Super Tornado' study, which had the lengthened ADV fuselage married to IDS/ECR features. The third ADV

Left: Early RAF squadrons have been marking their 75th anniversaries with special colour schemes, including No. 25, in September 1990. Names of campaigns in which the squadron has participated appear on the forward fuselage.

Below: Rattling the cast-iron roofs of Butterworth town, No. 29 Squadron operated from Malaysia in exercise 'Lima Bersatu' in 1988 as one feature of the 'Golden Eagle' round-the-world deployment of four Tornados led by Wing Commander Doble.

Royal Air Force

Tornado GR.Mk 1/1A

Of 385 Tornados covered by the original UK requirement, 220 were to be the GR.Mk 1 interdictor/strike version for home-based Strike Command and RAF Germany. Subsequently an order for a further nine attrition replacements has been confirmed, but a further 26 of the GR.Mk 4 mid-life update Tornados planned for Batch 8 are not now to be ordered. After allowance for diversions to Saudi Arabia and 'pay-backs', the order position is thus:

	Standard GR.Mk 1	Dual control	Reconnaissance	Total
Refurbished		1		1
Batch 1	11	12		23
Batch 2	39	16		55
Batch 3	60	8	*	68
Batch 4	45	8		53
Batch 5			2	2
Batch 7	7	6	14	27
Totals	**162**	**51**	**16**	**229**

*14 GR.Mk 1s subsequently converted for reconnaissance

Tornados were obtained to replace the Vulcan bomber force, partly to supplement the Jaguar and Buccaneer as interdictors and to replace reconnaissance Canberras in operational roles. Two planned maritime strike/attack squadrons were not formed and the earmarked aircraft were instead diverted to RAF Germany, where eight of the 11 operational squadrons are based. A further Reserve squadron would be formed in wartime from aircraft and crews of the weapons training unit. As an extension of the collaborative agreement that brought the Tornado into being, the four partner air arms (RAF, AMI, Luftwaffe and Marineflieger) agreed that all crew training should be undertaken in Britain for reasons of economy. However, although the TTTE formed to provide basic type conversion – and continues to perform that task successfully – West Germany objected to the proposed cost of a multi-national Tornado Weapons Conversion Unit at RAF Honington, with the result that this phase has always been a national responsibility.

Batch 1 aircraft were assigned to TTTE and those of Batch 2 (from April 1981 onwards) to the TWCU and the first home-based squadron, No. IX. Batch 3, beginning in July 1982, introduced the undernose laser rangefinder and marked target seeker, deliveries going mainly to the squadrons at Laarbruch, West Germany. Also brought in at this time was the Marconi ARI 18241/2 radar warning receiver to replace the Elettronica ARI 23284 equipment in Batch 1-2 aircraft. In 1987, a programme began to convert all to ARI 18241/1 (despite its suffix, a more advanced equipment) standard, as in the Tornado F.Mk 3.

With Batch 4, built from January 1984, came the Mk 103 version of RB.199 turbofan for squadrons at Brüggen, although Laarbruch aircraft were modified to this standard. Batch 5, all bar two of which went to Saudi Arabia, brought in a MIL STD 1553B digital databus, doubled (128K) computer power, ADA computer language in the missile control unit, integrated ECM transmitter, chaff/flare dispenser and RWR operation and (in West German navy aircraft) HARM missile capability.

The last Batch 4 aircraft for the RAF was delivered on 30 September 1985, the two Batch 5 machines following in December 1986 and January 1987, configured as GR.Mk 1A reconnaissance aircraft, but flew with regular squadrons until the recce squadron (No. 2) was ready to be re-formed. Only in 1989 did deliveries re-start of Batch 7 aircraft, the early examples of which were Mk 1As for the UK-based recce squadron, No.13. This formed in January 1990, thereby completing the force of 11 operational squadrons envisaged a decade and a half before.

Tornado GR.Mk 1/1As were all delivered in a wrap-round camouflage scheme of green and grey, to which units have been permitted to add decorative markings, in some cases involving removal of the fuselage side roundel from the cockpit area to the engine air intake. West German-based squadrons, with the exception of No. 2, are additionally marked with a two-letter code as dual identification of their squadron and individual in-house identity. A feature of the Tornado programme has been the construction of hardened aircraft shelters (HASs) at each new operational base, beginning with Honington, where the first set of Mk 3 HASs was handed over by the contractors in November 1981. Mk 3s can house two Tornados, although the normal complement is one, but in West Germany most are smaller, earlier-generation Mk 1s with accommodation for a single aircraft only.

All Tornado GR.Mk 1s are assigned to NATO. In the UK, Nos 27 and 617 Squadrons at Marham are allocated to SACEUR's Strategic Reserve (Air) and are believed to be assigned to strikes against specific, pre-assigned targets with WE177 nuclear bombs. RAF Germany is part of the 2nd Allied Tactical Air Force, itself one half of Allied Air Forces Central Europe, and tasked with nuclear and conventional roles directly and indirectly in support of Central Army Group. Approximately 110 Tornado GR.Mk 1s – half the number delivered – are based in RAF Germany.

For realistic low-level training, squadrons deploy to Goose Bay in Canada, where aircraft of other NATO nations are engaged in similar flying over sparsely-populated terrain which resembles that of Central Europe. The first RAF Tornado squadron at Goose was No. IX in October 1983, others following during the next two years. To reduce the disruption caused by ferrying aircraft over the Atlantic, it was decided to base nine or so in Canada for several months at a time, during which they would be flown by the crews of several squadrons taken to Canada in transport aircraft.

Long-term detachments began on 20-25 February 1986 with nine aircraft in the markings of Nos IX, 27 and 617 Squadrons, but their first duty was to fly in a 'Green Flag' exercise crewed by Nos 20, 31 and 617 Squadrons. Only in April 1986 did the remainder of No. 31 arrive at Goose to begin low-level flying. They were replaced on 10 May by No. 17, and on 21 June by No. 617. A replacement batch of nine Tornados in Nos 15, 16 and 20 Squadron insignia arrived on 9 July, giving training to No. 15's personnel from 1 August. Three more squadrons (Nos 16, 20 and 17) followed, and the aircraft were finally flown in a 'Red Flag' before returning to Europe. Similar deployments have been made in subsequent years.

The 1987 deployment began on 24-25 February and lasted until November; in 1988 an average of nine Tornados was away between 26-29 February and 24 November; and this was repeated in 1989 from 27 February to November – including a 'Maple Flag' exercise at Cold Lake, Canada, before the homecoming. Where previously aircraft were drawn from some three squadrons, who then borrowed Tornados from the units whilst they were in Canada, beginning in 1988, each in RAFG donated one or, at most, two machines to the detachment. From 1989 onwards, the 'Storm Trail' deployment has taken the Tornados and their tankers on a southerly route via the Azores and Bermuda.

Eleven operational squadrons, two conversion units and a trials flight are equipped with Tornado GR.Mk 1s. These are detailed below in order of formation.

Trinational Tornado Training Establishment

Crews of all four European air arms operating the Tornado IDS receive the first phase of their instruction at Cottesmore before progressing to weapons training units in their own countries. Cottesmore was chosen as the TTTE's base in 1975 and began receiving personnel in April 1978, followed by the first two aircraft (ZA320 and ZA322) on 1 July 1980. West German Tornados began arriving on 2 September 1980 (4305), the first Italian aircraft (MM55001) being received on 5 April 1982. Initial establishment was 22 German, 21 RAF and seven Italian Tornados, reflecting the national shares of 42.5, 40.0 and 17.5 per cent in the provision of funding and allocation of aircrew training places. TTTE is a component of No. 1 Group, Strike Command, and administered by a British station commander – originally Group Captain M.G. Simmonds – assisted by Senior National Representatives from the two other countries. Subsequent commanders have been Group Captains Terry Carlton, P.J. 'Sam' Goddard, Peter T. Squire and Ron D. Elder. Flying activities are assigned to the Tornado Operational Conversion Unit (TOCU), the commander of which is rotated on a national basis.

TOCU comprises four squadrons: 'A', 'B', 'C' and 'S'; the first three train students and the last (Standards Squadron) is responsible for providing instructors. Aircraft wear a squadron badge as a representative gesture only, as all are pooled, irrespective of nationality. In-house identity markings include a code number in the range 01-49 for dual control aircraft and 50-99 for standard IDS versions; this is prefixed by a single letter to indicate the aircraft's nationality – G-, B- or I-. The provision of instructors also conforms to the 42.5/40.0/17.5 formula, but by late 1989 a reduction in training requirements had cut the aircraft establishment to 16 RAF, 18 German and five Italian.

Instructors for the TOCU initially came from the Service Instructor Training Courses, which began at MBB's Manching plant on 5 May 1980 and provided a cadre of nine pilots and six navigators qualified to fly. The remainder of 1980 was spent in training other staff at Cottesmore before No. 1 Course arrived on 5 January 1981. The unit was officially inaugurated on 29 January. The Main Course for students lasts 13 weeks, including nine of flying, during which pilots are airborne for about 35 hours and navigators for 28 hours. The new crew flies together for the first time after some eight hours separately with instructors. Training takes the crew up to the standard of a simulated attack mission, including terrain-following, but without weapon release. By April 1990 the TOCU had trained 2,000 aircrew: 1,084 pilots and 916 navigators on 140 Main Courses. In addition, experienced personnel attend Cottesmore for shorter periods of training with either the Senior Officers' Course (familiarisation), Competent to Instruct Course (producing instructor pilots and navigators) or Instrument Rating Examiner Course.

In October 1985, the Saudi Arabian Training Flight formed to convert RSAF aircrew to the Tornado IDS. Because this was a wholly British responsibility, only RAF personnel and aircraft were used and the Saudi nationals took course places originally assigned to the RAF. The Flight closed early in 1987 after four courses, when the RSAF became responsible for its own training. As the initial service Tornado flying unit in any country, TOCU has several high-timed aircraft, including the first of each nation to reach 1,000 hours: ZA361 of the RAF on 10 October 1985, closely followed by 4305 of the Luftwaffe and, on 28 February 1986, Italy's MM55000. 4305 then took the lead, becoming late in 1989 the first Tornado to reach 2,000 hours. In search of improved weather during the winter, some TTTE aircraft are deployed to Scottish bases. Leuchars hosted the first detachment between October 1986 and March 1987, and Machrihanish and Lossiemouth have also been used.

TTTE conducts no squadron exchanges, but it saw a remarkable gathering of aircraft in October 1988 when 93 Tornados from 31 users gathered at their *alma mater* for a Panavia-sponsored symposium. Earlier, but smaller, events had previously been held at Büchel in 1986 and Brüggen in 1987.

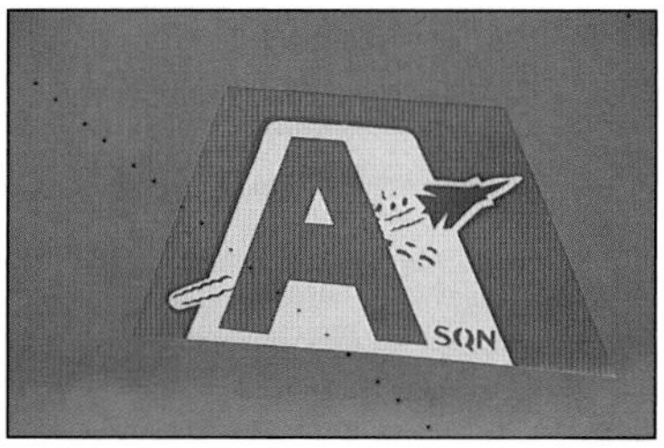

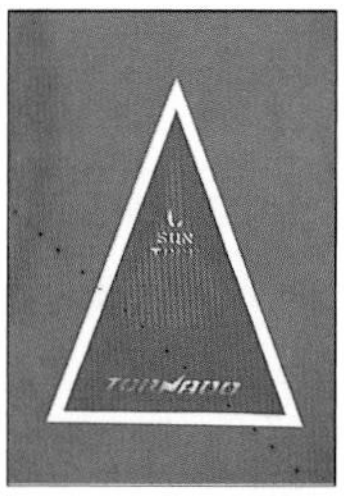

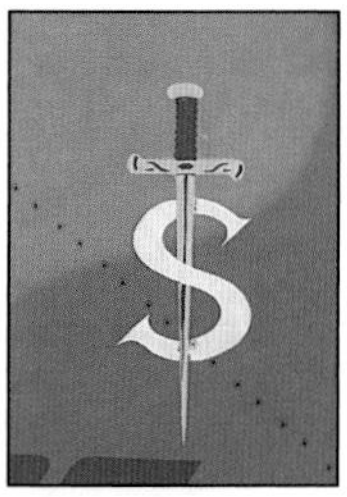

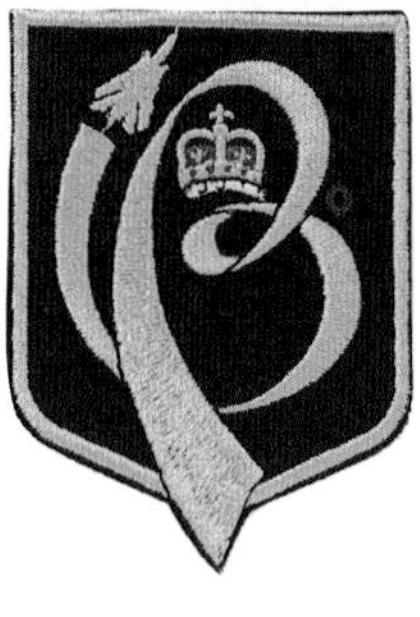

The TTTE consists of four separate squadrons. A, B, and C are responsible for conversion training for all West German, Italian and RAF IDS aircrew, while S (Standards) looks after instructor training and standardisation. Each has a separate badge.

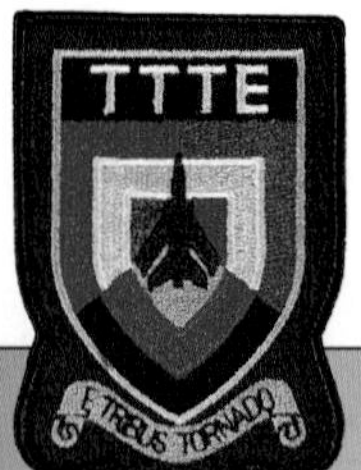

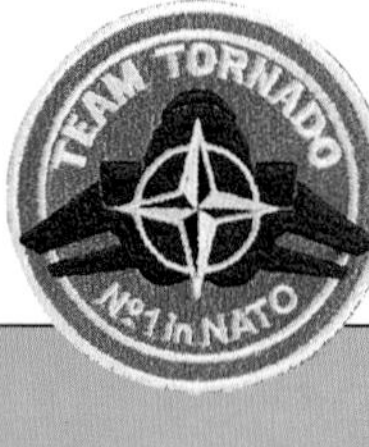

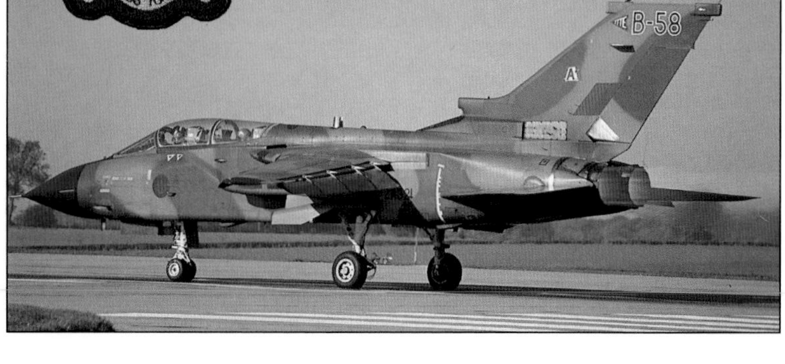

Tornado Weapons Conversion Unit/No. 45 (Reserve) Squadron

After learning to fly the Tornado GR.Mk 1 at TTTE, Cottesmore, RAF crews are posted to Honington to become familiar with the aircraft as a weapons system before joining an operational squadron. TWCU received its first aircraft, ZA542, from BAe on 29 June 1981 and was formed on 1 August under Wing Commander Duncan A. Griffiths. It had received an initial allocation of 16 aircraft by the end of the following November and flew the first overseas 'Ranger' sortie on 22-23 October. No. 1 Course for students began on 11 January 1982 and ended on 8 March, with No. 2 overlapping (22 February to 21 May). Establishment peaked at 25 Tornados from Batch 2 but, beginning on 20 September 1982 with ZA365, laser-equipped Batch 3 machines were delivered to replace some of the original equipment. TWCU provided aircraft for the first overseas RAF Tornado deployment when three GR.Mk 1s departed Honington on 10 May 1983 to accompany the Red Arrows on a tour of North America. The unit achieved 1,000 hours on 12 March 1982; 5,000 hours on 23 March 1983; 10,000 hours on 12 March 1984; and 45,000 hours on 10 April 1990 – this last figure having significance in that on 1 January 1984 the TWCU became No. 45 (Reserve) Squadron with an operational commitment in wartime. CO was Wing Commander G.I. McRobbie.

Training courses for novice crews last approximately 35 hours, during which they practise lay-down and loft bombing, tactical defence, terrain-following, low-level tactical formation flying, simulated attack profiles and low-level evasion. Half the airborne time is spent with instructors and the remaining period as a new crew. Experienced personnel may return to TWCU to become Qualified Weapons Instructors in a course including some 45 flying hours. By early 1990, the TWCU had 23 aircraft, including a single GR.Mk 1A, and was being led by Wing Commander Mal Prissick.

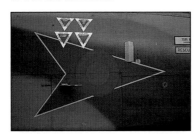

TWCU heraldry includes the 'Crown and Arrows' arms of Bury St Edmunds and the winged camel of the shadow unit, No. 45 Squadron.

No. IX Squadron

This famous bomber squadron disbanded with Vulcan B.Mk 2s at Scampton on 29 April 1982 and re-emerged at Honington on 1 June that year as the first operational Tornado IDS unit of any air force. Commanded by Wing Commander Peter Gooding, AFC, the unit had received its first aircraft on 6 January 1982 when ZA586 was delivered from BAe, this Tornado also gaining the less welcome distinction of being the first to crash in service when it was lost on 27 September 1983 after an electrical failure. Between 4 and 18 March 1985, No. IX became the first RAF squadron to take part in a USAF 'Green Flag' ECM training exercise at Nellis AFB, Nevada. As a pioneering squadron, No. IX took time to become combat-ready, not least because staggered orders for weapons and equipment caused severe disruption and there were always new items to investigate and test. This requirement receded after formation of the TOEU (now SAOEU) in September 1983, but a related inconvenience was operation from an HAS complex, which demanded additional manpower compared with the old system of servicing aircraft in a single hangar.

It had always been intended that the first UK Tornado squadron would eventually reinforce RAF Germany, and this occurred when No. IX transferred to Brüggen on 1 October 1986. In doing so, it relinquished its original batch of 'laser-less' aircraft and took over new equipment from Batch 4, the first of which had arrived in December 1985. In 1989, ZA609 was painted in special markings to celebrate the squadron's 75th anniversary. Establishment was increased from 12 to 18 aircraft from late 1989 onwards, at which time the squadron began receiving Tornados modified to carry the BAe ALARM anti-radar missile and TIALD thermal-imaging and laser designation pods. Delivery of TIALD was expected in 1990 following trials at Farnborough in a Buccaneer, but ALARM has been delayed until 1992, at which time the squadron will assume the roles of defence suppression and target-designation. COs in West Germany have been Wing Commanders A.L.

Below and right: A yellow-outlined green arrowhead on the nose and a bat silhouette on the fin adorn the aircraft of Brüggen-based No. IX Squadron. Code letters from 'AA' to 'AZ' are allocated.

Below: For the 75th anniversary in 1989, one aircraft was painted up in a more eye-catching colour scheme, with a yellow and green spine and tail stripe and with the unit's official badge replacing the stylised bat.

Tornado Operators

Ferguson, Rob Wright and Ivor Evans.
The squadron has an unprecedented record in the Salmond Trophy, which is awarded to RAFG squadrons for bombing and navigation accuracy plus ground crew support. In the first four years since Tornados began competing for the Trophy in 1986, No. IX has been placed first, second, second and first.

In an attempt to improve conspicuity at low level, one of No. IX Squadron's aircraft received an all-white fin. The experiment was not considered to be a success.

No. 617 Squadron

On 16 May 1983, 40 years to the day after the historic raid on the German dams, No. 617 re-formed as the RAF's second Tornado squadron, with Wing Commander Tony Harrison in command. Deliveries to this former Vulcan unit (disbanded 31 December 1981) began with ZA601 on 23 April 1982 – from which it will be seen that supply of aircraft was running well ahead of aircrew availability during the early 1980s. Marked at first with red codes beginning at '01' the aircraft soon adopted single letters, the same as those used by Lancasters on the

dams raid. Late in 1977, the squadron identification letter 'M' was added (e.g. 'MA') but was dropped by May 1989. Primary role is nuclear strike with WE177 bombs.
Supported by Victor K.Mk 2 tankers of co-located No. 55 Squadron, the 'Dam Busters' took part in the 1984 Strategic Air Command bombing competition in the USA, entering two teams, each of two crews. With spectacular success they achieved first and second places (98.7 per cent and 98.5 per cent) for the Le May Trophy for high- and

low-level bombing by an individual crew; first and third (90.45 per cent and 83.1 per cent) in the Meyer Trophy for highest damage expectancy from team bombing at low level; and second (96.05 per cent) in the Mathis Trophy awarded for the best high- and low-level teams.
Early in 1986, led by Wing Commander Peter Day, part of the squadron was back in the USA when it joined selected crews from Nos 20 and 31 Squadrons in a 'Green Flag' ECM exercise, flying against opposition from aggressor F-5s, F-15s and F-16s, plus

simulated Soviet SAMs. The squadron participated in a rapid redeployment to the Middle East when four aircraft, accompanied by a pair of Tornado F.Mk 2s of No. 229 OCU, flew to Oman on 25 November 1985 at the start of exercise 'Saif Sareea' (Swift Sword), refuelled for the 10¼-hour, 4,200-mile (6760-km) journey by VC10 and TriStar tankers. A new standard was presented to No. 617 by the Queen Mother in a ceremony on 13 January 1988. The current CO is Wing Commander Bob Iveson, who replaced Nigel Day in 1990.

No. 617 Squadron takes its 'Dam Busters' heritage seriously, although unit markings on the aircraft are confined to red lightning bolts against a black background.

No. 27 Squadron

The initial Tornado for the RAF's third squadron (ZA609) was delivered to Marham on 29 June 1982 – well in advance of its formation. Although No. 101 was expected to become a Tornado squadron, it instead was re-formed with VC10 tankers and the former Vulcan-equipped No. 27 Squadron (disbanded 31 March 1982), brought into being on 12 August 1983 as a replacement. Wing Commander John Grogan was the first CO and, unusually, called for his aircraft to be identified by numbers beginning with '01'. This was perpetuated until March 1989 when, under Wing Commander Bill Green, the present two-letter identification was adopted. Though appearing to be almost in sequence with the RAF Germany series, the letter 'J' actually represents 'Jumbo' – the squadron badge of an elephant.
No. 27 was the second Tornado squadron (after No. 617) to participate in the USAF's 'Giant Voice' bombing competition – known to the RAF as 'Prairie Vortex'. For the 1985 event, two teams of two crews each were entered, tanker support being provided by No. 57 Squadron's Victor K.Mk 2s. Flying against all SAC's B-52 and FB-111 units, plus Australian F-111s, the Tornado demonstrated a +/– 2 second timing accuracy during a 6½-hour sortie and a mean aiming error of less than 30 ft (9 m) at low level. No. 27 gained first and second places for the Le May Trophy and first and second for the Meyer Trophy, and was placed second for the Mathis Trophy only because of a mechanical fault which delayed the release of a practice bomb by one-third of a second.
Notable squadron exchanges have taken place with Canadian CF-18s in September 1987 and Spanish Phantoms in April 1988. In March 1989, two of No. 27's Tornados (in

reality, a pair of Mk 103-engined aircraft on loan from RAFG) made the type's first deployment to Malaysia to take part in air defence exercise 90-2 as interdictors and also to make a courtesy visit to Indonesia. Like its partner at Marham, the squadron is tasked with nuclear strike.
In June 1989 the squadron deployed to Villafranca, Italy, for an exchange with the F-104G-equipped 28° Stormo, while in May 1990 it exchanged with the Armée de l'Air's Jaguar-equipped Escadre de Chasse 3/7 at St Dizier. The commanding officer is Group Captain W.L. Green.

No. 27 Squadron's aircraft wear code letters in the range 'JA' to 'JZ'. One aircraft has received a 75th anniversary colour scheme.

Strike-Attack Operational Evaluation Unit

In order to accelerate development of operating procedures for the Tornado GR.Mk 1 force, Strike Command decided to form a specific trials unit of four aircraft at Marham, to where the aircraft were delivered from 11 November 1982 (ZA393) onwards. Instead, and after some delay, the Tornado Operational Evaluation Unit (TOEU) formed at Boscombe Down under Wing Commander John Lumsden on 1 September 1983, reporting jointly to the resident Aeroplane & Armament Experimental Establishment and the High Wycombe-based Central Tactics & Trials Organisation. An OEU was, itself, an experimental venture and it was accordingly given only a two-year charter during which it developed operating procedures for laser-guided bombs,

optimum methods for delivering JP233, improvements to the electronic warfare suite and assessed passive night flying operations with night vision goggles and forward-looking infra-red.

During a one-year extension, TOEU conducted ECM development and assessment of weapon delivery techniques, including a live drop of JP233 in the USA. The OEU was then made permanent, with a view to extending its areas of responsibility to the Harrier GR.Mk 5/7, its next CO being Wing Commander 'Raz' Ball. Re-titled SAOEU late in 1987, the unit accepted its first Harrier GR.Mk 5 in July 1988 and currently operates three Harriers, a Jaguar T.Mk 2A, two Tornado GR.Mk 1s and a GR.Mk 1A.

Right: No. XV Squadron's 'birthday ship' wears an attractive but subdued red and blue fin and spine stripe. Another aircraft, below, had an all-red fin for low-level high conspicuity trials.

Below: Laarbruch-based No. XV Squadron has replaced single letter codes with two-letter codes commencing 'EA'. The white 'XV' is still carried prominently on aircraft and flying suits!

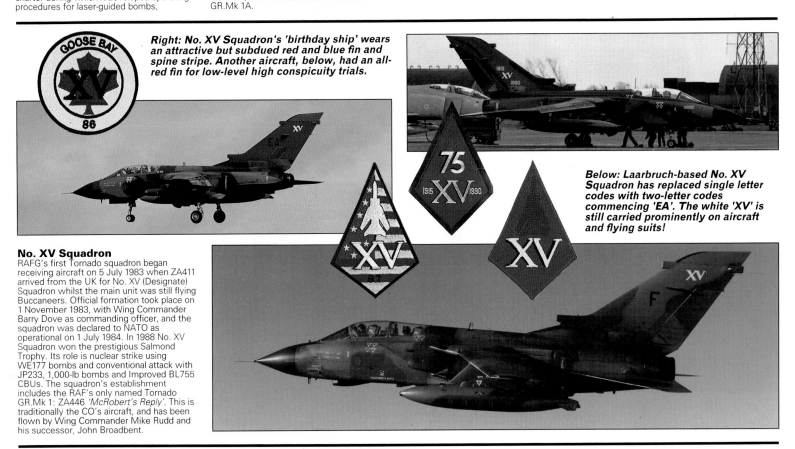

No. XV Squadron

RAFG's first Tornado squadron began receiving aircraft on 5 July 1983 when ZA411 arrived from the UK for No. XV (Designate) Squadron whilst the main unit was still flying Buccaneers. Official formation took place on 1 November 1983, with Wing Commander Barry Dove as commanding officer, and the squadron was declared to NATO as operational on 1 July 1984. In 1988 No. XV Squadron won the prestigious Salmond Trophy. Its role is nuclear strike using WE177 bombs and conventional attack with JP233, 1,000-lb bombs and Improved BL755 CBUs. The squadron's establishment includes the RAF's only named Tornado GR.Mk 1: ZA446 *'McRobert's Reply'*. This is traditionally the CO's aircraft, and has been flown by Wing Commander Mike Rudd and his successor, John Broadbent.

No. 16 Squadron

Another former Buccaneer squadron, No. 16 received its first aircraft, ZA458, on 13 December 1983 and became RAFG's second Tornado unit on 1 March 1984. Like No. XV, it is assigned to nuclear and conventional attack, but its specific weapons include the CPU-123B Paveway laser-guided bomb for precision attacks. For airborne designation services, the squadron relies on the Buccaneer S.Mk 2Bs of No. 237 OCU from Lossiemouth, which in wartime would be detached to RAF Germany with their Westinghouse AN/AVQ-23E Pave Spike laser pods. Highlights of No. 16's recent

Below: A stylised version of the unit's crossed keys badge is carried, along with the unofficial 'saint' insignia.

Above: Also based at RAF Laarbruch is No. 16 Squadron, whose aircraft carry codes between 'FA' and 'FZ'. These are in the squadron colours of black and gold, reflecting the unit's traditional day and night role, which continues to this day. Right: black and gold bars flank the roundel.

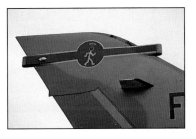

Tornado Operators

career include the achievement of Squadron Leader Rod Sargent, who on 6 May 1985 became the first service pilot in any air force to fly 1,000 hours on Tornados, and the painting of ZA591 in an all-black scheme in 1990 for the unit's 75th anniversary.

Black and gold keys signify the squadron's former Army co-op role, of unlocking the enemy's secrets by day and night. The 'saint' figure alludes to the formation at St Omer during World War II.

The third Laarbruch-based Tornado unit was No. 20, which wears codes between 'GA' and 'GZ', outlined in pale blue. Unit markings consist of pale blue, red and white stripes and a stylised version of the official badge of a talwar eagle, clutching a sword, in front of the rising sun. This commemorates the unit's long service in India and the Far East.

No. 20 Squadron
Equipped with Jaguars at Brüggen, No. 20 Squadron disbanded at that base on 29 June 1984, re-forming at the same moment at Laarbruch with Tornados. No. 20 (Designate) had received Tornado GR.Mk 1 ZA461 in March 1984 and begun flying on 2 May. As the fourth squadron on a previously three-squadron base, it had the privilege of operating from a newly-built complex of Mk 3 HASs. Weaponry includes WE177, JP233

Like many Tornado units, No. 20 Squadron uses a diamond-shaped flying suit patch.

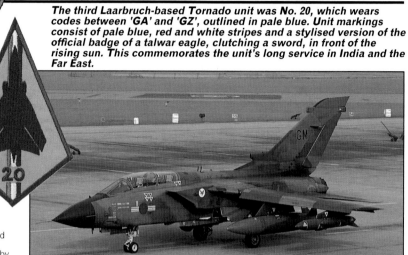

and 1,000-lb (454-kg) bombs and Improved BL755, plus CPU-123B Paveway laser-guided bombs with designation provided by No. 237 OCU's Buccaneers.

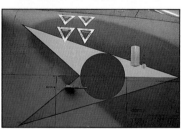

Left: A spate of collisions involving low-flying NATO tactical aircraft led to extended trials of high-conspicuity paint schemes and strobe lights. One aircraft from No. 31 wore a white fin during these trials. It is seen here with underfuselage practice bomb dispensers.

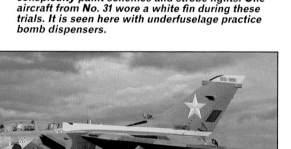

Right: To celebrate its 75th year, No. 31 Squadron decorated an aircraft with a coloured tailfin, spine and fuel tanks. The unit's mullet badge is carried in larger form on the decorated fin.

No. 31 Squadron
The first Tornado to arrive at Brüggen was ZD712 on 13 June 1984, assigned to No. 31 (Designate) Squadron. Formerly equipped with Jaguars, the squadron officially changed aircraft types on 1 November 1984, coming under the command of Wing Commander Dick Bogg – the first navigator to run a Tornado unit – and later, Wing Commander Pete Dunlop. In common with Nos 14 and 17 Squadrons, No. 31 is assigned to nuclear strike with WE177 bombs. It was winner of the Salmond Trophy in 1987. Liaison with NATO squadrons has included an exchange with Danish Drakens in 1988 and Italian Starfighters of 5° Stormo in May 1989. A 75th anniversary colour scheme was applied to ZA461 in 1990. The current CO is Wing Commander Jerry Witts.

Right: No. 31 Squadron, first of the Brüggen-based Tornado units, wears codes between 'DA' and 'DZ'. No. IX Squadron formed at Honington and didn't move to Brüggen until 1986.

No. 17 Squadron

Dedicated to nuclear strike with WE177 weapons, as well as airfield attacks with JP233, No. 17 Squadron came into being as a Tornado unit on 1 March 1985 under Wing Commander Grant McLeod, having formerly flown Jaguars. Its first aircraft (ZD742) was delivered to No. 17 (Designate) Squadron on 16 August 1984, and the squadron flew in its first 'Red Flag' late in 1986.

The black and white zig-zags once worn by Bristol Bulldogs and Gloster Gauntlets now decorate No. 17 Squadron's Brüggen-based Tornados, along with the unit's mailed hand insignia and 'CA' to 'CZ' codes.

No. 14 Squadron

The sixth and last Tornado strike/attack squadron to form in RAF Germany, No. 14 flew Jaguars until October 1985. On 11 April that year, aircraft had begun arriving at Brüggen for No. 14 (Designate) Squadron, the unit building up in parallel to the Jaguar operation until the Tornado element formally came into being on 1 November 1985. The squadron is tasked with nuclear strike using WE177 free-fall bombs and airfield attack with JP233 and other weapons. Its commanders since formation have been Wing Commanders Joe Whitfield and Vaughan Morris. Two aircraft received red fins early in 1989 for an unsuccessful visibility trial. Four of its aircraft were painted in 75th anniversary markings late in 1989.

No. 14 is based at RAF Brüggen and uses codes from 'BA' to 'BZ'. The Crusader badge reflects the unit's long service in the Near East.

Blue and white diamonds have been associated with No. 14 since the 1950s, when it flew Hawker Hunters.

No. 2 Squadron

Earmarked as the first Tornado GR.Mk 1A reconnaissance squadron, No. 2 flew its final operational sortie with the pod-equipped Jaguar GR.Mk 1A on 16 December 1988. Due to delays in delivery of sensors for the replacement Tornados, assigned aircraft had been allocated in small numbers to several other units in Britain and West Germany since April 1987, but they began to assemble in the squadron's HAS complex towards the end of 1988, the first test sortie being made on 30 September that year. Squadron CO is Wing Commander Al Threadgould. Structural work to permit installation of sensors had previously been undertaken at BAe's Warton plant, but fitment of the equipment itself was the responsibility of the RAF, in the form of No. 431 Maintenance Unit at Brüggen. No. 2 Squadron has a secondary attack role with bombs and BL755 cluster weapons, and for

most of 1989 this was all it was able to accomplish.

By October, the squadron was up to strength with 12 Mk 1As and a dual control Mk 1, and at about this time the side windows began to be fitted to its aircraft, indicating arrival of infra-red sensors, six of

which were fitted by the end of the year. Earlier in 1989, two aircraft received white fins as a visibility aid to reduce the risk of aerial collisions, but the trial proved unsuccessful and the aircraft reverted to standard markings. No. 2's Tornados carry individual letters which, when aircraft are

correctly placed in line, read 'SHINEY TWO II AC'. ('II' is one aircraft; 'AC' refers to a long-forsaken role of army co-operation; and a further dual-control Tornado is 'X'.)

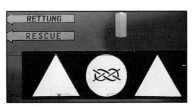

Black and white triangles and the 'Wake' knot have long been associated with No. 2 Squadron.

No. 13 Squadron

The last of the planned 11 operational Tornado IDS squadrons, No. 13 is also the second equipped with the reconnaissance configured GR.Mk 1A. The unit received its first aircraft, a dual-control Batch 1 aircraft (ZA357/'T'), in the autumn of 1989, closely followed by the first new-build Batch 7 GR.Mk 1A (ZG705) on 13 October 1989. The unit officially reformed on 1 January 1990 under Wing Commander Glenn L. Torpy. By the late summer of 1990, No. 13 had taken delivery of 10 of the planned total of 12 Batch 7 GR.Mk 1As and was expecting to complete the delivery of all reconnaissance equipment. The sideways-looking infra-red and infra-red linescan were described as producing ''first class real-time imagery.'' By August all aircraft were also fitted with laser ranger and marked target seekers, and the squadron was expecting to be declared attack operational on 1 January 1991. In the secondary attack role the squadron could use 1,000-lb free-fall or retarded bombs, laser guided bombs or BL755 CBUs. All aircraft are ALARM-capable and can carry two AIM-9 Sidewinders.

No. 13 Squadron's badge is a lynx head in front of a dagger, denoting vigilance. A blue and gold tail stripe and nose markings have been adopted.

Royal Air Force
Tornado F.Mk 3

Revitalisation of No. 11 Group's interceptor force was completed in 1990 with formation of the eighth and last Tornado F. Mk 3 unit: seven squadrons and an OCU with a reserve front-line commitment. Two squadrons were formerly equipped with Lightnings, two had Phantom FGR.Mk 2s and two flew Phantom FG.Mk 1s, while the remaining two are additional to Strike Command strength. With the exception of the OCU and No. 11 Squadron, all units operate from hardened shelters. The bases at Coningsby and Leuchars formerly housed Phantoms, but Leeming had previously been a training station and underwent a major re-building programme to fit it for its new role. The station re-opened on 11 January 1988. As part of the uni-directional defence policy, it was announced in 1981 that Stornoway in the Hebrides would receive new taxiways and dispersals (and eventually nine HASs, work on which began in March 1989) to act as a forward dispersal base for Tornados. Brawdy performs a similar role for aircraft defending the South-western Approaches.

In this connection, Nos 11 and 43 Squadrons are dedicated to SACLANT for defence of naval units, whereas the remainder of the force is under the permanent control of SACEUR with responsibility for defending the UK Air Defence Region (UKADR). This is divided into two areas: Sector 1, north of 55°N, is controlled by the Sector Operations Centre at Buchan and policed by Leeming and Leuchars Tornados; Sector 2, in the south, where there are fewer unannounced intrusions, is the responsibility for Coningsby Tornados and the SOC at Neatishead.

All Tornado interceptors in current RAF service are F.Mk 3s. A requirement for radar updating has resulted in some interchange of aircraft and re-issue of new Tornados to certain squadrons only shortly after their re-equipment. The latest standard of AI.Mk 24 Foxhunter radar is Stage 1, which was in use at Coningsby by early 1990 and was delivered off the production line to Leuchars squadrons. The Leeming Wing will be last to have its radars upgraded.

RAF requirements for the interceptor Tornado initially totalled 165, the first three of which were retrospectively added to Batch 1 production as prototypes. Of 92 called-for in Batch 6, 24 were diverted to Saudi Arabia and replaced out of Batch 7. It had been intended to order 15 further F.Mk 3s in Batch 8, but seven of these were cancelled on 18 June 1990 as an economy measure. Frequent changes in standards of radar resulted in differences of capability even between aircraft of the same production Batch, and thus Block numbers assumed importance with regard to which Tornados were assigned to a squadron. The position is as below, Batch 4 aircraft being F.Mk 2s.

		Standard	Dual control	Total	First flight
Batch 1	Block 1	2	1	3	27 Oct 79
Batch 4	Block 8	0	6	6	12 Apr 84
Batch 4	Block 9	10	2	12	11 Jan 85
Batch 5	Block 10	12	6	18	20 Nov 85
Batch 5	Block 11	22	12	34	26 Aug 86
Batch 6	Block 12	39	7	46	Sep 87
Batch 6	Block 13	12	10	22	1 Dec 88
Batch 7	Block 14	7	0	7	90
Batch 7	Block 15	17	0	17	91
Totals		**121**	**44**	**165**	

On 27 September 1987, a Tornado became the first British fighter to make an unrefuelled transatlantic crossing when a BAe development aircraft was flown by Peter Gordon-Johnson and Les Hurst from Goose Bay to Warton, fitted with two 2250-litre and two 1500-litre external tanks.

The eight Mk 3 operating squadrons and single trials flight are detailed below in order of formation.

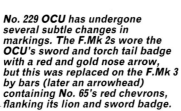

No. 229 Operational Conversion Unit/No. 65 (Reserve) Squadron

By contrast with the GR.Mk 1 syllabus, aircrew destined for the interceptor Tornado are trained at a single unit which is responsible for both conversion to the aircraft and teaching combat techniques. No. 229 'unofficially' formed at Coningsby on 1 November 1984 in order to take delivery of its first pair of Tornado F.Mk 2s (ZA901 and ZA903) on 5 November, although it was 4 February 1985 before the first instructors began their training courses with BAe at Warton. The OCU was officially constituted on 1 May 1985 with Wing Commander R.S. 'Rick' Peacock-Edwards in command, and introduced itself to the public on that year's air show circuit with a co-ordinated display by a Tornado and a Spitfire of the co-located Battle of Britain Memorial Flight.

The initial build-up was completed on 21 October 1985 with the arrival of the 16th F.Mk 2, and on the same day the Tornado made its first participation in an air defence exercise when OCU crews took part in 'Priory 85/2'. A further event of note was the provision of nine aircraft to overfly London for the Queen's official birthday on 14 June 1986, the unit repeating this with 16 on 16 June 1990. Not until the autumn of 1986 was the target of 18 instructor crews achieved for 'A' and 'B' Flights – 'C' Flight being the standards section for instructor training and 'D' Flight, the ground school. Delivery of Tornado F. Mk 3s began with ZE159 on 28 July 1986 and some F.Mk 2s were dispatched to storage without having trained a single student, the last of them departing in January 1988.

First crews for No. 29 Squadron arrived on 1 December 1986 to begin conversion. Those with no air defence experience receive the Long Course, which includes 61.35 hours for the pilot and 48.45 for the navigator over six months. Because most of this time is spent with instructors, 105.00 hours of airborne time is needed to produce a crew. The Short Course lasts three months, but at 60.00 hours and 48.55 hours for pilot and navigator appears to be almost exactly the same length. However, because of earlier teaming-up, only 82.45 hours are needed per crew. Training aids include a Tornado Air Interception Trainer, operational since October 1985 for pilots and navigators to practise use of Foxhunter radar; a mission simulator; and a twin-dome combat simulator which was commissioned on 4 December 1987.

Delays with delivery of radars resulted in many aircraft flying with lead ballast in the nose until late in 1986 and also caused abandonment of plans to form a new squadron at Coningsby as the first operational Tornado interceptor unit. Instead, the RAF took the unusual step of assigning a reserve role to the OCU before any other squadrons had converted, and the title of No. 65 Squadron was awarded on 1 January 1987. Aircraft now wear OCU insignia on the fin and No. 65's on the

No. 229 OCU has undergone several subtle changes in markings. The F.Mk 2s wore the OCU's sword and torch tail badge with a red and gold nose arrow, but this was replaced on the F.Mk 3 by bars (later an arrowhead) containing No. 65's red chevrons, flanking its lion and sword badge.

A handful of F.Mk 3s have regained the red and yellow arrowhead worn by the unit's F.Mk 2s, although this has always been worn at the top of the fin on the newer variant. The torch and sword badge have remained constant.

One No. 229 OCU F.Mk 3 is used as the RAF's Tornado display aircraft, and as such wears a striking red and white tailfin, with a red spine and red lines under fuselage and wings.

forward fuselage. By the beginning of 1990, the unit was operating 28 Tornado F.Mk 3s, although this number was expected to be reduced following completion of training for No. 111 Squadron at the end of that year. Interesting squadron exchanges were conducted with Canadian CF-18 Hornets in April 1988 and Swedish JA 37 Viggens in August 1989. For the 1990 air display season, aerobatic pilot Flight Lieutenant Fred Grundy flew a specially marked No. 229 OCU aircraft celebrating the 50th anniversary of the Battle of Britain.

Tornado F.Mk 3 Operational Evaluation Unit

This was formed with four Block 11 aircraft on 1 April 1987, under the command of Wing Commander Mal Gleave, as a lodger unit at RAF Coningsby. The establishment of four aircraft must always represent the latest production standard, especially insofar as radar is concerned. Accordingly, the unit has a high turnover of aircraft. Block 12 aircraft arrived from 21 December 1987, and Block 13 from February 1989. The F3OEU, as it is known in short, is one of the flying arms of the Central Tactics and Trials Organisation (CTTO). The role of the unit is to develop tactics and operational doctrine for the Tornado F.Mk 3 force, and it accomplishes this by conducting trials to evaluate F.Mk 3 aircraft and weapons systems as well as by spearheading tactical thinking. It liaises closely with the front-line squadrons, British Aerospace, GEC-Ferranti, EASAMS and other interested parties. Advanced radar trials, night operations with NVGs and advanced tactical evaluations have occupied much time lately, and in the summer of 1990 the F3OEU was at the forefront of operational test and evaluation during 'Operation Granby', the deployment of British forces to counter the Iraqi invasion of Kuwait.

Above: The F.Mk 3 OEU, like the SAOEU, uses the three-sword and circle badge of the CTTO.

The F.Mk 3 Operational Evaluation Unit tests and evaluates new tactics and equipment, like the unidentified pods seen left.

No. 29 Squadron

Chosen to be the first squadron (after the OCU) to receive Tornado F.Mk 3s, No. 29 formerly flew Phantom FGR.Mk 2s at Coningsby. On 1 December 1986 it stood down from operational commitments and formally disbanded as a Phantom squadron on 31 March 1987. In the meantime, the first batch of aircrew for the 'new' No. 29 began their ground school training with the OCU in December 1986. Wing Commander Lloyd Doble was appointed CO on 25 April 1987 and the squadron returned to operational status on 1 November that year. Since 1 January 1980, No. 29 had been assigned to SACLANT for maritime defence, that commitment being picked up once more with the Tornado. The squadron is additionally responsible for out-of-area (i.e. non-NATO) interceptor commitments: this was part of the reason for it being chosen for Operation Golden Eagle, an ambitious circumnavigation of the globe. Between 21 August and 26 October 1988 four aircraft participated in a Malaysian air defence exercise, operated with the Royal Thai Air Force, visited air forces in South East Asia and took part in air shows in Sydney (for the Australian bicentennial celebrations) and Harrisburg, Pennsylvania. At the latter, Flight Lieutenant Fred Grundy gave the first Tornado aerobatic display in the American continent. Detachments were made to Akrotiri for APC in February-March 1988 and March-April 1989.

No. 5 Squadron

As indicated by the 'C' prefix to its code letters, No. 5 was the third Tornado interceptor unit to form. Stood-down from operational commitments as a Lightning F.Mk 6 squadron at Binbrook on 31 October 1987 and flying its final sortie on 10 December, it took up residence at Coningsby on 1 January 1988, led by Wing Commander Euan Black. A trial of the squadron's new markings had been made on ZE256 in June 1987, but its first aircraft was ZE292, which arrived from BAe on 25 September 1987. As soon as possible, however, the Batch 5 aircraft that initially equipped the squadron were exchanged for Batch 6 machines. No. 5 became operational on 1 May 1988 and conducted APC in Cyprus during July-August 1988 and May-June 1989. Four of its aircraft operated from Tanagra, Greece, on a one-way exchange in August 1989. In 1990 it was chosen to provide a defending force of four aircraft to participate in the Malaysian air defence exercise ADEX 90-2. Deployed to RMAFB Butterworth in March of that year, it flew sorties directed by local fighter controllers, extending its CAPs by refuelling from two VC10 K.Mk 2s of No. 101 Squadron.

No. 5 Squadron's maple leaf badge is worn with great pride. It dates from World War I, when the unit played an active part supporting the Canadian Corps on the Western Front.

Above: What might have been. No. 5 Squadron's first aircraft was initially painted up in this less-than-striking colour scheme, with markings restricted to the same sort of small fin flash worn on some of the unit's last Lightnings. Fortunately someone came up with the rather bolder colour scheme that is worn today.

Tornado Operators

Right: This aircraft is one of those sent to Dhahran, Saudi Arabia, in the wake of Iraq's invasion of Kuwait. The detachment at Dhahran, which contained aircrew and aircraft from No. 29, and aircrew from No. 11, was known as No. 5 (Composite) Squadron under the command of Euan Black.

No. 11 Squadron

Stood-down at Binbrook as a Lightning F.Mk 6 squadron on 30 April 1988, No. 11 flew its final sortie on 30 June. Meanwhile, No. 11 (Designate) Squadron was established at Coningsby on 1 May 1988 under Wing Commander David Hamilton. Its first F.Mk 3, ZE764, had arrived at Coningsby on 25 April and became the CO's aircraft. On 1 July 1988, the official date of formation, it and two others flew to Leeming to take up residence. (The station had received its first Tornado when ZE761 arrived on short-term loan for engineering familiarisation on 28 March 1988.) Declared operational on 1 November 1988, the squadron celebrated its new status by taking off before dawn to fly to Akrotiri for an armament practice camp. In December, shortly after returning, it was subjected to its first Taceval. Coincident with becoming operational, the squadron assumed the maritime defence task until then held by No. 43 Squadron, at that time Phantom-equipped. Accordingly, No. 11 operates from a large Type C hangar at Leeming, and in time of war would re-deploy to Stornoway or elsewhere. Its first squadron exchange was with Danish F-16s of Esk 726 in 1989.

No. 11 Squadron's badge consists of two eagles, and commemorates the unit's origins as a two-seat fighter squadron. It is worn with pride, and renewed relevance, by today's Tornado aircrew, and on the fins of their aircraft.

No. 23 Squadron

The first of two additional air defence squadrons stationed at Leeming was established on 1 November 1988 under Wing Commander Neil Taylor, whose aircraft, ZE809, had been the first arrival, on 5 August 1988. Thereafter, deliveries from Warton were made directly to Leeming, and not via Coningsby, as had been the case with No. 11 Squadron. Housed in the first of two new HAS complexes, No. 23 undertook its initial armament practice camp at Akrotiri, Cyprus, in June/July 1989 before being declared operational on 1 August 1989. Celebration of that fact was muted by the loss on 21 July of the RAF's first Tornado interceptor (ZE833), which crashed into the North Sea. A second APC was conducted in May 1990.

Above: No. 23 Squadron's official badge is an eagle preying on a smaller bird. The prey is omitted on the version carried on the fins of the unit's Tornados, to avoid confusion with No. 29's rather similar insignia.

Above: The squadron flying suit patch comes complete with unit nickname.

Below: This Tornado F.Mk 3 wears standard No. 23 Squadron markings and is allocated to one of the flight commanders, Squadron Leader Tony Paxton, who photographed the specially painted 75th anniversary aircraft above.

No. 25 Squadron

The third and last Leeming squadron was also the second at that base to be re-formed from scratch, although the unit was until 30 September 1989 an operator of the Bloodhound Mk 2 SAM. No. 25 (Designate) Squadron was established at Leeming on 1 July 1989 and officially came into being on 1 October, commanded by Wing Commander A.M. 'Mick' Martin. Its first Tornado (ZE858) had been received at Leeming as long before as 15 December 1988, however, after being used at Coningsby for working up, it and five others made a symbolic arrival at their new base on 3 July 1989. No. 25 was

declared operational on 1 January 1990 and two days later had its readiness tested by a Taceval. ZE838 was painted in special colours for the squadron's 75th anniversary in 1990.

No. 25 Squadron's official badge portrays a hawk rising from a gauntlet, and is worn on the tailfins of the squadron's Tornados.

No. 25 Squadron's markings recall the parallel black bars worn in the 1920s and 1930s.

No. 43 Squadron

The busiest of the RAF's fighter bases in terms of Soviet aircraft interceptions, Leuchars was the last to receive Tornado F.Mk 3s. First to arrive on the station, for technical familiarisation, was ZE963, which was received from Warton on 23 August 1989. No. 43 Squadron, equipped with Phantom FG.Mk 1s, was stood-down on 30 June 1989 and flew its final operational sortie on 31 July. Its first two aircraft, ZE961 and ZE962, were delivered from Coningsby

on 23 September and the squadron then began re-forming under Wing Commander Andy Moir, whose aircraft, ZE966, delivered on 9 January 1990, is the 800th production Tornado and 160th ADV. It is also the squadron commander's aircraft, its tail letters 'GF' being the initials of the squadron motto – *Gloria Finis* (Glory to the End). It differs from the squadron aircraft in that it also has a black/white chequer flash at the tip of the fin. The squadron is now fully operational, having declared on 1 July 1990.

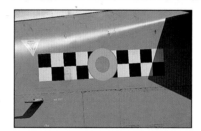

No. 43 Squadron's traditional black and white checks and fighting cock emblem are alive and well.

Left: Treble-One's badge comprises a Palestine cross, three seaxes, and two crossed swords. These signify various bases used by the unit in the past.

Below: No. 111 Squadron's Tornados carry codes between 'HA' and 'HZ', and wear a distinctive black and gold lightning flash that runs forward from the engine intakes. The squadron is the newest RAF Tornado ADV unit.

No. 111 Squadron

Companion to No. 43 Squadron, this unit flew its final operational Phantom FG.Mk 1 sortie on 31 October 1989, following which the Quick Reaction Alert (Interceptor) task within Sector 1 passed entirely to the Leeming Wing for the duration of re-equipment. No. 111 continued to fly the Phantom for aircrew currency training until the end of January 1990. A new No. 111 Squadron was in process of formation during mid-1990 with Wing Commander P.B. Walker as its first CO. The first flight with the new aircraft took place on 1 May 1990, and the squadron expects to complete training with the Tornado F.Mk 3 and become fully combat-ready by the end of 1990.

Aeroplane & Armament Experimental Establishment

A&AEE is assigned to exploration of military developments of aircraft from its base at Boscombe Down. Its first Tornado, P.12/XZ630, was received on 3 February 1978 and was followed by several others, but only a GR.Mk 1A and an F.Mk 2 were in use by mid-1990.

Empire Test Pilots' School

Not strictly involved with trials, the ETPS is, however, responsible for producing many of the pilots and flight engineers who will be involved with testing new aircraft. Based at Boscombe Down, its varied fleet was augmented early in 1988 by a Tornado F.Mk 2.

Below: RAe Bedford's 'raspberry ripple' Tornado was nearly written off after a fire, but was repaired and allocated to the MoD (PE).

Royal Aerospace Establishment

The RAE – known until 1 May 1988 as the Royal Aircraft Establishment – concerns itself with research, rather than the military applications of aircraft. Since 1983 its Flight Systems Department has operated from Bedford a Tornado GR.Mk 1 in a high-visibility red, white and blue colour scheme (known as 'raspberry ripple') on a number of programmes, including advanced terrain-following techniques, stores carriage and release, and investigation of low-level turbulence. On 24 April 1988, an F.Mk 2 was delivered to Farnborough for use by 'A' Flight of the Experimental Flying Squadron. After an extensive fitting-out programme, it is due to return to the air in 1991.

Luftwaffe der Deutschen Bundesrepublik

The Luftwaffe was one of the two Federal German armed forces with a requirement for the Tornado. Eventually, this was to cover 212 aircraft (plus 112 for the navy) to which have been added 35 (reduced from a target of 40) more in ECR configuration from Batch 7. There is a stated need for 35 IDS Tornados in Batch 8, whilst long-term plans have examined the prospect of up to 60 more, but unification of East and West Germany make it unlikely that these options will be adopted. Firm Luftwaffe Tornado orders are:

	Standard	Dual control	ECR	Total
Prototypes	2			2
Batch 1	3	11		14
Batch 2	15	11		26
Batch 3	24	12		36
Batch 4	56	8		64
Batch 5	31			31
Batch 6	26	13		39
Batch 7			35	35
Totals	**157**	**55**	**35**	**247**

Aircraft have been built alongside those for the navy, using a single batch of serial numbers beginning at 4301, which first flew at Manching on 27 July 1979. The last of the original 210 production aircraft, 4622, was completed in October 1989, and the first ECR (4623) flew on the 26th of the same month, piloted by H. Hickel. The Luftwaffe intended to have 53 dual control aircraft, but later increased this to 55 at the expense of standard IDS versions. Production rates were slowed in the early 1980s for reasons of short-term economy, and instead of building up from 46 to 63 per year between 1981 and 1983 West Germany received 44, 44 and 42 respectively. A similar move was made by the UK.

Tornados have replaced the Lockheed F-104G Starfighter in service with four combat wings (each of two squadrons) and a single-squadron training wing (JBG 38) is currently adding a second component equipped with 18 of the ECR. Usual complement of a wing (Geschwader) is 38 aircraft including four dual control, or 32 (14 dual) in the case of

JBG 38. An individual squadron (Staffel) draws aircraft from the base pool as required, and therefore the badge appearing on Tornados is of the wing only. Squadrons are numbered as a function of their wing, with (for example) JBG 31 possessing 311 and 312 Squadrons in NATO parlance – or 1/JBG 31 and 2/JBG 31 in the traditional Luftwaffe manner. Tornados based at Cottesmore with the TTTE have the 'shadow' identity of JBG 39. In the unlikely event that the previously planned 35 Batch 8 Tornado IDSs are ordered, they will go to Husum in 1995, where JBG 41 will re-equip from Alpha Jets and become JBG 37.

The first Tornado camouflage scheme was grey, green and black with light grey undersides, this changing with aircraft 4391 to a three-tone green scheme overall. Earlier aircraft have adopted the new markings when being overhauled. Detachable refuelling probes are fitted when aircraft are ferried to Goose Bay, Canada, to undergo low-level training. As West Germany has no large tanker aircraft, USAF KC-135s or KC-10s provide support, fitting refuelling drogues to their 'flying booms'. Tornados occasionally act as target tugs for aerial gunnery practice, carrying a Dornier Aerial Target System 3 in the form of a winch-pod on the port underfuselage pylon and a dart-shaped target suspended from the centre and starboard pylons until the time of launch. The first experimental flight of the equipment was made at Erprobungsstelle 61 on 12 September 1984.

A further Tornado 'operating' unit is Technischeschule der Luftwaffe 1 at Kaufbeuren, which since 1982 has kept two non-flying but fully serviceable aircraft for technical training. They are exchanged at regular intervals to ensure even utilisation.

Tornado crews are trained at RAF Cottesmore and then with JBG 38 at Jever. Navigators undergo basic instruction in Dornier Do 28D Skyservants of 3/JBG 49 and then Boeing T-43s in the USA, before being literally 'brought up to speed' by a short fast-jet familiarisation course in the back seats of Alpha Jets of 2/JBG 49 at Fürstenfeldbruck. Only then do they go to TTTE for the Tornado phase. 2/JBG 49 is also responsible for Alpha Jet pilot conversion, but such was the urgent requirement for Tornado weapon systems officers (known in West Germany as Kampfbeobachter – Combat Observer) in the mid-1980s that it was completely preoccupied with this task.

Five Luftwaffe fighter-bomber wings are equipped with Tornados, as listed in order of formation.

Jagdbombergeschwader 38 'Friesland'

Following the decision to undertake its own weapons training instead of participating in a joint unit at Honington, the Luftwaffe made preparations to adapt the Starfighter weapons school, Waffenschule 10, at Jever. Initially, however, a small unit was established as part of the maintenance unit (*Luftwaffenversorgungsregiment* 1) at Erding. Within *LsVersRgt* 1, *Technische-gruppe* 11 was responsible for acceptance checking of Tornados, and it was an offshoot of this, the Weapons Training Component (*Waffenausbildungs-komponente* – WaKo), which received its first aircraft (4328) for training on 9 November 1981.

When commissioned on 16 February 1982 WaKo had received nine of its allocated 16 machines, deliveries continuing with 4040 on 31 March 1982 as the 100th Tornado delivered to a service unit. Three WaKo Tornados were the first in West Germany to undertake night bombing, using the range at Munsingers. Moved to Jever on 1 July 1983, having trained 170 pilots and navigators, the unit took over from WS 10, which had flown its last Starfighter mission in the previous May.

On 26 August 1983 it became JBG 38 under Oberstleutnant Hans Klaffenbach, with 24 aircraft, subsequently adding a further eight, including six during 1989 in preparation for formation of a second squadron (382) with 18 Tornado ECRs,

deliveries of which began in January 1990. The ECRs are to Block 14 standard, but will be upgraded with Block 15 improvements after deliveries of the remainder of the 35 on order are made to JBG 32.

At Jever, new crews arriving from Cottesmore fly some 30 hours, together or each with an instructor, learning how to use the aircraft as a weapon system (for example, by dropping practice bombs and training in air combat manoeuvring). At Cottesmore, all the West German aircraft are Luftwaffe machines, and this is almost true at Jever. However, 4379 arrived from MFG 1 on 9 April 1984 in the naval colour scheme for five years' loan, and there have been a limited number of shorter-term interchanges since then.

JBG 38 is also responsible for conducting QFI and QWI training courses for the West German air force and navy Tornado force, and holds electronic warfare courses for all fighter types in the West German inventory. JBG 38 also functions as the West German Tornado Operational Evaluation Unit.

Right, above: The Geschwader badge of JBG 38, as worn on the unit's aircraft, with the badges of the wing's constituent units, 381 Staffel (centre) and 382 Staffel (right). The aircraft pictured (right) wears the old-style grey and green camouflage.

Jagdbombergeschwader 31 'Boelcke'

After equipping the TTTE at Cottesmore and a training unit (later to become JBG 38), production Tornados from MBB were next issued to the navy's MFG 1. JBG 31 thus became the second combat unit to form, having flown its final Starfighter sortie on 30 April 1983. Crew training then began at Cottesmore, and in the meantime 4393 arrived on 26 July 1983 as the wing's first Tornado. Transition to the new aircraft officially began on 1 August 1983 and was scheduled to last a year, the first CO being Oberstleutnant Böttcher. JBG 31 had the minor distinction of receiving the 100th West German production Tornado (4400) on 24 August 1983, this aircraft later receiving a special colour scheme for the wing's 30th anniversary in 1988. In November 1989 JBG 31 took part in Red Flag with JBG 32. This was the first participation by German Tornados. The wing is presently commanded by Oberst D. Reiners, and flew its 50,000th Tornado hour on 23 August 1990, the first German wing to achieve such a total. JBG 31 also has a Tornado flying

German Staffel badges are rarely seen, since they are worn by aircrew but not by aircraft, which are not allocated to individual squadrons but pooled in the wing. JBG 31 has taken the traditions of the Boelcke Geschwader.

display team.

Trained initially for nuclear strike duties, JBG 31 received its first MW-1 pods on 22 November 1984. In May 1986, one of its aircraft, accompanied by another from JBG 38, flew from Beja (Portugal) to St Johns (Canada) in the course of the first non-stop Tornado transatlantic flight to use 'buddy'

refuelling (in the form of two other JBG 31 aircraft). At Eglin AFB, Florida, two live drops of the MW-1 bomblets were demonstrated, and the aircraft appeared at Andrews AFB open day before returning. Having meanwhile received clearance for refuelling from KC-135 tankers, nine JBG 31 aircraft flew from Nörvenich to Goose Bay

in six hours 20 minutes at the start of a training detachment. Liaison with the RAF has included squadron exchanges with TWCU in 1986 and Tornado F.Mk 3s of No. 29 Squadron in May 1989. The wing, currently in the hands of Oberst D. Reiners, flew its 40,000th Tornado hour on 28th July 1989.

JBG 32's badge incorporates the traditional blue checkers of Bavaria with a diving eagle and the NATO star.

Jagdbombergeschwader 32

West German Tornado re-equipment plans envisaged conversion of one wing per year, and thus on 18 April 1984 JBG 32 flew its final Starfighter mission and began the Tornado conversion process. Its first aircraft, 4436, was received on 27 July and the unit officially re-formed on 1 August, taking a year to become operational. In 1988 it celebrated its 30th anniversary by decorating 4450 in a special colour scheme.

JBG 32 comprises 321 and 322 Squadrons with Tornados and 323 with Hansa Jets in the ECM training role. There is no fourth Staffel, although the wing parents the joint military/civilian calibration unit, the GFMS (*Gemeinsame Flugvermessungsstelle*) Fachbereich IV with BAe 125s and HS.748s. When Tornado ECRs are received from May 1991, they will re-equip 321 Squadron, and the unit's current Tornado IDS aircraft will be re-distributed to other units. The other units will continue in its attack role. JBG 32 has a purely conventional assignment, and is the only front-line German Tornado wing never to have had a nuclear strike commitment. JBG 32 won the flight safety trophy in 1989, and the Prinz Heinrich Preis for the best overall performance by a flying wing.

Left: One JBG 32 Tornado was painted up in this eye-catching colour scheme to celebrate the unit's 30th anniversary.

Jagdbombergeschwader 33 Büchel

Third of the air force wings to re-equip, JBG 33 relinquished its final Starfighter on 30 May 1985 in preparation for Tornados. Delivery of the first, 4472, took place in August 1985, the wing having received its full complement a year later. Like other Luftwaffe wings, JBG 33 has the dual roles of nuclear strike and conventional attack.

Below: After starting with a green and sea grey camouflage, with light grey undersides, most Luftwaffe Tornados now wear an overall two-tone dark green lizard camouflage, and unit markings and codes are small. Occasionally a colourful touch may be added, such as the shark's mouth applied to the chaff dispenser carried by this JBG 33 aircraft.

Above: The diving-eagle badge of JBG 33 now incorporates the silhouette of a Tornado. It is otherwise identical to the badges carried by the unit's F-104Gs and F-84s.

Jagdbombergeschwader 34 Memmingen

After JBG 33, the navy's second wing received Tornados, so JBG 34 was required to wait until 16 October 1987 to fly its last Starfighter mission. Delivery of new equipment began immediately with 4560, the wing being declared operational in June 1988. The final aircraft (4603) arrived in August 1988, although four dual-control Tornados were later received to replace a similar number delivered earlier. By August 1988 West German Tornados of both air arms had flown over 160,000 hours for the loss of eight aircraft.

The Geschwader badge of JBG 34 is flanked by the badges of the unit's two squadrons: 1/JBG 34 'Grunherz' and 2/JBG 34 'Edelweiss'.

Marineflieger

In common with the Luftwaffe, West German naval aviation required the Tornado to replace its Starfighters in the strike/attack role, but also to undertake reconnaissance. As it had not benefitted from the interim purchase of McDonnell Douglas F-4 Phantoms – as had the air force when it became clear that the Tornado would not meet its in-service target of 1975 – the navy had priority for the first combat-assigned Tornados produced by MBB. Responsible, with Denmark, for representing NATO in the Baltic and its approaches, West Germany assigns its Tornados partly to anti-shipping attack.

Conversion to the Tornado was a major undertaking for the Marineflieger. Not only would it have to learn how to operate the first front-line examples of the aircraft, but it also needed to train from scratch a new class of flier: the fast-jet weapon systems officer. The air force had at least tackled this problem when it received Phantoms; for the navy it was an entirely new experience. Fortunately, training of crews in the UK and with a Luftwaffe-run weapons school eased the burden.

After a few small problems were overcome with computer software (for example, some attack procedures were too complicated), the Tornado settled down to be a potent and highly reliable all-weather combat aircraft. The Navy's requirement was originally for 112 aircraft, including 10 with dual control, to equip two wings, each of two squadrons, but in the event 12 'twin-stick' machines were obtained. Both wings were issued with 48 aircraft when re-equipped, and only in 1989 did they receive the balance of the Marineflieger order. Deliveries were:

	Standard	Dual control	Total
Batch 2	12	5	17
Batch 3	32		32
Batch 5	34	5	39
Batch 6	22	2	24
Totals	**100**	**12**	**112**

Prime Tornado anti-shipping weapon is the MBB Kormoran missile, the Mk 1s having been taken over from Starfighters. Kormoran Mk 2 was issued to squadrons in 1989, requirements being for 174 of this variant to follow the 350 Mk 1s. Up to four Kormorans are carried, the Mk 2 having multiple-launch capability. As well as self-protection AIM-9L Sidewinders, Tornados are receiving the Texas Instruments AGM-88A HARM (High-speed Anti-Radiation Missile), of which 556 have been ordered from 944 required. Two or four HARMs are carried on anti-shipping missions, it being possible to fit two plus a pair of Kormorans for maximum flexibility. The Tornado's HI-LO-LO-HI mission radius of 1575 km allows it to cover the entire Baltic from its home bases, but for a long-range mission entirely at low level a Sargent-Fletcher 28-300 'buddy' system has been acquired, together with the same firm's 'clip-on' semi-retracting receiver probe. The navy received 73 pods, although 96 aircraft are equipped to carry them.

MFG 1's aircraft were delivered in a colour scheme of bluish-grey upper surfaces with white beneath. In 1985, 4385 was re-painted in a new disruptive pattern camouflage scheme of three-tone grey, but when aircraft for MFG 2 were delivered from August 1986 it was found that this had been rejected in favour of a two-tone grey disruptive scheme covering the whole aircraft. Some MFG 1 aircraft have been similarly painted subsequently.

Marinefliegergeschwader 1

The first Marineflieger Tornado was a trials aircraft, 4327, delivered to Erprobungsstelle 61 late in 1981. On 29 October that year, MFG 1 flew its final Starfighter mission and stood down for re-training at Cottesmore. Deliveries began to MFG 1 at Schleswig-Jagel on 2 July 1982, the unit building up over the next 12 months to 48 aircraft, of which five were dual-control. In its first six months, the wing flew 1,000 hours, and by early 1983 it was the first unit with the Multiple Weapon Carrier System of three underfuselage weapon attachments. The first CO was Kapitän zur See Waldemar Scholz, who had been replaced by KzS Klaus-Jurgen Wewetzer by the time the wing was declared operational on 1 January 1984.

On 20 July 1984, two aircraft flew from Beja, Portugal, to the Azores across 980 miles (1580 km) of featureless ocean and landed 2 hours 40 minutes later with a mean navigation system error of 6 feet (2 metres). Liaison with RAF Tornado

operations has included a squadron exchange to No. 229 OCU at Coningsby in August 1987, whilst on 24 May 1989 MFG 1 under KzS L.-U. Klöckner became the first Tornado wing to complete 50,000 hours. MFG 1 is armed with Kormoran, BL755 CBUs and conventional bombs and progresses rapidly in HARM integration.

This MFG 1 Tornado wears the original grey and white colour scheme and carries a buddy refuelling pod on the centreline. Most Marineflieger Tornados are now camouflaged.

Marinefliegergeschwader 2

MFG 2 was the fifth West German Tornado wing, arrival of its first aircraft taking place on 11 September 1986, although the last Starfighter sortie was not flown until May 1987. Aircraft issued were five dual-control and 43 standard models, those of 1/MFG 2 equipped with a 380-kg MBB-Aeritalia tactical reconnaissance pod on the centreline. West Germany ordered 26 of these units, each containing two Zeiss visual spectrum cameras and a Texas Instruments RS-710 infra-red linescan for all-weather photography. The 1 Staffel aircraft fly the daily 'Eastern Express' mission into the Baltic, photographing all shipping movements and anything else of interest. Tornados of 2 Staffel have a strike/attack tasking using the same weapons as MFG 1, with the addition of HARM. Unlike the Luftwaffe, which regards HARM as self-protection on all but the ECR, the navy uses the weapon offensively in anti-shipping

missions. In 1988, four MFG 2 aircraft staged to the US West Coast and back in an 11-day mission, supported for their transatlantic journey from the Azores to Newfoundland by two 'buddy' tanker Tornados.

MFG 2's Tornados are equipped to carry an MBB/Aeritalia reconnaissance pod, and those of the second Staffel are wired for the HARM anti-radiation missile.

Wehrtechnische Dienststelle für Luftfahrtzeuge 61

Based at Manching, WTD 61 was known until 1987 as Erprobungsstelle 61. Involvement with Tornado flying began with the prototypes and has continued through to the present-day development of the ECR version, using several Luftwaffe and Marineflieger aircraft. In

addition to testing new weapons and equipment, ESt 61 undertook acceptance trials of an early-production machine, 4319, delivered on 2 July 1981. For this, the Tornado Introduction team was formed to conduct a 315-hour/18-month four-phase test programme undertaken partly at Manching and partly by operational units.

Aeronautica Militare Italiana

In common with West Germany, Italy had no experience of supersonic combat aircraft design when it joined the Panavia consortium, both nations having previously relied upon licensed manufacture of Starfighters to equip their air arms. The Italian preference for a single-seat Tornado was an indication that the AMI saw its new aircraft as a less sophisticated fighting machine, and it, like the West German navy, had to start training 'back-seaters' when the Tornado arrived. Unfortunately, this should have begun *before* the aircraft became available, so some Italian navigator places at Cottesmore went unfilled in the early days.

Italy chose to introduce the Tornado slightly later than its companions, so none was ordered in Batch 1 production. One pre-series aircraft was refurbished to join 99 series-built, including 12 with dual controls. The latter have serials MM50000-50011, while standard IDS versions are MM7001-7088. Italy did not slow its production rates in the early 1980s as did Britain and West Germany, the plan being for it to accept eight, 23, 24, 23 and 11 aircraft in 1982-86 respectively.

	Standard	Dual control	Total
Refurbished	1		1
Batch 2	10	5	15
Batch 3	23	5	28
Batch 4	27		27
Batch 5	27	2	29
Totals	**88**	**12**	**100**

The first Batch 2 aircraft built by Aeritalia, MM50000, was rolled out on 1 July 1981 and first flew on 25 September. Fourth off the line, MM7003, was first in service hands when it was delivered to Cameri-Novara on 17 May 1982 for 1° Centro Manutenzione Principale. The 1° CMP had formed on 1 November 1981 with responsibility for Tornado third-level overhauls and repairs, its single aircraft being assigned for familiarisation. Meanwhile, urgent steps were being taken to provide a cadre of navigators with fast-jet experience by flying those newly trained in the back seats of TF-104G Starfighters or West German F-4 Phantoms.

The AMI formally assigned only 54 Tornados to combat squadrons, but a further 36 are designated as in-use reserves and the remainder either went to Cottesmore or trials' units. Three fighter-bomber squadrons (*Gruppi Caccia-Bombardieri*) operate the aircraft, each attached to a different wing (Stormo) and the insignia of each is normally applied to aircraft. Squadrons comprise four flights (Squadriglie) for administrative purposes.

Italy's first overseas deployment took place in June 1987 when six aircraft of all three squadrons staged via Cottesmore and Goose Bay to Selfridge ANGB, refuelled by RAF VC10s, for exercise 'Sentry Wolverine' with the Michigan ANG. The Tornados flew 137

Three Tornados of the 154° Gruppo, 6° Stormo near their base at Brescia-Ghedi, the first of Italy's three Tornado IDS units. Italian Tornados serve with only three front-line units, and with the TTTE at Cottesmore. Ninety were ordered, 36 of them to serve as in-use reserves. Italy requires 16 of the new ECR variant, which was jointly developed with Germany.

simulated combat missions and 360 hours, including maritime attack over Lake Michigan. They returned in the same manner late in July, but in 1990 the first of four AMI Boeing 707 tankers became available, giving Italy autonomy in its refuelling support.

For the future, Italy has joined with West Germany in a Tornado mid-life update programme, the details of which are being worked upon, and in development of the ECR version, of which 16 are required. The three operating squadrons, in order of re-equipment, are detailed overleaf.

Tornado Operators

154° Gruppo Caccia-Bombardieri Brescia-Ghedi (6° Stormo 'Alfredo Fusca')

Previously equipped with F-104G Starfighters, the 154° Gruppo (comprising 380ª, 391ª, 305ª and 396ª Squadriglie) stood down early in 1982 for conversion to Tornados. On completion of training at RAF Cottesmore, the Wing CO, Lieutenant-Colonel Gabriele Ingrosso, delivered MM7006 to Ghedi on 27 August to begin the building-up of an instructor cadre for the AMI's Tornado force. That done, No. 154 Squadron was re-formed in February 1983 and formally commissioned on 20 May that year with a unit establishment of 18 aircraft. Training of new personnel to expand the force was hampered by the irregular supply of spares; late completion of base infrastructure; and delays in the training of technicians, with the result that pilots were only able to manage 120-130 flying hours per month instead of the NATO-specified minimum of 180. One positive feature of these early days was that, despite its novelty, the Tornado was delivering better serviceability per maintenance hour than the Starfighter.

In 1984, Tornados participated in Exercise 'Mare Aperto' as 'Orange' forces attacking Italian naval vessels while Starfighters (unsuccessfully) attempted to intercept. Only in spring 1985 could No. 154 Squadron

be declared operational, after crews had completed their own in-house weapons training. An early squadron exchange was made with No. 27 Squadron at RAF Marham in April 1986. Participation in 'Red Flag' had included six aircraft flown out to Nellis AFB via Cottesmore in October 1989. The squadron presently has some 36 aircraft on strength.

The 154° Gruppo marks its aircraft with a bold red lightning flash on the tailfin, on which is superimposed the 6° Stormo's devil badge.

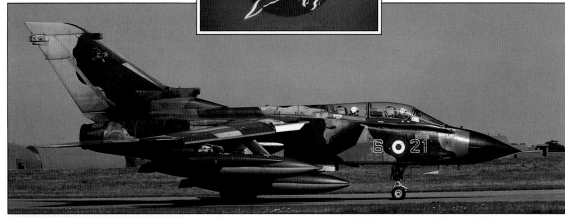

156° Gruppo Caccia-Bombardieri Gioia del Colle (36° Stormo 'Helmut Seidl')

Italy's second Tornado squadron was a previous operator of the F-104S Starfighter in a two-squadron wing whose second component (12° Gruppo) continues to fly this aircraft. Components of the squadron are the 381ª, 382ª, 383ª and 384ª Squadriglie. After training at RAF Cottesmore and with its own aircraft at Ghedi, No. 156 Squadron returned to its home base in May 1984 with 18 aircraft, including two dual-control, and became operational in August, commanded by Colonello Massimo Tommaso Ferro. Roles of the unit are ground attack and anti-shipping with Kormoran missiles. It was operating 24 Tornados in 1990.

Right: 156° Gruppo Tornados carry the 36° Stormo eagle badge superimposed on a yellow lightning flash on the fin.

The 156° Gruppo's lynx's-head badge is carried on the engine intake. The intakes of Italian Tornados are edged in red, for safety reasons. The unit has an anti-shipping commitment.

155° Gruppo Caccia-Bombardieri Piacenza (50° Stormo 'Giorgio Graffer')

In its previous incarnation, No. 155 Squadron (361ª, 364ª, 365ª and 378ª Squadriglie) was an F-104S Starfighter unit under 51° Stormo at Istrana. Stood-down to begin Tornado conversion in September 1984, it was transferred to Ghedi on 1 January 1985, making 6° Stormo a two-squadron wing. Training was completed during the year and the squadron remained with its new parent unit until 1 December 1989 when 50° Stormo was re-activated at Piacenza. Transfer of the aircraft to Piacenza did not begin until the following spring, however. No. 155 Squadron's roles include tactical reconnaissance with the Aeritalia-MBB sensor pod, its current strength being 16 aircraft.

The 155° Gruppo originated as the second Gruppo of the 6° Stormo at Ghedi, and its aircraft thus wore 6- codes and the red devil badge, but with a blue tail marking and the Gruppo badge on the intake.

Reparto Sperimentale di Volo

Having the alternative designation, 311° Gruppo (535ª and 536ª Squadriglie) of the Italian air force, the RSV is responsible for trials of aircraft for all three armed services. Aircraft of its permanent fleet, based at Pratica di Mare, have identity numbers prefixed 'RS-', two Tornados being in use during 1990.

A number of Tornados have been used by the Reparto Sperimentale di Volo for test and trials work.

Al Quwwat al Jawwiya as Sa'udiya

The Royal Saudi Air Force has been a long-term patron of the UK aircraft industry, and of Warton's products in particular, having previously bought Lightnings and Strikemasters. Although narrowly the second export customer, it was the first non-European recipient due to the postponement and eventual cancellation of Oman's order. Despite being a sizeable air arm in the region, the RSAF is far from self-supporting and requires the services of an expatriate workforce for instruction and technical support.

Early delivery of an initial batch of 20 aircraft was included in the terms of the first Saudi Tornado order for 48 IDSs and 24 ADVs, signed on 26 September 1985. Accordingly the RAF relinquished the last 18 of its final 20 GR.Mk 1s, these including four with dual control. As the RSAF required six in this configuration, two airframes originally to have been for West Germany in Batch 7 were brought forward on the line and completed in Batch 5 production. The eventual order position is currently:

	Standard IDS	Dual IDS	Standard ADV	Dual ADV	Total
Batch 5	14	4			18
Batch 7(5)		2			2
Batch 6			18	6	24
Batch 7	20	8			28
Totals	**34**	**14**	**18**	**6**	**72**

Similarly with the ADV interceptors, 24 RAF F.Mk 3s were set aside for completion to RSAF contracts. All were single-stick Tornados, but as will be seen above, six were completed with dual control. Batch 7 includes 'pay-backs' for the RAF as well as further new production for the RSAF. Provisional agreement was reached on an additional 12 IDS and 36 ADV Tornados, but no formal order was signed.

Tornado squadrons have been formed in numerical order, as indicated below.

7 Squadron

Formerly equipped with Northrop F-5E Tiger IIs, No. 7 Squadron was selected as the first RSAF Tornado unit, equipped with IDS attack versions. The first, originally laid down for the RAF as ZD997, made its first flight on 7 February 1986 and was delivered as RSAF 701 on 26-27 March 1986 in company with three others, one of them dual-control. The first local pilots trained at RAF Cottesmore were to fly the aircraft in Saudi Arabia. Two more 'two-stickers' followed in April, but no further deliveries took place until the following year. No. 7 Squadron received its 20th Tornado in October 1987, but completion had to wait until late 1989 when four more dual aircraft were supplied. All IDS versions have an overall disruptive camouflage scheme of sand, green and brown.

A Tornado IDS of No. 7 Squadron before delivery. These moved from Dhahran to Taif after the invasion of Kuwait to make room for USAF F-15s and RAF Tornado ADVs.

29 Squadron

Twelve of the Tornado ADV interceptors ordered by Saudi Arabia are allocated to No. 29 Squadron, all having been originally laid down as F.Mk 3s for the RAF. The first, notionally ZE859, flew on 1 December 1988, 1988, was handed over on 9 February 1989 and delivered to the RSAF as 2905 on 20 March 1989, accompanied by three others. Equipment of the squadron, which includes four dual-control aircraft, was completed on 20 September 1989.

34 Squadron

Also with Tornado ADVs diverted from the RAF, No. 34 Squadron's first aircraft was delivered to Dhahran on 14-15 November 1989 where it was initially assigned to No. 29 Squadron. Completion of the unit is due in 1990. RSAF Tornado ADVs will partner McDonnell Douglas F-15 Eagles in the defence of Saudi airspace, operating in conjunction with Boeing E-3A Sentry AWACS aircraft.

66 Squadron

The second RSAF Tornado IDS attack squadron will be No. 66, which is due to begin forming in 1990 at a base yet to be disclosed. The unit is allocated 24 aircraft, four of them dual-control. Equipment will include some reconnaissance equivalents to the RAF's GR.Mk 1A, plus appropriate ground interpretation facilities.

The serial 2903 identifies this aircraft as belonging to No. 29 Squadron based at Dhahran. In August 1990 the unit was commanded by Colonel Yahya Zahrani.

Al Quwwat al Jawwiya al Sultanat Oman

The Sultan of Oman's Air Force intended to purchase eight Tornado ADVs from the UK assembly line, all to be dual-control. The contract, placed on 14 August 1985, was deferred and then cancelled, but the aircraft may be built for the RAF as attrition replacements.

Al Quwwat al Jawwiya al Malakiya al Urduniya

Jordan's requirements for Tornados concerned eight IDS attack aircraft, including three with dual control, to be built in the prospective Batch 8. All were cancelled due to financial stringency.

Falcons on Guard

Once thought of as a poor relation of the active duty Air Force, flying ancient 'hand-me-downs', the Air National Guard can now boast a combat fleet with a similar average age to the regular force. At the heart of this rejuvenation is the introduction of the General Dynamics F-16 Fighting Falcon, now serving in both interceptor and tactical roles.

Nine ANG units employ their F-16s on dual-role tactical duties, involving both air-to-surface attack and battlefield air superiority. This four-ship is from the 157th Tactical Fighter Squadron, 169th TFG, South Carolina ANG, based at McEntire ANGB.

Above: The purposeful shape of the General Dynamics F-16 Fighting Falcon is known the world over, and increasingly so in Air National Guard units. Recent transferrals from the active-duty force and the retirement of F-4 Phantoms now make it the most numerous type in ANG service, with over 350 examples on strength, split between tactical and interceptor duties.

Left: The 'Green Mountain Boys' of the Vermont Air National Guard were famous as the operators of the Martin EB-57 defence systems evaluation platform, but their role today is to defend the north-eastern seaboard of the United States. The single F-16A squadron (134th FIS, 158th FIG) is based at Burlington International Airport, but a four-aircraft alert detachment is maintained at Bangor in Maine.

Right: Air National Guard F-16s now form the bulk of the US air defence network, falling under the command of TAC's 1st Air Force. Guarding the eastern seaboard and its vast population centres are the 119th Fighter Interceptor Squadron, 177th Fighter Interceptor Group of the New Jersey Air National Guard, the famed 'Jersey Devils' from Atlantic City International Airport.

Above: *Flying from Andrews AFB in Maryland, the 121st TFS, 113th TFW flies F-16A/Bs on tactical duties with the District of Columbia ANG.*

Left: *The 'Boys from Syracuse' of the 138th TFS, 174th TF, New York ANG transferred to the F-16A from the A-10A. They retain a specialist gunnery mission, their aircraft equipped with an underfuselage cannon pod.*

Below: *The 182nd TFS of the Texas ANG flies from Kelly AFB.*

Above: Another Texas ANG F-16 unit is the 111th TFS, 147th FIG, an air defence squadron flying from Ellington Field near Houston.

Right: The 'Flying Razorbacks' of the Arkansas ANG base their tactical-dedicated F-16s at Fort Smith. The unit is the 184th TFS.

Above: Several of the air defence units previously flew the graceful Convair F-106 Delta Dart, New Jersey being the last to convert to the F-16.

Below: 186th FIS, 120th FIG aircraft of the Montana ANG help defend the northern states of the US, other units being North Dakota, Minnesota and Michigan ANGs.

Above: The Kansas ANG 'Jayhawks' at McConnell AFB are one of two main F-16 training units dedicated to tactical forces. While front-line units usually have one F-16B two-seater attached for continuation training/orientation purposes, the training units naturally have several on strength. The squadron is the 161st Tactical Fighter Training Squadron, 184th TFG.

Above left: Training for the ANG F-16 air defence force is handled by the 114th TFTS, part of the Oregon ANG based at Kingsley Field. Another Oregon squadron flies the F-15 Eagle for interception duties, one of two squadrons to do so.

Left: The blue stripe and lightning flash of the 159th FIS, 125th FIG, used to adorn the F-106s of the Florida ANG, but is now to be seen on F-16As. Guarding the south-eastern states, the unit flies from Jacksonville International Airport.

Left: *The 162nd Tactical Fighter Group, Arizona ANG, at Tucson is the second Replacement Training Unit for the Guard F-16 fleet, with one squadron assigned (148th TFTS). Dutch F-16 pilots are also trained by the Group, and A-7D Corsair IIs are attached (195th TFTS), making it one of the largest ANG units.*

Left: *A Guardsman holds his F-16 steady during a refuelling, illustrating the superb all-round view available to him thanks to the bulbous one-piece canopy of the Fighting Falcon. ANG personnel regularly prove their ability in air force exercises, often flying away with the top prizes. Being 'part-time' soldiers in no way decreases the fighting ability of the Guardsmen.*

Above: *The Alabama ANG has two squadrons, both featuring a stylish modification to the nose camouflage. One squadron flies the RF-4C tactical reconnaissance platform, while the 160th TFS, 187th TFG flies the F-16A on tactical duties from Dannelly Field, Montgomery.*

Below: *The western seaboard is not so heavily defended as the east, relying on the Oregon and California Guards. The latter fly the F-16 ADF with the 194th FIS, 144th FIW from Fresno. The ADF variant has Sparrow and AMRAAM compatibility, improved radar, IFF and communications, and can be identified by the fairing on the fin/fuselage box.*

P-3 Orion Briefing

In continuous production for 30 years, the first P3V-1 having flown in April 1961 and the 644th and last P-3C being scheduled for delivery in September 1991, the Lockheed Orion will still be in front-line service a quarter of a century from now. This longevity, coupled with virtually unchanged airframe and powerplant installation, clearly evidences the soundness of the basic design. Moreover, the fact that the P-3C Update III is still setting the standard against which other land-based ASW aircraft are compared further confirms that the Orion's original design concept incorporated what it took to cope with the ever more sophisticated threat of quieter submarines.

Quite remarkably, the turboprop-powered Electra airliner from which this superb ASW aircraft was derived had initially experienced major structural and powerplant difficulties. Quickly rendered obsolete in the eyes of travellers by the introduction of pure-jet trans-

ports, it remained in production for only four years and was rapidly withdrawn from use by most major carriers. Fortunately for Lockheed, the Electra's technical difficulties were easily resolved and, unlike airlines, the US Navy and several foreign air forces found considerable

Left: The airframe may have stayed the same, but the current Orion features a considerably upgraded avionics suite compared with the first variants. The P-3C Update III represents the state of the art as far as sub-hunting goes.

Above: A trio of P3V-1s from VP-8 show off the lines of the then-new maritime patroller. They were the first unit to receive the type, and were soon in action during the blockade of Cuba during the 1962 missile crisis.

Left: Lockheed Electra N1883 was used as an aerodynamic prototype for the Orion, featuring dummy MAD boom and weapons bay projection. It is seen here before having the fuselage shortened to Orion dimensions.

merits in turboprops, as the ASW and maritime patrol missions for which the Orion was derived from the Electra favoured long loitering capability over higher cruising speed.

Development of the Electra to provide the Navy with replacements for its land-based Lockheed P2V Neptunes and water-based Martin P5M Marlins was initiated in 1957, before the first flight of the turboprop-powered airliner, when Lockheed submitted a formal proposal. With its design meeting fully the requirements of Navy Type Specification No. 146, Lockheed easily won the design competition, was awarded an initial research and development contract in May 1958, and first flew the Orion's aerodynamic prototype – the third Electra (c/n 188-1003, N1883) which had been used for static tests of the airliner – on 19 August 1958.

Equipment installation

Whereas this aerodynamic prototype was initially flown with only limited modifications – including the installation of a dummy magnetic anomaly detector (MAD) boom and of a fairing which projected beneath the forward fuselage to simulate the proposed weapons bay – it was fitted in 1959 with a forward fuselage shortened by 7 ft (2.13 m) to represent more accurately the production configuration of the maritime patrol air-

craft. At that time, most of the avionics equipment was installed and the aircraft was officially redesignated YP3V-1. It became the YP-3A in September 1962 and was later redesignated NP-3A. After completion of sundry tests for the manufacturer and the Navy, the aircraft was transferred to NASA in 1967. With this organisation it was first numbered NASA 927 but in August 1969 it was registered N927NA. Twenty-one years later, the aircraft was still operated by NASA.

Production contract

In October 1960, following successful evaluation of the YP3V-1, the Navy awarded an initial production contract for seven P3V-1s (BuNos 148883/148889). Retaining the Allison propeller turbines of the Electra, these P3V-1s had the shortened fuselage and MAD boom of the YP3V-1, and had accommodation for a crew of 12. The offensive load – including conventional or nuclear depth bombs, torpedoes, mines

and/or rockets – was carried in the forward fuselage bay and on 10 underwing racks, while sonobuoys and markers were carried in the aft fuselage. Fuel tank arrangements were revised to boost internal capacity from 5,450 US gal (20631 litres) for the Model 188A Electra to 9,200 gal (34826 litres) for the Model 185 Orion, with the fuel being carried in one fuselage tank and four wing tanks (an arrangement which has remained unchanged during the entire production).

One of the unique design features of the P3V-1 and subsequent maritime patrol versions of the Orion was their dual radar installation (with a forward-facing AN/APS-80 under a nose radome and an aft-facing AN/APS-80 in a tail radome ahead of the MAD boom to provide full 360-degree coverage; dual AN/APS-115 installation is provided in the P-3C), whereas their Western competitors, the BAe Nimrod and Dassault-Breguet Atlantique, were fitted respectively with a single Thorn-EMI Searchwater in a nose radome and a Thomson-CSF Iguane in a

The Orion can carry a wide variety of stores, covering the entire anti-ship/anti-sub spectrum. Illustrated in front of this Australian P-3C are Harpoon missiles, torpedoes, sonobuoys and smoke markers.

The Orion's mission is global, flying from many detachments around the world. This pair of aircraft is involved in a regular task: shadowing Soviet ships as they transit across the Atlantic to Cuba.

Designed to patrol for long hours over the ocean, the Orion is also very fast and surprisingly manoeuvrable, allowing it to undertake attacks against both surface and submarine targets and to dodge defences.

ventral radome.

BuNo 148883, the first production P3V-1, was flown on 15 April 1961, and BIS trials were conducted by the Service Test and Flight Test Divi-

The Orion has become the standard maritime surveillance aircraft of many 'Western' nations. Japan is a major user of the type, the P-3C having replaced P-2 Neptunes on the patrol squadrons. This aircraft flies with VX-51.

sions at NATC Patuxent River beginning on 15 April 1962, a total of 2,521 hours being flown in 585 flights. The Orion's service life began on 23 July 1962 when P3V-1s were delivered to Patrol Squadron Eight (VP-8) at NAS Patuxent River, Maryland. Soon after entering service, P-3As from VP-8, VP-44 and VX-1 took part in the quarantine of Cuba during the autumn of 1962, and in mid-1963 P-3As began operating abroad (the first overseas station was Kindley AFB, which became NAS Bermuda on 1 July 1970 upon being transferred to USN control). During the war in South East Asia, P-3As (later supplemented by P-3Bs) provided night radar coverage

of the Gulf of Tonkin, undertook 'Market Time' patrol to prevent seaborne infiltration of arms and ammunition to the Viet Cong, and took part in routine, open-ocean patrols and shipping surveillance flights.

These three primary types of mission were flown from NS Sangley Point in the Philippines until this station was turned over to the Philippine government on 31 August 1971, and from Tan Son Nhut AB and then from NAF Cam Ranh Bay as part of the Vietnam Air Patrol Unit. When NAF Cam Ranh Bay was disestablished on 2 December 1971, the PATRON detachments were redeployed to NAS Cubi Point in the Philippines, from where they operated until hostilities ended.

Since then, Orions of the US Navy have been and continue to be used regularly for such missions as ASW patrol, mining, over-the-horizon targetting, surface surveillance, direct submarine support, weather modification (for which rain-

Above: The P-3C is the standard production model, but it currently serves in five distinct variants, shortly to be joined by a sixth in the shape of 'Update IV'. This is one of the baseline models, serving with VP-50.

producing silver iodide cartridges are carried in place of chaff/flare cartridges in the ejection system beneath the tail of the Orion) and SAR. Today, they do so not only from their home stations but also during regular deployments to bases in Alaska and abroad (NAS Adak, NAS Agana, NAF Atsugi, NAS Bermuda, NAS Cubi Point, NAF Diego Garcia, MCAS Futenma, NAS Guantanamo Bay, MCAS Iwakuni, NAF Kadena, NAS Keflavik, NAF Lajes, NAF Midway, NAF Mildenhall, NAF Misawa, NAVSUPPACT Naples, NS Roosevelt Roads, NS Rota and NAS Sigonella) and during multinational exercises such as UNITAS when, every year, they operate from various air stations in Latin America (UNITAS XXX, the 30th five-month multi-national exercise, was held between 19 July and 10 December 1989).

Bravo deliveries

Deliveries of P-3Bs began in January 1966, when VP-9 at NAS Moffett Field and VP-26 at NAS Brunswick exchanged their Neptunes for Orions, and ended during the summer of 1968, when the last Bravo went to VP-30 at NAS Patuxent River. In turn this improved version, which featured more powerful engines and incorporated avionics and electronics improvements progressively introduced during the course of P-3A production, was followed by P-3C variants. 'Baseline' P-3Cs were first delivered to VP-56 at NAS Patuxent River in June 1969 and first deployed overseas by VP-49 during the autumn and winter of 1970, P-3C Update I aircraft first went to VX-1 at the same station in early 1975, and the first production Update II Orions were delivered to NAS Patuxent River in September 1977, one aircraft being used by NATC's Antisubmarine Aircraft Test

Directorate for the Navy Technical Evaluation (NTE) of this new variant while another went to VX-1 for operational tests. Update II.5 and Update III aircraft followed in 1981 and 1984, the last production P-3C Update III for the USN was delivered on 17 April 1990, and Update IV aircraft modified from Update II airframes will enter fleet service during FY 94.

With the Naval Air Reserve, Orions made their debut in July 1970 when five P-3As were delivered to the Naval Air Reserve Detachment (NARDET) at NAS Moffett Field, California. Four months later, this unit was commissioned as VP-91 to become the first of 13 reserve squadrons to fly Orions. Today, 12 of these squadrons fly P-3B TACNAVMOD Orions (with two to convert to 'Charlies') and one is already equipped with P-3Cs, while two Master Augment Units (VP-MAUs) operate a mix of TP-3As and P-3Cs.

New Zealand became the first export customer for the Orion when in 1966 it ordered

five P-3Bs to replace antiquated Short Sunderland MR.5 flying-boats equipping No. 5 Squadron at Hobsonville, Auckland, and Lauthala Bay, Fiji. Following crew training at NAS Moffett

Among the more remarkable of the special mission variants are the EP-3A (EATS) aircraft which fly with the Pacific Missile Test Center at NAS Point Mugu. The Extended Area Test System, comprising a phased-array antenna in the fin projection, is used for range support.

Field, the five RNZAF Orions were ferried to No. 5 Squadron's new base at Whenuapai where they were joined 20 years later by an ex-RAAF P-3B. In Australia, No. 11 Squadron at RAAF Edinburgh, NSW, operated 10 P-3Bs from 1968 until 1984 when it was re-equipped with 10 Orions from a second batch of Australian P-3C Update IIs. Also based at RAAF Edinburgh, No. 10 Squadron has flown the first 10 Australian P-3C Update IIs since 1978. Currently, all 20 Australian P-3Cs are about to be fitted with Israel Aircraft Industries ESM (electronic support measures) systems as part of an update pro-gramme managed by Australia's AWA Defence Industries. The Kongelige Norske Luftforsvaret (RNoAF) first acquired five new P-3Bs in 1968 and supplemented them with two ex-USN P-3Bs ordered in 1980; the RNoAF has now re-placed five of its P-3Bs with four P-3C Update IIIs fitted to carry Penguin anti-ship missiles and has demilitarised the other two for SAR and fishery patrol duties with the P-3N designation. The next foreign customer for the Orion was the Imperial Iranian Air Force, which took delivery of six P-3Fs in 1975. Two or three P-3Fs are believed extant with the Iranian Islamic Revo-lutionary Air Force.

Seen under Lockheed tests, the first CP-140 Aurora is based on the Orion airframe but incorporates the anti-submarine warfare suite from the S-3A Viking. Specific Canadian equipment includes survival kit.

Above: An unusual civilian use of the Orion is firefighting. Six P-3As fly with Aero Union at Chico, California, modified with a 3,000-US gal ventral tank.

Below: A pair of P-3 AEW 'Blue Sentinel' aircraft fly with the US Customs Service, dedicated to detecting smuggling operations from Davis-Monthan AFB and New Orleans.

In 1976, after a protracted evaluation, Canada ordered 18 CP-140 Aurora maritime patrol aircraft combining P-3C airframes with S-3A avionics and data processing systems. The Auroras are currently distributed among four squadrons of No. 140 Wing, Canadian Forces, and will be supplemented in 1991 by three CP-140A Arcturus. Japan, which in 1978 selected the Orion as a replacement for Neptunes serving with its Maritime Self Defence Force, acquired a manufacturing licence and will eventually supplement three Lockheed-built Update IIs and four similar aircraft assembled in Japan from Lockheed kits, with at least 93 Kawasaki-built P-3Cs. Currently, some 60 P-3Cs equip six operational squadrons and a test and development squadron (51 Kokutai). Two of the Japanese Orions, and probably others, will be modified as EP-3C electronic warfare platforms. The last customers to order new Orions were the Netherlands, which acquired 13 P-3C Update IIs to equip Nos 320 and 321 Squadrons at Leiden-Valkenburg, and Pakistan, which will receive three P-3C Update II.5.

So far, Portugal, Spain and Thailand are the only nations to have acquired only second-hand Orions but other air arms will eventually obtain ex-USN P-3s. In the case of Portugal, six ex-RAAF P-3Bs have been modernised as P-3Ps for service with 601 Esquadra at Lajes. Spain, which first obtained three ex-USN P-3As in 1973, is having two ex-USN P-3As and five ex-RNoAF P-3Bs upgraded to a common configuration for service with Escuadrón 221 at Jerez de la Frontera. Finally, Thailand is to receive two ex-USNR P-3B TACNAVMOD Orions.

Although it has been in service for nearly 30 years, the story of the Orion is far from over. The cancellation of the follow-on P-7A may lead to further P-3 orders, while the existing aircraft will be subject to further improvements.

Lockheed P-3 Orion variants

PRINCIPAL ASW VARIANTS

Even before the Orion's entry into service, airborne detection of submerged submarines relied increasingly on monitoring sound waves emitted during underwater transit as improved designs enabled submarines to spend more time below the surface. Today's diesel submarines have improved engines, generators, batteries and air purification equipment, which permit them to travel submerged for greatly extended periods. Nuclear-powered submarines have no practical limit on time spent underwater. Hence, as submerged submarines cannot be detected visually, by radar or by ESM, acoustic sensing has become the only reliable method for initial detection. However, considerable advances have been made in reducing the noise made by the submarine equipment and propellers, rendering necessary the development of more sensitive sonobuoys and faster acoustic data-processing equipment and their integration in steadily more capable versions of the Orion, from the P-3A, which entered service in 1962, to the P-3C Update IV, which will join the fleet in four years.

P-3A

(Designated P3V-1 prior to September 1962)

Powered by four 4,500-eshp Allison T56-A-10Ws, early production Orions were fitted with dual AN/APS-80 radar, AN/ASQ-10 MAD gear and AN/ASR-3 detector to sniff the diesel exhaust released by the snorkel of submerged submarines. Their acoustic signal processors and data recorders were the AN/AQA-3 or AQA-4(V) 'Jezebel' which permitted a single operator to examine only four acoustic chart recordings in very limited modes. First tested on the 35th production Orion, Delayed Time Compression (DELTIC) was a major ASW system improvement which was incorporated in the AN/AQA-5 'Jezebel', as installed on the 110th P-3A and retrofitted to most earlier aircraft. Other items retrofitted in early production P-3As were 4,910-eshp T56-A-14 turboprops, a fuselage-mounted APU (Auxiliary Power Unit) forward of the weapons bay, and provision for two Martin Bullpup missiles beneath each wing.

Development of a TACNAVMOD (Tactical Navigation Modernization) package was sponsored in 1975 by NATC to replace the inertial navigation and tactical display systems with a new very-low-frequency navigation system and a general-purpose digital computer to enable modernised P-3As (and later P-3Bs) to stabilise a sonobuoy pattern as effectively as more modern P-3Cs. This package was fitted mostly to P-3As and P-3Bs after their transfer to reserve units.

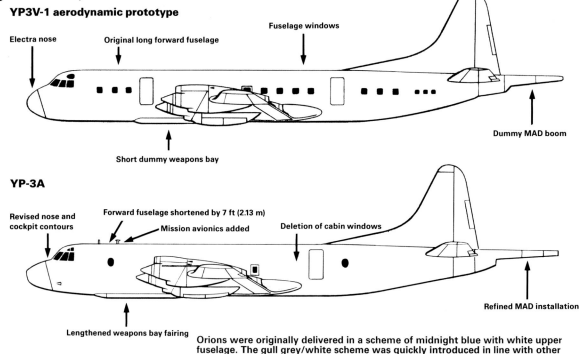

YP3V-1 aerodynamic prototype

Electra nose
Original long forward fuselage
Fuselage windows
Short dummy weapons bay
Dummy MAD boom

YP-3A

Revised nose and cockpit contours
Forward fuselage shortened by 7 ft (2.13 m)
Mission avionics added
Deletion of cabin windows
Lengthened weapons bay fairing
Refined MAD installation

Orions were originally delivered in a scheme of midnight blue with white upper fuselage. The gull grey/white scheme was quickly introduced in line with other Navy types.

After replacement by P-3Bs and Cs, many P-3As served with the US Navy Reserve, such as this example of VP-65 seen at Hill AFB. Today the Reserve is largely P-3B-equipped.

A VP-91 P-3A climbs out of McClellan AFB, illustrating the large searchlight carried under the starboard wingtip. The Reserve P-3As had the TACNAVMOD update, with precise navigation equipment.

P-3B

Beginning with the 158th Orion, Lockheed switched to the P-3B version which incorporated most of the improvements – including T56-A-14 engines and DELTIC equipment introduced during the course of P-3A production – and was fitted with the AN/AQH-1 analogue tape recorder to enhance inflight and post-flight acoustic signal analysis. A substantial portion of the 124 P-3Bs built for the USN were retrofitted to carry and launch Bullpup missiles and many received the TACNAVMOD package. P-3Bs were also built for the RAAF, the RNoAF and the RNZAF.

One of the P-3Bs (BuNo 152758) operated by the Antisubmarine Aircraft Test Directorate at NATC Patuxent River had a black rectangle painted above its fuselage, just aft of the cockpit, when in 1978 it was used for air refuelling trials with a USAF-style boom, simulated contacts being made with a KC-135A, a KC-130F and another P-3.

The P-3B was essentially a rationalisation of the improvements made during P-3A production, incorporating the more powerful engines and DELTIC equipment. This searchlight-carrying aircraft flew with VP-46, a regular Pacific Fleet squadron. Like most Orion units, it was regularly deployed overseas, this example being seen at Kadena on Okinawa, a major Orion base for the US Navy.

P-3B (P-3A similar)

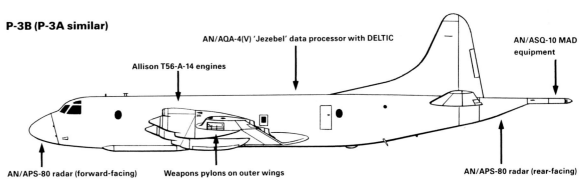

AN/AQA-4(V) 'Jezebel' data processor with DELTIC

Allison T56-A-14 engines

AN/ASQ-10 MAD equipment

AN/APS-80 radar (forward-facing)

Weapons pylons on outer wings

AN/APS-80 radar (rear-facing)

A retrofit applied to many P-3Bs was the ability to launch the Bullpup guided missile against surface targets. This VP-47 aircraft carries the normal quota of four missiles on its outer pylons.

Not all Orions are what they appear to be! This P-3B is masquerading with P-3C squadron badges and a spurious serial during Far East operations. The additional aerials may suggest an electronic reconnaissance role.

P-3C

Retaining the airframe and powerplant installation of the P-3B, the 'baseline' P-3Cs were preceded by the 240th Orion airframe which, built in a batch of P-3Bs and first flown on 18 September 1968, was designated YP-3C (BuNo 153443 was later modified as the sole RP-3C for service with VXN-8). They were fitted with the 'A-New' integrated ASW and navigation avionics with AN/ASQ-114 computer system, thus becoming the world's first ASW aircraft with a centralised computer, and with the AN/AQA-7 acoustic processors and display system. Significantly, the AN/AQA-7 system featured (1) DIFAR (Directional Low Frequency Analysis and Recording) passive acoustic signal processing and display; (2) dual-operator acoustic station, with both gram and video displays at each sensor station to quadruple the number of sonobuoys which could be processed at any given time; (3) a computer-controlled miniature sonobuoy receiver group; (4) an acoustic test signal generator; and (5) an updated analogue tape recorder.

'Baseline' P-3Cs are being brought up to Update III standards by Lockheed modification teams at NAS Jacksonville and NAS Moffett Field. The work notably entails the installation of LTN-72 inertial navigation, LTN-211 Omega, Harpoon air-to-surface missiles, MAD compensation group adapter, IACS (Integrated Acoustic Communication System) and KY-75 secure HF voice communication set. Installation of the first Update III retrofit kit in a P-3C belonging to VP-31 was completed in March 1987 and kits have been or are being installed in a total of 133 early-model 'Charlies.'

The YP-3C 'prototype' for the major Orion production series was a converted P-3B, Bu No 153443. Seen with its weapon bay doors open, it shows to advantage the sonobuoy launching tubes under the rear fuselage.

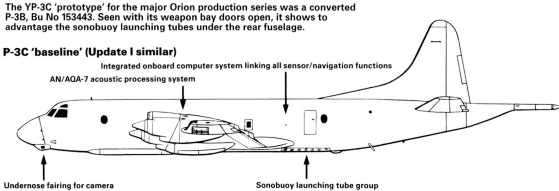

P-3C 'baseline' (Update I similar)

Integrated onboard computer system linking all sensor/navigation functions

AN/AQA-7 acoustic processing system

Undernose fairing for camera

Sonobuoy launching tube group

'Baseline' and Update I P-3Cs can be distinguished by the undernose camera fairing with windows. This aircraft is from VP-47 'Golden Swordsmen', part of the Pacific Fleet and now flying the Update III variant. Photographed during the mid-1970s, the aircraft wears Bicentennial markings.

P-3C Update I

By the mid-1970s, new avionics were ready for incorporation into the P-3C, but the computer memory and access channels were saturated. Update I removed these limitations and introduced (1) a seven-fold increase in computer memory; (2) an Omega navigation system; (3) significant improvements in DIFAR; (4) an additional tactical display at sensor stations 1 and 2; and (5) a new operational programme providing computer-aided acoustic analysis, ESM signal sorting and refinement of Omega nav signals.

P-3C Update II

Update II Orions, which were delivered beginning in August 1977, introduced another set of major improvements including (1) installation of an Infrared Detection System (IRDS, a turret-mounted FLIR); (2) provision for carrying and launching Harpoon anti-ship missiles; (3) incorporation of a 28-track acoustic tape recording system; and (4) mounting of a Sonobuoy Reference System (SRS) for continuous monitoring of sonobuoy positions.

Before retaining the AN/AAS-36 IRDS to equip Update II and Update III Orions, the Navy evaluated three systems to improve the night detecting capability of its land-based ASW aircraft. The programme, called Project PASS for Patrol Advanced Surveillance System, was undertaken in 1971-72 at NATC.

BuNo 160290 was the first of the Update II aircraft featuring, among other improvements, a turret-mounted FLIR under the nose. This replaced the camera fairing of the 'baseline' P-3C.

Pod-mounted under the wing of a P-3C of the Weapons System Test Division, the three systems were the General Electric Active Low Light Level Television (ALLLTV) and FLIRs from Hughes and Texas Instrument, the winning system being that developed by Hughes.

In 1972-73, prior to the development of the Update II version, the Naval Missile Center at NAS Point Mugu was responsible for a series of tests during the initial development phase for the air-launched version of the Harpoon anti-ship missile. P-3As were used by NMC first for free-fall separation tests in May and June 1972, then for captive Harpoon engine tests in June, and finally for air launches beginning on 17 October. The first full-guidance test was made on 20 December 1972, with the Harpoon launched from a P-3A impacting on the decommissioned destroyer *Ingersoll* (DD-652) riding at anchor off the coast of California, and the first successful Harpoon hit on a moving patrol boat target was obtained in November 1973. Subsequently Harpoons were adapted for launch from several types of aircraft including the P-3C Update II and Update III, the first operational launch being made in the autumn of 1979 from a P-3C Update II of VP-23. Since AGM-84A Harpoons have been added to its armament, the Orion also has a secondary surface warfare role and can sink surface warships some 60 miles (96 km) away. However, Harpoons have been fitted not so much to turn the P-3 into an anti-surface vessel strike aircraft as to enhance further its effectiveness in the ASW role by enabling it to take

A pair of regular P-3C Update IIs from VP-10 (above) and VP-23 (right), both based at NAS Brunswick, Maine, as part of PATWING 5.

out electronic surveillance trawlers shadowing battle groups or convoys for Soviet submarines and warning them of P-3 activities.

The Australian P-3C Update II aircraft differ from USN aircraft in a number of details and, notably, are fitted with the Anglo-Australian Barra acoustic data processor and carry Australian-developed SSQ-801 Barra passive directional sonobuoys.

P-3C Update II.5

Appearing in 1981, the Update II.5 version saw (1) selected systems (e.g. INS, Doppler, VHF, VOR/ILS, TACAN, ESM, etc) replaced by more reliable and/or more easily maintained systems; (2) IACS added to provide a communication link with friendly submerged submarines; (3) the installation of a MAD compensation group adaptor; (4) the standardisation of wing pylons; and (5) improvements being made in fuel tank venting. In other respects, Update II.5 aircraft are similar to Update II Orions.

In addition to their regular roles, the P-3 can be called upon to sow mines, as evidenced by this Update II.5 of VP-16, climbing away from its base at Jacksonville.

P-3C Update III

The last production version of the Orion, delivery of which began in May 1984, introduced an entirely new underwater acoustic monitoring system based on the Proteus analyser unit. The AN/UYS-1 Advanced Signal Processor (ASP) detecting set and the AN/USQ-78 ASP display and control set render the P-3C Update III's system twice as effective as that of the Update II.5 by doubling the number of sonobuoys that can be monitored concurrently. Accompanying

the entirely new acoustic signal receiving, processing, display and control system are improvements in the air conditioning system to ensure that

the densely packed avionics are adequately cooled. A redesigned Transparent Logic Unit is also incorporated to form the basis for future

Retractable forward-looking infra-red turret under chin

AN/ASQ-114 central digital computer and AN/AYA-8 data processing system (UIII only)

Additional antennas along spine

Aft-facing camera for battle-damage

P-3C Update III (Updates II and II.5 similar)

Pylons available for many stores, including AGM-84A Harpoon missiles

Extra sensors (including AN/ALQ-78 ESM) carried under central pylons

Lockheed P-3 Orion variants

VP-62 'Broadarrows' were the first Reserve unit to receive the Update III, these being new-build aircraft. The squadron shares its Jacksonville base with the active-duty aircraft of PATWING 11.

VP-40 'Fighting Marlins' wore their badge loud and proud on the fin, and added some style to the cockpit area. The adoption of the TPS grey has rendered the Orions the most anonymous of all warplanes.

modernisation of the data processing system.

Modifications introduced during the past three years to enhance the Orion's ability to cope with current and future threats include (1) the installation of AN/ALQ-157, a so-called 'infra-red survivability and vulnerability enhancement device' (one must seriously doubt that the Navy really means 'vulnerability enhancement' . . .), on both sides of the rear fuselage, and (2) the adoption of the all-grey Tactical Paint Scheme (TPS) to reduce the aircraft's IR signature. In addition, to endow the P-3 with some self-defence capability against shore-based fighters or Soviet Yak-38 'Forger' naval VTOL fighters, NATC Patuxent River has initiated tests with a P-3C modified to carry AIM-9L Sidewinder missiles beneath the wing's outboard panels.

The flight crew of the P-3C Update III consists of a pilot, co-pilot, flight engineer, and NAV/COMM. For most

ASW or maritime patrol sorties, its mission crew includes a tactical co-ordinator (TACCO), two acoustic sensor operators (SENSOs), a magnetic field sensor operator, an ordnanceman (ORD), and an inflight technician (IFT). The ORD also acts as loading ordnance crew chief and, as also does the IFT, doubles up as an observer. The most senior naval aviator or naval flight officer on board normally operates as mission commander (MC); however, when a mission commander is not assigned, his responsibilities and duties are assumed by the pilot. If required, up to 13 additional crew members can be accommodated either as observers on operational/training sorties, or as passengers during ferry missions. Pressurisation, air conditioning, two bunks, a galley, a small dining area, and an airline-type lavatory are fitted in the rear fuselage of the P-3C to provide the crew with the comfort required during long-duration sorties.

To perform its primary ASW mission – search, localisation and destruction of enemy submarines – the P-3C is equipped with a broad array of acoustic and electronic sensing devices, enabling its crew to determine the existence of targets and then pinpoint their location. The data handling system of P-3C Update III aircraft is based on the AN/ASQ-114 central digital computer and AN/AYA-8 data processing equipment, which receives input from the various sensing devices and then organises, stores, times, and sequences them. The integrated data are displayed to the pilot, the TACCO, and three of the sensor operators.

The P-3C weapon system consists of kill stores (the armament subsystem) and search stores (the ordnance subsystem). The maximum weapon load of the P-3C is 19,250 lb (8730 kg) with kill stores being carried in a bomb bay and on 10 wing stations. The bomb bay, located beneath the main deck in the forward fuselage, is designed to carry various arrangements of weapons with a maximum of eight stations available at one time. The heaviest store it can accommodate is the 2,197-lb (997-g) Mk 55 mine. Other internally carried stores include Mk 82 and Mk 83 bombs; Mk 25, Mk 36, Mk 52, Mk 55, and Mk 56 mines; Mk 36 and Mk 40 destructors; and Mk 46 torpedoes. In addition, the P-3C Update III has been cleared to carry up to three B57 nuclear depth bombs, but nuclear stores are not carried by non-US aircraft. These anti-submarine special stores are drogue-retarded, fin-stabilised nuclear weapons weighing 510 lb (231 kg). They must be released at an indicated air speed of between 140 and 330 knots (260 and 610 km/h) and at an altitude not exceeding 1,000 ft (305 m). Stores can be carried in different combinations depending upon mission requirements, but the basic internal load consists of one B57 nuclear depth bomb and four

Mk 46 torpedoes.

Various weapons and search stores, as well as the AN/ALQ-78 ESM pod, are carried on 10 wing stations, three under each outer panel and two on the inboard panels, between the fuselage and the inner engines. Kill stores carried externally include Mk 25, Mk 36, Mk 52, Mk 55, and Mk 60 mines; Mk 36, Mk 40, and Mk 41 destructors; Mk 20 Rockeye cluster bombs; AGM-84A Harpoon air-to-surface anti-ship missiles; LAU-10, LAU-61, LAU-68, and LAU-69 FFAR pods; and SUU-53 dispensers. For training purposes, Mk 76, Mk 106 and BDU-33D/B practice bombs can be used to simulate conventional stores. The B57 nuclear depth bomb is simulated with either the BDU-20/C, which duplicates the aerodynamic characteristics of the weapon, or the non-expendable BDU-11A/E, which is used to train personnel in the use of the aircraft monitor and control system (AMAC), as a training tool for special weapons handling and loading procedures, and to simulate the aircraft's response when carrying special weapons.

Search stores include sonobuoys, Mk 25 and Mk 58 smoke markers, bathythermograph buoys, and Mk 64 and Mk 84 Sound Underwater Signals (SUS). Size A sonobuoys (AN/SSQ-36, -41A, -41B, -47B, -50, -50A, -53, -53A, -57A, -62, -71, and -83) are carried in 48 unpressurised sonobuoy launch tubes (SLT) which must be loaded on the ground. A freefall chute and three pressurised SLTs are accessible in flight and are used to launch 36 size A sonobuoys stowed in the aft cabin. Several types of pyrotechnic devices (e.g., Mk 24, Mk 45 and LUU-2 parachute flares in SUU-44/A dispensers on wing pylons) are also carried for illumination, signals and rescue work. In addition, the P-3C is equipped with an aft-facing KB-18 camera for damage assessment.

This VP-31 P-3C displays the open weapons bay and AN/ALQ-78 pod under the centre section. This equipment provides automatic passive detection and classification of hostile radars.

Orion as bomber: this P-3C of VP-45 carries Mk 36 destructors under the wing. The outer wing pylons can carry a variety of stores, including various mines, depth charges, bombs and missiles. Torpedoes are usually carried internally.

P-3C Update IV

Development of the Update IV was initiated in July 1987 when Boeing was selected over Lockheed to integrate advanced systems, including AN/APS-137(V) radar and AN/ALR-77 ESM, to enable the Orion to detect quieter submarines which will enter service during the mid to late 1990s. No P-3s will be delivered with Update IV avionics, but about 80 Update II aircraft will be retrofitted to equip the six PATRONs at NAS Brunswick beginning during FY 94.

P-3F

When in 1975 the Imperial Iranian Air Force placed an order for six maritime patrol aircraft, Iran was not initially allowed to acquire aircraft fitted to the then current P-3C 'baseline' or Update I standards. However, this embargo was quickly removed and on delivery the P-3Fs differed from the P-3C 'baseline' configuration only in being fitted with a boom receptacle for inflight-refuelling by Boeing 707-3J9C tankers of the IIAF.

Notable for their unusual camouflage, the Iranian P-3Fs played an important part in the Gulf war with Iraq, flying from Bandar Abbas. Due to chronic spares shortages, it is thought that only one or two are left airworthy.

P-3G

The P-3G designation was briefly used to identify the proposed development of the Orion being developed to meet Navy requirements for an advanced Long-Range, Air Antisubmarine warfare-Capable Aircraft (LRAACA). In October 1988, the Navy selected Lockheed to develop the LRAACA and 11 months later assigned to it the P-7A designation. The P-7A was derived from the P-3C but incorporating new materials and manufacturing technologies, will be powered by the 5,150-shp General Electric GE38 turboprop engine. The programme was cancelled in 1990.

P-3N

Designation identifying two Norwegian P-3Bs modified for Coast Guard duties with most of their ASW equipment removed.

Portugal's ex-US Navy P-3B Orions are designated P-3P to signify some local modifications.

P-3P

This designation identifies six ex-RAAF P-3Bs which have been modernised for service with the Força Aérea Portuguesa. The first was modified by Lockheed in California and the others by Oficinas Gerais de Material Aeronautico (Central Aeronautical Material Workshops) in Portugal.

CP-140 Aurora

In July 1976, the Canadian Armed Forces announced the selection of an Orion derivative as its new Long Range Patrol Aircraft (LRPA) to replace Canadair Argus maritime patrol aircraft. Designated CP-140 and named Aurora, the new aircraft was to combine the airframe and powerplants of the P-3C with the avionics system and data processing capability of the Lockheed S-3A Viking (including dual AN/APS-126 search radar, AN/ASQ-501 MAD, and AN/AYK-10 computer). Eighteen CP-140s with revised interior arrangement to meet specific CAF needs and weapons bay adapted to carry and drop the Canadian-developed SKAD/BR search and rescue kit were delivered between May 1980 and March 1981.

CP-140A Arcturus

To supplement its 18 CP-140s before Lockheed closes the Orion production line, the CF has ordered three 'white tail' P-3Cs. To be delivered without much of their operational equipment, the CP-140As will be fitted in Canada with removable equipment in the weapons bay to undertake alternative civil tasks such as aerial surveys, pollution control and resources location.

Canada's CP-140 fleet numbers 18 aircraft, most of which serve with three squadrons at Greenwood in Nova Scotia. The remaining squadron covers the West Coast from Comox, British Columbia. Externally similar to other Orions, the Auroras have a different sensor fit, although the basic configuration of fore- and aft-facing radars, MAD boom and centralised computer remains the same.

ELECTRONIC WARFARE VARIANTS

EP-3A

This designation has been given to a number of aircraft modified as electronic research platforms. BuNo 149673, originally delivered as a P-3A, was modified for electronic reconnaissance experiments, with its MAD boom being deleted and specialised equipment fitted within radomes beneath the forward fuselage and wing centre-section. This EP-3A was successively operated by the Naval Air Test Center, the Naval Weapons Laboratory, and Air Test and Evaluation Squadron One (VX-1). BuNo 149674, which had started life as a P-3A and had been successively modified as a WP-3A and NP-3A, was designated EP-3A when assigned to the Naval Research Laboratory. BuNo 150529 was modified to serve in the electronic

Testing of electronic reconnaissance equipment is the role for VX-1's EP-3A. Seen here at Fallon, it displays a blunt nose, wingtip pods and EP-3E-style ventral radome for a 360° coverage antenna. VX-1 is headquartered at Patuxent River.

aggressor role with VAQ-33 and has served with that squadron since 1983.
The EP-3A (EATS) and EP-3A (SMILS) versions are described under the 'Special Purpose' heading.

A single EP-3A operates in an electronic aggressor role with VAQ-33, the Key West-based Atlantic Fleet EW squadron. Operating alongside ERA-3Bs and EA-6As, it provides electronic threats during fleet exercises.

EP-3B

Under the guidance of the US Naval Avionics Facility, Lockheed modified two P-3As (BuNos 149669 and 149678) as 'Batrack' electronic surveillance aircraft with direction-finding sets, radar signal analyser, and communications interception and recording equipment replacing standard ASW gear and housed in a retractable ventral radome, dorsal and ventral 'canoe' fairings, and modified tail cone. The EP-3Bs were operated by VQ-1 beginning in June 1969 and flew combat support missions from Da Nang AB during the South East Asia War. They were later brought up to EP-3E standards.

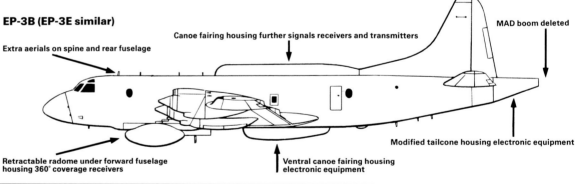

EP-3B (EP-3E similar)

Canoe fairing housing further signals receivers and transmitters

Extra aerials on spine and rear fuselage

MAD boom deleted

Retractable radome under forward fuselage housing 360° coverage receivers

Ventral canoe fairing housing electronic equipment

Modified tailcone housing electronic equipment

A pair of EP-3B 'Batrack' aircraft were modified to augment Lockheed EC-121s on fleet electronic reconnaissance duties with VQ-1. Originally flown in midnight blue and white, the pair was assigned to missions in the South East Asia war zone, flying alongside EA-3B Skywarriors, Air Force RC-135s and Army Neptunes in the constant monitoring of North Vietnamese radio and radar traffic.

EP-3C

Two Japanese P-3Cs are being modified by Kawasaki as electronic warfare prototypes for evaluation by the JMSDF beginning in the spring of 1991.

EP-3E

Ten P-3As (BuNos 148887/148888, 149668, 150494, 150497/150498, 150501/150503 and 150505) were modified to the 'Aries' electronic surveillance configuration and the two EP-3Bs were brought up to the same standard. In these aircraft the dual AN/APS-115 radar installation is retained but the remainder of the ASW equipment is replaced by electronic monitoring devices including AN/ALD-8 direction-finding set, AN/ALQ-76 noise jamming pod, AN/ALQ-78 automatic ESM system, AN/ALQ-108 IFF jammer, AN/ALQ-110 radar signal analyser, AN/ALR-52 instantaneous frequency measuring equipment, AN/ALR-60 communications interception and recording system, and AN/ALR-132 infra-red jammer. Most of the antennas for these systems are housed in a retractable ventral radome, dorsal and ventral 'canoe' fairings, and in the modified tail cone.

The EP-3E flight crew is led by the Electronic Warfare Aircraft Commander (EWAC), who is always a pilot, while overall command rests with the Mission Commander (MC), who is either a pilot or an NFO. The 15-person mission crew includes two NFOs, the Electronic Warfare Tactical Evaluator (EVAL) and the Electronic Warfare Navigator (EWAN), and enlisted naval aircrewmen including flight engineer, radioman, airborne electronic supervisor, and electronic warfare operators.

To replace the 12 EP-3Es that are fast reaching the end of their airframe lives, 12 P-3Cs are being converted by Lockheed Aeromod Center, Inc. (LACI) in Greenville, South Carolina, to EP-3E standard under a CILOP (Conversion-In-Lieu-Of-Procurement) programme. Most of their mission equipment will come from the first batch of EP-3Es as these aircraft are phased out. However, some new equipment will be incorporated if funding can be provided.

On approach to Atsugi, this VQ-1 EP-3E 'Aries' graphically displays the underfuselage radome containing receivers for the onboard electronic suite. The positioning of the radome allows 360° coverage. Other equipment fills large canoe fairings above and below the rear fuselage. Electronic fingerprinting of naval vessels is a speciality. The airframes are sorely in need of replacement, although the reconnaissance equipment is state-of-the-art.

Both Fleet Air Reconnaissance Squadrons have six EP-3Es each (VQ-1 illustrated), with utility aircraft attached to serve as 'bounce bird' trainers and hacks.

P-3 AEW&C

Over the past eight years Lockheed has fought a costly battle to develop an airborne early warning and control aircraft utilising either existing or new Orion airframes. An aerodynamic prototype, with dorsal rotodome but without radar and other specialised AEW equipment, was obtained by modifying an ex-RAAF P-3B and first flew in June 1984. Unfortunately, no export customers have yet been found and only two Orion AEW&C aircraft have been sold to the US Customs Service for use in anti-smuggling operations in the Caribbean and Gulf of Mexico. Fitted with an AN/APS-125 radar with antenna in a 24-ft (7.32-m) diameter rotodome, the first AEW&C 'Blue Sentinel' was delivered in June 1988 and was instrumental in the seizure of $75 million in contraband drugs during its first 10 months of service. A second 'Blue Sentinel' with an AN/APS-139 radar providing better coverage in land clutter was delivered to the Customs Service in April 1989.

P-3 AEW&C

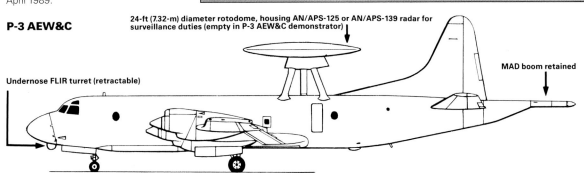

24-ft (7.32-m) diameter rotodome, housing AN/APS-125 or AN/APS-139 radar for surveillance duties (empty in P-3 AEW&C demonstrator)

Undernose FLIR turret (retractable)

MAD boom retained

N91LC was the aerodynamic prototype for the P-3 AEW version, featuring a large rotodome on the rear fuselage. Lockheed tried long and hard to sell the aircraft to numerous customers (including the RAF and Armée de l'Air), but was defeated by the tried and trusted E-2 Hawkeye and E-3 Sentry. So far only the US Customs Service has bought the type (with two different radars), but its results against smuggling have been spectacular.

SPECIAL PURPOSE VARIANTS

P-3A (CS)

Preceding the AEW&C 'Blue Sentinel' in Customs service, four ex-USN Orions (BuNos 150514, 151390, 151395 and 152170) were fitted with an AN/APG-63 in place of the nose-mounted AN/APS-80 of the P-3A to improve their ability to detect aircraft flying illegally into the United States. These P-3A (CS) aircraft were provided with associated radar operator positions and displays in the fuselage and were fitted with a new inertial navigation system. Multi-frequency radios (with numerous blade antennas beneath the rear fuselage) are provided for communications with US Customs ground stations, Coast Guard vessels and civilian law enforcement agencies.

EP-3A (EATS)

Three P-3As (BuNos 150499, 150521 and 150522) were modified by Hayes International Corporation and Tracor as Extended Area Test System (EATS) airborne instrumentation stations for use at the Pacific Missile Test Center, NAS Point Mugu, California. All ASW equipment was removed before installation of a Raytheon Rotman-lens phased array antenna in a distinctive extension of the vertical fin.

Right: The EP-3A (EATS) aircraft were modified by Tracor at Mojave, California. This aircraft carries extensive wool-tufting on the fin and antenna fairing to test airflow patterns.

Below: Two of the three EATS aircraft in PMTC service. These provide accurate instrumentation of missile tests over the Pacific Range.

EP-3A (SMILS)

The Sonobuoy Missile Impact Locating System (SMILS) was developed to provide support for tests of Navy submarine-launched ballistic missiles by determining accurately the impact point of strategic re-entry bodies and rating the accuracy of missiles and trajectories. Two P-3As were so modified and after evaluation by VX-1 were delivered to NAS Point Mugu, where they currently serve with PMTC.

The Pacific Missile Test Center operates a large array of types to support its objectives. In addition to F-14, F-18, A-7 and A-6 launch aircraft, it has a large fleet of drones, including QF-4 Phantoms. Orions and Skywarriors fly on support duties, the two EP-3A (SMILS) machines being used to monitor SLBM warhead tests. RP-3A aircraft are also on strength for monitoring duties.

NP-3A, NP-3B & NP-3C

The N prefix identifies a number of Orions which have been modified so extensively for use as equipment testbeds that they cannot be brought back to operational standards.

Most of the NP-3 fleet have served with the Naval Research Laboratory at Patuxent River, Maryland. This much-modified aircraft is typical of the test fleet engaged on a myriad of trials and research programmes.

NP-3A N428NA serves with NASA at Wallops Island. It was the first Orion to be built, having had its MAD boom replaced. NASA also operates an Electra.

RP-3A

Two P-3As (BuNos 149667 'El Coyote', and 150500 'Arctic Fox') were modified for Oceanographic Development Squadron Eight (VXN-8) at NAS Patuxent River to study the acoustic and thermal characteristics of oceans (Project 'Outpost Seascan') and collect environmental and polar ice data (Project 'Birdseye').

Right: RP-3A BuNo 150500 was modified with special equipment to collect environmental data and perform polar research, with particular emphasis on the changes in the ice cap. Operating under the 'Project Birdseye' programme, it was fittingly named 'Arctic Fox'.

Below: 'Project Seascan' is aimed at the nature of the oceans, and employs the other RP-3A, BuNo 149667 'El Coyote'. The VXN-8 fleet wears this characteristic orange/white scheme for conspicuity over the polar regions.

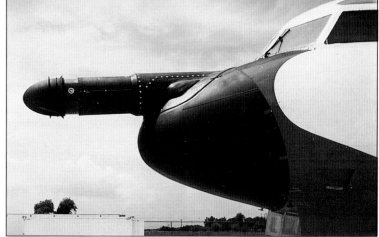

Right: Photographed in June 1983, RP-3A BuNo 150500 'Arctic Fox' is seen with this unusual and unidentified sensor projecting from the nose. VXN-8 aircraft have occasionally picked up different sensor fits for various phases of their programmes.

RP-3C

The YP-3C (BuNo 153443) was modified for use by VXN-8 as a replacement for the RP-3A 'El Coyote' and was given the same nickname. It is currently active with VXN-8.

After its evaluation as the first P-3C, BuNo 153443 was modified as the replacement aircraft on the 'Seascan' project, retaining the 'El Coyote' nickname. Behind, and wearing the unit's 'JB' codes, is a UP-3A, used by VXN-8 as a utility support aircraft.

RP-3D

The 51st P-3C, BuNo 150528 'Paisanos Tres' was modified to be used by VXN-8 in collecting worldwide magnetic data required for ASW and sundry scientific programmes (Project Magnet). All ASW equipment was replaced by specialised gear for atmospheric research and magnetic survey and a 1,200-US gal (4543-litre) was added in the weapons bay. It is still in service.

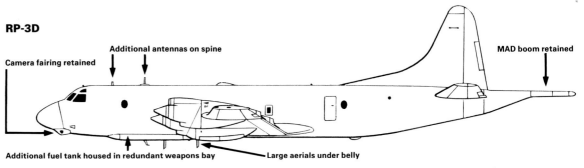

RP-3D

Camera fairing retained

Additional antennas on spine

MAD boom retained

Additional fuel tank housed in redundant weapons bay

Large aerials under belly

The third of VXN-8's major tasks is 'Project Magnet', a long-running investigation into atmospheric and earth magnetic fields. The RP-3D 'Paisanos Tres' is the aircraft assigned to this mission, a converted 'baseline' P-3C with ASW equipment removed but retaining the undernose camera fairing. VXN (Oceanographic Development Squadron)-8 is based at NAS Patuxent River alongside the NRL, with whom it shares much research data. Its nickname, the 'World Travelers', denotes the global nature of its work, which entails its aircraft being detached on survey work to many parts of the world.

TRAINING, TRANSPORT AND UTILITY VARIANTS

TP-3A

To avoid damaging the delicate avionics of P-3Cs during repeated touch-and-go training activities, 12 obsolete P-3As were modified by LAS as TP-3A pilot trainers. All ASW equipment was removed and the cockpit brought up to P-3C Update II.5 standards. The TP-3A prototype was handed back to the US Navy in December 1985 and these trainers are currently operated by the two Fleet Replacement Squadrons (VP-30 and VP-31) and the two Master Augment Units.

UP-3A

This designation identifies a number of P-3As from which the ASW equipment has been removed and which are used as utility transport. Personnel accommodation is rather spartan and cargo is carried in the Orion's weapons bay.

VP-3A

Designation given to three WP-3As and two P-3As modified as flag officer/staff transports with airline-type seats and other VIP amenities.

Above: Several early Orions have been 'de-modded' for use as hacks. This smart UP-3A serves at Naval Air Station Keflavik on Atlantic Fleet support duties. Keflavik is a major Orion operating location, allowing detached aircraft to cover the vital North Atlantic area.

Right: Wearing VXN-8-style colours, this UP-3A is bailed to the General Offshore Corporation/Offshore Systems Inc. for sonobuoy development work. The aircraft is based at Brunswick, Maine.

The VP-3A is an early Orion with all mission equipment removed and a staff transport interior installed. Below is the transport of the CNO (Chief of Naval Operations), while below right is an aircraft of VC-1, based at NAS Barbers Point.

WEATHER RECONNAISSANCE VERSIONS

WP-3A

As part of its Replacement Weather Reconnaissance Aircraft Test (RWRAT), the US Navy evaluated the C-130 and the P-3 during heavy weather tests conducted in Bermuda in 1969. The Orion was selected as the airframe most suitable to replace the Lockheed WC-121N, and a contract for the modification of four P-3As (BuNos 149674/149676 and 150496) into WP-3As was placed with Lockheed Aircraft Service. Modified in Ontario, California, the first WP-3A underwent BIS at Patuxent River and Roosevelt Roads during the winter of 1970 and was delivered to VW-4 in July 1971. The WP-3As were characterised by the removal of most of the ASW equipment, the installation of weather reconnaissance radar (in a ventral radome which extended 18 inches in flight) and meteorological systems, and their shorter tail boom (from which the MAD was deleted). After VW-4 was disestablished in April 1975, BuNo 149674 became an NP-3A and the three other WP-3As were modified as VP-3A staff transports.

Only four WP-3A weather reconnaisance aircraft were converted, serving with VW-4. The main sensor was a 360° radar in an extendable underbelly radome.

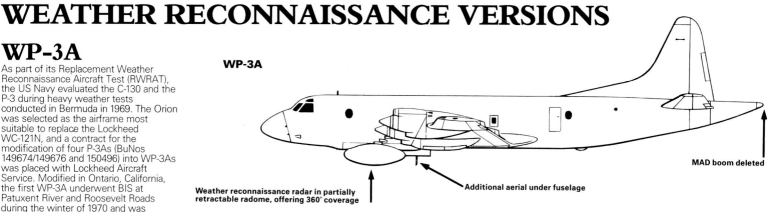

WP-3A

Weather reconnaissance radar in partially retractable radome, offering 360° coverage

Additional aerial under fuselage

MAD boom deleted

WP-3D

Utilising the basic airframe and powerplant installation of the P-3C, two WP-3Ds were built for the National Oceanic and Atmospheric Administration (NOAA), a civilian agency coming under the US Department of Commerce, to undertake atmospheric research and weather modification experiments. Given BuNos 159773 and 159875 for contractual purposes, these two aircraft became NOAA 42 and NOAA 43 and were given civil registrations N42RF and N43RF.

The WP-3Ds, which are still operating from Miami, Florida, carry a flight crew of four and a mission crew of 12 to 17 scientists, technicians and observers. They are fitted with a pitot static boom beneath the port wingtip and a probe extending from the forward fuselage to measure gust velocity relative to the aircraft and incremental changes in the angles of attack and side slip. A 12-ft

(3.05-m) wide, C-Band dish antenna is housed in a belly radome in place of the weapons bay; it can be rotated 360 degrees in a horizontal plane and tipped 10 degrees up or down. A 4 ft×6 ft (1.22 m×1.83 m) X-band radar antenna is installed parallel with the centreline of the aircraft in an aft radome replacing the AN/APS-115 of the patrol aircraft; it can be rotated 360 degrees around the centreline.

In addition to their usual weather research/modification tasks, the WP-3Ds are used to monitor hurricanes in the Caribbean, flying right through the storm systems to plot the track and developing nature of the cyclone.

WP-3D

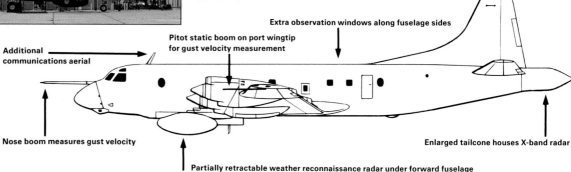

A pair of WP-3Ds is based at Miami with the NOAA, this positioning reflecting the most common hurricane area in the United States. Sophisticated radars and airflow indicators are the main sensors, although visual observations are also important, hence the additional windows at individual crew stations.

Additional communications aerial

Pitot static boom on port wingtip for gust velocity measurement

Extra observation windows along fuselage sides

Nose boom measures gust velocity

Partially retractable weather reconnaissance radar under forward fuselage

Enlarged tailcone houses X-band radar

Lockheed P-3 Orion Operators

Patrol Squadrons of the US Navy

The Maritime Patrol Aviation (MPA) force is composed of 25 active duty squadrons and 15 reserve units. The active squadrons come under the Commander Patrol Wings Atlantic (COMPATWINGSLANT), who oversees the six squadrons of PATWING Five at NAS Brunswick, Maine, and the six squadrons (plus VP-30, a Fleet Replacement Squadron) of PATWING Eleven at NAS Jacksonville, Florida, and under the Commander Patrol Wings Pacific (COMPATWINGSPAC), who owns the five squadrons of PATWING Two at NAS Barbers Point, Hawaii, and the eight squadrons (including an FRS, VP-31) of PATWING Ten at NAS Moffett Field, California. Seven reserve squadrons and a squadron-sized Master Augment Unit (MAU) comes under the Commander Reserve Patrol Wing Atlantic (COMRESPATWINGLANT), while six squadrons and an MAU are under the Commander Reserve Patrol Wing Pacific (COMRESPATWINGPAC).

Following the 1986 raid on Libya, the US Navy Orion fleet began to lose its once-colourful squadron markings. Virtually none remain today, and many aircraft now wear the dreaded grey.

Commander Patrol Wings Atlantic (COMPATWINGSLANT)
Patrol Wing Five (PATWING 5), NAS Brunswick, Maine

VP-8 'Tigers'	P-3C UII.5 (to receive P-3C UIV)
VP-10 'Red Lancers'	P-3C UII (to receive P-3C UIV)
VP-11 'Pegasus'	P-3C UII.5 (to receive P-3C UIV)
VP-23 'Sea Hawks'	P-3C UIII (to receive P-3C UIV)
VP-26 'Tridents'	P-3C UII (to receive P-3C UIV)
VP-44 'Golden Pelicans'	P-3C UII (to receive P-3C UIV)

Patrol Wing Eleven (PATWING 11), NAS Jacksonville, Florida

VP-5 'Mad Foxes'	P-3C UIIIR
VP-16 'Eagles'	P-3C UII.5 (to receive P-3C UIIIR)
VP-24 'Batmen'	P-3C (to receive P-3C UIIIR)
VP-30 'Pros'	TP-3A, P-3C UII.5 and IIIR
VP-45 'Pelicans'	P-3C UIIIR
VP-49 'Woodpeckers'	P-3C UIIIR
VP-56 'Dragons'	P-3C (to receive P-3C UIIIR)

VP-16 'Eagles'

VP-11 'Pegasus' is scheduled to receive the improved Update IV.

VP-30 is the Atlantic Fleet training squadron.

VP-49 'Woodpeckers'

A VP-44 P-3C flies past Mount Etna on Sicily.

Commander Patrol Wings Pacific (COMPATWINGSPAC)

Patrol Wing Two (PATWING 2), NAS Barbers Point, Hawaii
VP-1 'Screaming Eagles'	P-3C (to receive P-3C UI)
VP-4 'Skinny Dragons'	P-3C (to receive P-3C UI)
VP-6 'Blue Sharks'	P-3B (to receive P-3C UII.5)
VP-17 'White Lightnings'	P-3C (to receive P-3C UI)
VP-22 'Blue Geese'	P-3C UII.5

Patrol Wing Ten (PATWING 10), NAS Moffett Field, California
VP-9 'Golden Eagles'	P-3C UI (to receive P-3C UIIIR)
VP-19 'Big Red'	P-3C UI (to receive P-3C UIIIR)
VP-31 'Black Lightnings'	TP-3A, P-3C UI and III
VP-40 'Fighting Marlins'	P-3C UIII
VP-46 'Grey Knights'	P-3C UI (to receive P-3C UIIIR)
VP-47 'Golden Swordsmen'	P-3C UIII
VP-48 'Boomerangers'	P-3C UIIIR
VP-50 'Blue Dragons'	P-3C UIIIR

VP-46 is part of PATWING 10 at Moffett Field.

VP-1 'Screaming Eagles'

VP-6 'Blue Sharks'

VP-19 'Big Red'

Pacific Fleet Orions regularly operate from Japan. Misawa, where this VP-40 Update III aircraft gets a wash, is in the north of the country, allowing the Soviet Pacific Fleet to be monitored closely.

VP-31 'Black Lightnings'

VP-47 'Golden Swordsmen'

Naval Air Reserve Force

In addition to contributing 13 combat-ready patrol squadrons, the Naval Air Reserve must upon mobilisation also provide trained aircrews and maintenance personnel to fill wartime slots in fleet squadrons. To that end, NAVAIRES established in 1984 Squadron Augmentation Units (SAUs) in Fleet Replacement Squadrons (VP-30 and VP-31) to train individual reservists in the Orions that they would operate and support if mobilised, and two Master Augment Units (VP-MAUs), the 'Northern Sabres' at NAS Brunswick and the 'Rolling Thunders' at NAS Moffett Field, to train complete crews. Organised as other reserve squadrons, the VP-MAUs will, upon mobilisation, break up and their crews and maintenance personnel will be distributed to fleet squadrons. The VP-MAU reservists spend two weeks' active duty per year with their gaining squadrons, usually while these squadrons are deployed. Currently, VP-MAUs are assigned the same Orion versions as co-located active squadrons. Anticipated military budget reductions may result in the withdrawal of all aircraft from the two VP-MAUs, these units then borrowing aircraft from fleet squadrons.

VP-68 'Blackhawks'

VP-Master Augment Unit, NAS Brunswick

Commander Reserve Patrol Wing Atlantic (COMRESPATWINGLANT)

VP-62 'Broadarrows', NAS Jacksonville, Florida	P-3C UIII
VP-64 'Condors', NAS Willow Grove, Pennsylvania	P-3B TACNAVMOD
VP-66 'Liberty Bell', NAS Willow Grove, Pennsylvania	P-3B TACNAVMOD
VP-68 'Blackhawks', NAF Washington, Maryland	P-3B TACNAVMOD
VP-92 'Minutemen', NAS South Weymouth, Massachusetts	P-3B TACNAVMOD
VP-93 'Executioners', Selfridge ANGB, Michigan	P-3B TACNAVMOD
VP-94 'Crawfishers', NAS New Orleans, Louisiana	P-3B TACNAVMOD
VP-MAU 'Northern Sabres', NAS Brunswick, Maine	TP-3A, P-3C UII

VP-69 'Totems'

VP-92 'Minutemen'

VP-94 'Crawfishers'

Commander Reserve Patrol Wing Pacific (COMRESPATWINGPAC)

VP-60 'Cobras', NAS Glenview, Illinois	P-3B TACNAVMOD
VP-65 'Tridents', NAS Point Mugu, California	P-3B TACNAVMOD (to receive P-3C)
VP-67 'Golden Hawks', NAS Memphis, Tennessee	P-3B TACNAVMOD
VP-69 'Totems', NAS Whidbey Island, Washington	P-3B TACNAVMOD
VP-90 'Lions', NAS Glenview, Illinois	P-3B TACNAVMOD
VP-91 'Stingers', NAS Moffett Field, California	P-3B TACNAVMOD (to receive P-3C UIII)
VP-MAU 'Rolling Thunders', NAS Moffett Field, California	TP-3A, P-3C UIII

P-3B of VP-92 in the Tactical Paint Scheme.

The 'Peter Rabbit' codes and bat insignia adorn the fin of VQ-1 'World Watchers' EP-3Es.

Miscellaneous USN units

CINCAFSE, NAS Sigonella, Sicily, Italy	UP-3A
CINCLANTFLT, NAS Norfolk, Virginia	VP-3A
CINCPACFLT, NAS Barbers Point, Hawaii	VP-3A
CNO, NAF Washington, Maryland	VP-3A
NADC, NADC Warminster, Pennsylvania	NP-3A, UP-3A, P-3C
NAS Bermuda, Bermuda	UP-3A
NS Keflavik, Iceland	UP-3A
NATC, NAS Patuxent River, Maryland	P-3B, P-3C
NRL, NAS Patuxent River, Maryland	P-3A, NP-3A
PMTC, NAS Point Mugu, California	P-3A, EP-3A (EATS), EP-3A (SMILS), RP-3A
VAQ-33 'Firebirds', NAS Key West, Florida	EP-3A
VC-1 'Blue Alii', NAS Barbers Point, Hawaii	VP-3A
VQ-1 'World Watchers', NAS Agana, Guam	EP-3E
VQ-2 'Batmen', NS Rota, Spain	EP-3E
VX-1 'Pioneers', NAS Patuxent River, Maryland	P-3C UIII
VXN-8 'World Travelers', NAS Patuxent River, Maryland	RP-3A, RP-3C, RP-3D, UP-3A

Left: This colourful marking is used by VX-1 'Pioneers'.

Above: The 'JQ' codes denote the 'Batmen' of VQ-2 from Rota, flying the EP-3E Sigint gatherer.

Other US operators

National Oceanographic and Atmospheric Administration/ Department of Commerce, Miami, Florida	WP-3D
General Offshore Corp., Brunswick, Maine	UP-3A
NASA, Wallops Station, Wallops Island, Virginia	NP-3A
US Customs Service, Davis-Monthan AFB, Arizona, and NAS New Orleans, Louisiana	P-3A (CS), P-3 AEW&C
US Forestry Service/Aero Union, various fire bases	P-3A

Foreign Operators

Australia
Royal Australian Air Force

No. 10 Sqn, No. 92 Wing, Edinburgh, NSW	P-3C UII
No. 11 Sqn, No. 92 Wing, Edinburgh, NSW	P-3C UII

(The 20 P-3C Update IIs in RAAF service are to be fitted with Israel Aircraft Industries ESM systems as part of an update programme managed by Australia's AWA Defence Industries)

Australia previously flew P-3B Orions, but has now replaced these with P-3C Update IIs, albeit with some local modifications. These include the Barra passive buoy.

Canada
Canadian Forces

No. 404 Sqn, No. 140 Wing, Greenwood, Nova Scotia	CP-140
No. 405 Sqn, No. 140 Wing, Greenwood, Nova Scotia	CP-140
No. 407 Sqn, No. 140 Wing, Comox, British Columbia	CP-140
No. 415 Sqn, No. 140 Wing, Greenwood, Nova Scotia	CP-140

(The 18 CP-140 Auroras are to be supplemented with three CP-140A Arcturus patrol aircraft. After completion in Palmdale, the three CP-140As will be modified to the Arcturus configuration in Canada to serve in the military, environmental, maritime and Arctic surveillance roles and for fishery patrol)

Iran
Iranian Islamic Revolutionary Air Force

Maritime Command, Bandar Abbas	P-3F

Japan
Nihon Kaijyo Jieitai

1 Kokutai, 1 Kokugun, Kanoya, Kyushu	P-3C UII
2 Kokutai, 2 Kokugun, Hachinohe, Honshu	P-3C UII
3 Kokutai, 4 Kokugun, Atsugi, Honshu	P-3C UII
4 Kokutai, 2 Kokugun, Hachinohe, Honshu	P-3C UII
5 Kokutai, 5 Kokugun, Naha, Okinawa	P-3C UII
6 Kokutai, 4 Kokugun, Atsugi, Honshu	P-3C UII
51 Kokutai, Atsugi, Honshu	P-3C UII

(Japan will eventually acquire a total of 100 P-3Cs. The first three were built by Lockheed, the next four were assembled in Japan from Lockheed kits, and the others have been or are being built in Japan. Two P-3Cs are being modified by Kawasaki as EP-3C electronic warfare platforms with first flight in the autumn of 1990 and delivery to the JMSDF in March 1991; other EP-3C conversions are likely)

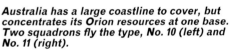

Australia has a large coastline to cover, but concentrates its Orion resources at one base. Two squadrons fly the type, No. 10 (left) and No. 11 (right).

Canada's Auroras have received this dark grey scheme in line with the greater emphasis on camouflage. Below is the badge of No. 407 Squadron.

Japanese units are officially known as kokutai, but crews use the US-style VP designations. This is a VP-2 P-3C Update II.

A VP-3 aircraft leaves Iruma AB. This unit flies under the aegis of 4 Kokugun, based at Atsugi on Honshu island.

Above: 6 Kokutai is the second Atsugi-based squadron.

Right: The first P-3C Update II for Japan is seen during Lockheed trials. Although the first three were built by the parent company, the remainder of the Japanese order is being built by Kawasaki.

Netherlands
Marine Luchtvaart Dienst
  No. 320 Sqn, Leiden-Valkenburg   P-3C UII
  No. 321 Sqn, Leiden-Valkenburg   P-3C UII

Dutch responsibilities include patrolling the North Sea, using P-3C Update II aircraft. One aircraft is detached to Keflavik in Iceland.

Norway
Kongelige Norske Luftforsvaret
  Skv 333, Andøya   P-3C UIII &
                      P-3N

(The four P-3C Update IIIs are fitted to carry Penguin Mk 3 anti-ship missiles. Most of the ASW equipment has been removed from the two P-3Ns which are operated on Coast Guard duties)

Two of Norway's elderly P-3Bs have been reworked as P-3Ns for Coast Guard duties. P-3Cs now undertake the main ASW mission.

Pakistan
Pakistan Air Force
  No. 29 Sqn, Sharea Faisal   P-3C UII.5

(Three new P-3C Update II.5s will enter service in late 1990/ early 1991 with No. 29 Squadron, Pakistan Air Force, but will bear the legend 'Pakistan Navy' on their fuselage)

Portugal
Força Aérea Portuguesa
  601 Esquadra, Grupo Operacional 41, BA 4
    Lajes, Azores   P-3P

Originally delivered in white and grey, the P-3Ps of 601 Esquadra now feature this unique two-tone grey scheme. From their base at Lajes, they patrol the central Atlantic region.

New Zealand
Royal New Zealand Air Force
  No. 5 Sqn, Whenuapai, New Zealand   P-3B

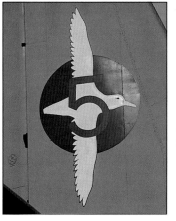

Below: The albatross insignia of No. 5 Sqn RNZAF's P-3Bs is appropriate for a long-range patroller of the southern seas.

Spain
Ejército del Aire Español
  Escuadrón 221, Ala de Patrulla 22, Jerez de
    la Frontera   P-3A & P-3B
(Two ex-USN P-3As and five ex-RNoAF P-3Bs are being upgraded under a programme managed by Boeing)

Thailand
Royal Thai Navy
  No. 2 Sqn, RTNAF U Tapao, Sattahip   P-3B
                                     TACNAVMOD
(Two ex-USNR Orions are being procured to replace Grumman S-2As in service with No. 2 Squadron)

Lockheed P-3 Orion

Characteristics and performance of the Lockheed P-3C Update III

Span, 99 ft 8 in (30.38 m); length, 116 ft 10 in (35.61 m); height, 33 ft 8½ in (5.18 m); wing area, 1,300 sq ft (120.77 sq m)

Empty weight, 61,491 lb (27892 kg); normal take-off weight, 139,760 lb (63395 kg); maximum gross take-off weight, 142,000 lb (64410 kg); wing loading, 103.8 lb/sq ft (507 kg/sq m); power loading, 6.9 lb/eshp (3.1 kg/eshp)

Max speed, 405 kts (750 km/h) at 13,000 ft (3960 m); long-range cruising speed, 350 kts (648 km/h) at 25,000 ft (7620 m); loiter speed, 209 kts (387 km/h) at 1,500 ft (450 m); rate of climb at sea level, 2,600 ft/min (13 m/sec); service ceiling, 34,000 ft (10365 m); max maritime surveillance mission radius, 2,000 naut miles (3700 km); max endurance at 1,500 ft (450 m) on two engines, 14.5 hours; ferry range, 4,500 naut miles (8335 km)

Right: In addition to pre-loaded sensors, sonobuoys can be loaded into tubes during flight to meet varying operational requirements. Buoys are ejected backwards to fall exactly under the aircraft's position at the point of launching.

The P-3 pilot has a well-designed cockpit, with an excellent outside view. At his control is a powerful and responsive aircraft.

The heart of the mission system is the Tactical Co-ordinator (Tacco) station. Information from all the sensors is displayed on the large screen.

Lockheed P-3C Orion cutaway key

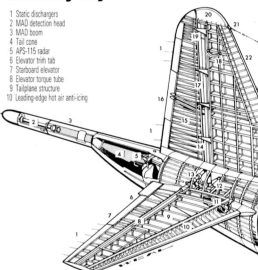

1 Static dischargers
2 MAD detection head
3 MAD boom
4 Tail cone
5 APS-115 radar
6 Elevator trim tab
7 Starboard elevator
8 Elevator torque tube
9 Tailplane structure
10 Leading-edge hot air anti-icing

11 Elevator (starboard) and rudder (port) hydraulic booster units
12 Rudder linkage
13 Elevator tube universal joint
14 Rudder lower hinge
15 Rudder structure
16 Rudder trim tab
17 Rudder post
18 Antenna
19 Rudder upper hinge
20 Fin tip
21 Aerial attachment
22 Fin leading-edge
23 Port elevator
24 Port tailplane
25 Fin root fairing
26 Integral fin/rear fuselage
27 Aft pressure bulkhead
28 Tail unit anti-icing timer
29 Bunk (hinged: in-flight maintenance work bench beneath)
30 Elevator trim tab servo
31 Avionics bay (K2)
32 Avionics bay (K1)
33 Refuse bins (2)
34 KB-18 ventral camera (strike assessment)
35 Avionics bay (J2)
36 Avionics bay (J1)
37 Galley
38 Bunk (hinged)
39 Four-place dinette
40 Window ports
41 Lavatory
42 Avionics bay (H3)
43 Coat closet
44 Avionics bay (H2)
45 Avionics bay (H1)
46 Port observation station (screened compartment)

47 Starboard observation station (screened compartment)
48 Observation window
49 'A'-stores angle of release
50 'B'-store launchers (3)
51 'A'-store launchers (3)
52 Guard rail
53 Under-deck 'A'-store launchers (48)
54 Entry ladder (stowed inflight position)
55 Main entrance door
56 Avionics bay (G2)
57 Avionics bay (G1)
58 Life-raft stowage (port)
59 Avionics bay (F2)
60 'A'-store stowage racks (36 stores)
61 Under-deck hydraulics service centre
62 Wing root fairing
63 Ventral KA-74 camera
64 Avionics bay (F1)
65 Emergency exit (port)
66 Avionics bay (E2)
67 Avionics bay (E1)
68 Life-raft stowage (starboard)
69 Emergency exit (starboard)
70 Main electrical load centre (starboard)
71 Operators' seats
72 Sensor station 2 (acoustic)
73 Sensor station 1 (acoustic)
74 No. 2 fuel tank
75 Engine aft nacelles
76 Jet-pipe cooling-air inlets
77 Jet-pipe exhausts
78 HF aerial
79 Fowler-type flaps
80 Aileron trim tab
81 Static dischargers
82 Port aileron
83 Wingtip fairing
84 Port navigation light
85 Formation/identification light

Glossary

ALLTV Active Low Light Level Television
AMAC Aircraft Monitor and Control
APU Auxiliary Power Unit
ASW Anti-Submarine Warfare
BA Base Aérea
BIS Board of Inspection and Survey
CAF Canadian Armed Forces
CILOP Conversion-In-Lieu-Of-Procurement
CINCAFSE Commander-in-Chief, Allied Forces Southern Europe
CINCLANTFLT Commander-in-Chief, Atlantic Fleet
CINCPACFLT Commander-in-Chief, Pacific Fleet
CNO Chief of Naval Operations
COMPATWINGSLANT Commander Patrol Wings Atlantic
COMPATWINGSPAC Commander Patrol Wings Pacific
COMRESPATWINGSLANT Commander Reserve Patrol Wings Atlantic
COMRESPATWINGSPAC Commander Reserve Patrol Wings Pacific
DELTIC Delayed Time Compression
DIFAR Directional Frequency Analysis and Recording
EATS Extended Area Test System
ESM Electronic Support Measures
EVAL Electronic Warfare Tactical Evaluator
EWAC Electronic Warfare Aircraft Commander
EWAN Electronic Warfare Navigator
FFAR Folded-Fin Aerial Rocket
FLIR Forward Looking Infra-red
FRS Fleet Replacement Squadron
FY Fiscal Year
IACS Integrated Acoustic Communication System
IFT Inflight Technician
INS Inertial Navigation System
IR Infra-red
IRDS Infra-red Detection Set
JMSDF Japanese Maritime Self Defence Force
LACI Lockheed Aeromod Center, Inc.
LAS Lockheed Aircraft Service Company
LRAACA Long-Range, Air Antisubmarine warfare-Capable Aircraft
LRPA Long Range Patrol Aircraft
MAD Magnetic Anomaly Detector
MAU Master Augment Unit

MC Mission Commander
MCAS Marine Corps Air Station
MPA Maritime Patrol Aviation
NADC Naval Air Development Center
NAF Naval Air Facility
NAVSUPPACT Naval Support Activity
NARDET Naval Air Reserve Detachment
NAS Naval Air Station
NASA National Aeronautics and Space Administration
NATC Naval Air Test Center
NAV/COMM Navigation/Communications
NFO Naval Flight Officer
NRL Naval Research Laboratory
NS Naval Station
NTE Navy Technical Evaluation
NWEF Naval Weapons Evaluation Facility
NWL Naval Weapons Laboratory
PASS Patrol Advanced Surveillance System
PATWING Patrol Wing
PMTC Pacific Missile Test Center
RAAF Royal Australian Air Force
RNoAF Royal Norwegian Air Force
RNZAF Royal New Zealand Air Force
RTNAF Royal Thai Naval Air Facility
RWRAT Replacement Weather Reconnaissance Aircraft Test
SAR Search and Rescue
SLT Sonobuoy Launch Tube
SMILS Sonobuoy Missile Impact Location System
SRS Sonobuoy Reference System
SUS Sound Underwater Signal
SUU Suspended Underwing Unit
TACAN Tactical Air Navigation
TACCO Tactical Co-ordinator
TACNAVMOD Tactical Navigation Modernization
TPS Tactical Paint Scheme
VAQ Tactical Electronic Warfare Squadron
VHF Very High Frequency
VOR/ILS VHF Omnidirectional Radio/Instrument Landing System
VP Patrol Squadron
VPU Patrol Special Projects Squadron
VQ Fleet Air Reconnaissance Squadron
VW Airborne Early Warning Squadron/Weather Reconnaissance Squadron
VX Air Development Squadron
VXN Oceanographic Development Squadron

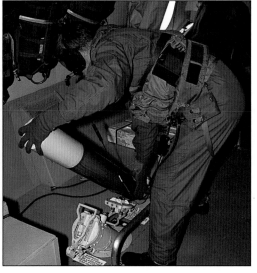

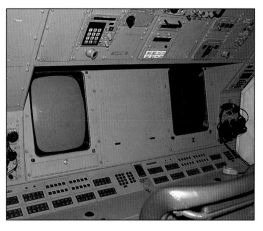

The acoustic sensor stations are positioned over the aircraft's wing, behind the non-acoustic station.

Sitting opposite the Tacco, the nav/comms station is on the starboard side of the cabin, immediately behind the flight deck.

86 No. 1 fuel tank
87 Integrally stiffened machined skin panels
88 Hot-air tapered ejector tubes ('piccolo' tubes)
89 Engine bleed air shut-off valve
90 Engine firewall
91 Nacelle cowling

105 Sensor compartment centre-aisle curtain
106 Operator's seat
107 Window port
108 Sensor station 3 (non-acoustic)
109 Avionics bay (D2) (computer)
110 Avionics bay (D1)
111 Ditching station (13 places)
112 Avionics bay (B3)
113 Avionics bay (B2)
114 Avionics bay (B1)
115 Avionics bay (C3)
116 Avionics bay (C2)
117 Avionics bay (C1)
118 Observation window
119 Nav/com station
120 Nav/com console
121 Tacco seat
122 Tacco station
123 Antenna

124 Curtains/doorway to flightdeck
125 Flight crew emergency exit
126 Avionics bay (A1)
127 Pilot's seat
128 Flight engineer's seat
129 Overhead instrument console
130 Windshield
131 Instrument panel shroud
132 Control column
133 Forward pressure bulkhead
134 Radar support
135 Nose cone
136 APS-115 radar
137 Retractable FLIR
138 Pitot head
139 Nosewheel well beams
140 Rudder pedal
141 Nosewheel retraction jack
142 Nosewheel doors
143 Forward-retracting twin nosewheels
144 Nosewheel leg torque link
145 Nosewheel leg pivot
146 Co-pilot's seat

147 Forward electrical load centre
148 Under-deck APU compartment
149 Under-deck weapons bay
150 Weapons bay doors
151 Bomb load (eight bombs)
152 Spinners
153 Four-blade propellers
154 Engine air intake
155 Intake trunking
156 Engine bearers ('V'-frame)
157 Oil tank

158 Inboard leading-edge section
159 Wing root fillet
160 Fuselage fuel cell (no. 5 bag)
161 Water-alcohol tank
162 Wing centre-section front beam
163 Centre-section integral fuel tank (No. 5)
164 Centre-section end rib
165 No. 3 fuel tank
166 Flap structure

173 Mainwheel leg pivot
174 Retraction jack
175 Mainwheel well forward doors
176 Engine air intake
177 Propeller reduction gear box
178 Oil cooler intake
179 Engine support struts
180 Drive shaft housing
181 Allison T56-A-10 turboprop engine compressor section
182 Combustion section
183 Turbine section
184 Jet pipe
185 Stainless-steel heat-resistant trough
186 Aileron control linkage
187 Twin (fail-safe) trim actuators
188 Aileron trim tab
189 Static dischargers
190 Starboard aileron
191 Starboard navigation light

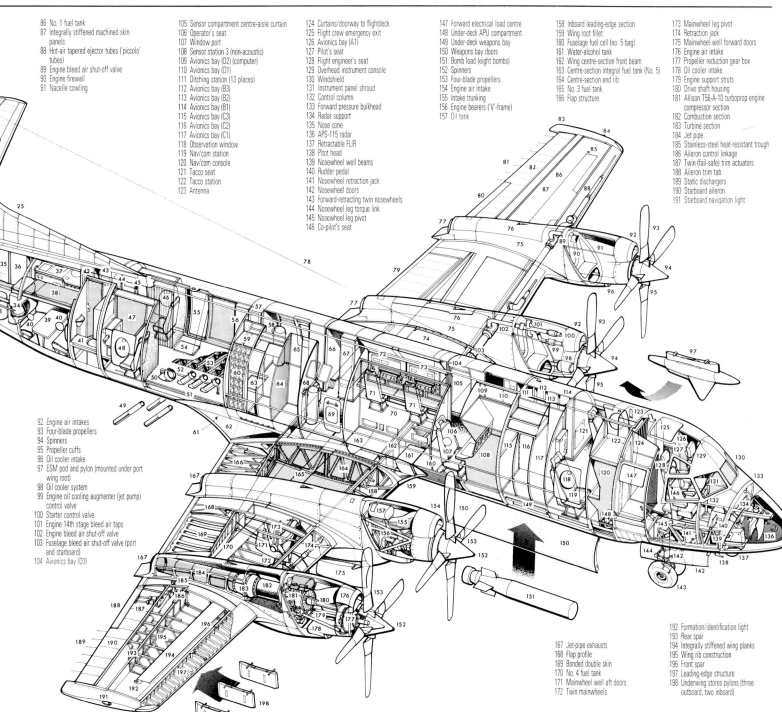

92 Engine air intakes
93 Four-blade propellers
94 Spinners
95 Propeller cuffs
96 Oil cooler intake
97 ESM pod and pylon (mounted under port wing root)
98 Oil cooler system
99 Engine oil cooling augmenter (jet pump) control valve
100 Starter control valve
101 Engine 14th stage bleed air taps
102 Engine bleed air shut-off valve
103 Fuselage bleed air shut-off valve (port and starboard)
104 Avionics bay (D3)

167 Jet-pipe exhausts
168 Flap profile
169 Bonded double skin
170 No. 4 fuel tank
171 Mainwheel well aft doors
172 Twin mainwheels

192 Formation/identification light
193 Rear spar
194 Integrally stiffened wing planks
195 Wing rib construction
196 Front spar
197 Leading-edge structure
198 Underwing stores pylons (three outboard, two inboard)

Força Aérea Portuguesa

Photographs by Peter Steinemann

Main picture: Rebuilt from US Navy surplus A-7As, LTV A-7P Corsairs are the prime attack aircraft of the FAP, serving with two squadrons. One has a detachment on the Azores – an important Atlantic staging-post for NATO.

Below: The venerable Fiat G91R/4 fought in Portugal's African wars, but surviving aircraft are of the very slightly newer R/3 version, obtained from West German surplus. The same source has promised Alpha Jets to supplant these workhorses.

Força Aérea Portuguesa

Above: Ten tandem-seat Fiat G91T/1s are used for training by Esquadra de Ataque 301 at Montijo, now the sole G91 operator. Note the tiger's-head badge.

Below: Ageing Lockheed T-33As are still used by the FAP. Following abandonment of the Boeing Skyfox, it is hoped to replace them with the Jet Squalus.

Above: *A mixed formation of T-33s and Northrop T-38A Talons, all from Esquadra de Instrucão 103. T-33s are used for instructor training, refresher flying and instrument rating, while the Talons provide the final 80 hours of pilot training before personnel convert to operational aircraft types at squadron level.*

Left: *Two batches of Corsairs, totalling 50 aircraft (six of them TA-7P trainers), are shared by Esquadras de Ataque 302 and 304, both based at Monte Real. Fitted with A-7E avionics, the aircraft are assigned to maritime attack and close air support, but have a secondary air defence commitment, using AIM-9P Sidewinder AAMs.*

Right: *In the absence of anything more suitable, eight of the dozen T-38A Talons are declared to NATO as Portugal's air defence force, fitted with Sidewinders and backed by similarly armed A-7s and G91s. Substantial upgrading of the FAP is in prospect with the placing of an order for 20 General Dynamics F-16A/B Fighting Falcons.*

123

Above: Smartly attired in the national colours worn by the Asas de Portugal aerobatic team, a pair of Cessna T-37C 'Tweets' crosses the Atlantic coastline. Two dozen T-37s of Esquadra de Instrucão 102 at Sintra provide student pilots with 60 hours of basic instruction between the Epsilon and T-38 stages of the syllabus. Delivered in 1962-4, the T-37s will fly for many more years.

Left: After the 1977 withdrawal of Lockheed Neptunes, the FAP was forced to use Hercules for maritime surveillance. An anti-submarine capability has once more been acquired in the form of six Lockheed P-3B Orions from Norway in 1987. Conversion to P-3P standard, with Update II avionics, has been delayed by funding shortages, however. The aircraft serve with 601 Squadron.

*Right: Neighbouring Spain was the source of 24 **CASA C.212** Aviocars for the FAP, most in light transport configuration. Esquadra de Transporte 502 operates from the mainland base of Tancos (part of Grupo 31), while inter-island airlift on the Azores is entrusted to Esq de Transporte 503, within Grupo 41 at Lajes. The latter is also tasked with maritime surveillance and weather reconnaissance.*

*Below: Befitting their name, the five **Lockheed C-130H Hercules** of Esquadra de Transporte 501 at Montijo are assigned diverse labours. In addition to airlift within Portugal and the Azores, the aircraft have a secondary maritime surveillance or **SAR** role and may be fitted with a **MAFFS** (Military Airborne Fire-Fighting System) for attacking forest fires. One is permanently detached to Lisbon.*

*Above, right: The **Reims-Cessna FTB337G** is another aircraft obtained for colonial wars, although delivery took place after the African possessions were relinquished. Sixteen delivered to Milirole standard as **COIN** aircraft are no longer armed; the others are eight photo-recce versions and eight trainers. Roles are transport, army co-operation, liaison, medevac and training.*

*Right: Portuguese variations on the Aviocar theme comprise two for **ECM** training, two with mapping cameras, a navigation trainer and this 'earth resources' exploration aircraft fitted with a magnetometer in an extended tailboom for geological survey. Aviocars were received between 1974 and 1976 as **Douglas C-47** replacements, the original requirement being for up to 40, some to be based in Africa.*

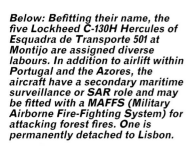

Força Aérea Portuguesa

Above: In 1985, 504 Squadron received three second-hand Dassault Falcon 20 executive jets: two for calibration/general transport and one with VIP fittings.

Below: Three Aerostructure (Fournier) RF-10 powered sailplanes are based with 802 Squadron at the Air Force Academy, Sintra.

Left: Some 30 Aérospatiale Alouette III utility helicopters remain from 142, obtained mainly for the colonial wars. They retain the option of carrying 70-mm rocket pods and 7.62-mm machine-guns. Main operator is Esq de Transporte 552 at Tancos, although some are detached to other bases for rescue and liaison and a few are assigned to co-located Esq de Instrucão 111 for helicopter pilot conversion.

Right: The North American T-6G/J Texan has retired from FAP service, but this example is one of two maintained in airworthy condition by the Museu do Ar. Built in Canada during 1952, it is a T-6J which saw service in the Luftwaffe before transferring to Portugal in the early 1960s. Located at Alverca, near Lisbon, the museum has 80 aircraft on display or in storage.

Above: *Ten DH Chipmunks were obtained from Britain in 1951, followed by 66 built locally by OGMA under licence. Having given primary instruction to generations of FAP pilots, they have only recently been replaced by Aérospatiale/SOCATA Epsilons.*

Below: *Aérospatiale's Puma is the primary SAR helicopter, fitted with flotation bags for over-water operation with Esq de Busca e Salvamento 751 at Montijo and 752 in the Azores. Some Pumas have received a prominent OMERA ORB-31 Hercules nose radar.*

The Last of the Whales

The heaviest and largest aircraft ever to have made an arrested landing aboard a carrier, the Douglas Skywarrior had early on been nicknamed the 'Whale' by air bosses and members of the roof gang who found it difficult to spot on the small deck of 'Hancock'-class carriers. Casting aside the derogatory connotation of this nickname, members of the A-3 community soon used it with pride and in recent years have conspicuously displayed 'Save the Whale' bumper stickers and T-shirts. Notwithstanding this call for preservation, the flying Whale is now on the list of endangered species.

Thirty years after it was accepted by the US Navy, TA-3B BuNo 144862 is still active with VAQ-33, continuing to train new crews for the Skywarrior. Seen on approach to Key West, the prominent tail bumper is deployed to avoid damage to the rear fuselage in the case of over-rotation.

First flown on 28 October 1952 and making its squadron debut on 31 March 1956, the Skywarrior first served in the strategic bombing role (50 A3D-1s and 164 A3D-2s, which became A-3As and A-3Bs respectively in September 1962) and soon added reconnaissance (one YA3D-1P modified from the seventh A3D-1 airframe and 30 A3D-2Ps/RA-3Bs), ELINT/SIGINT/COMINT (five A3D-1Qs/EA-3As modified from A3D-1 airframes and 25 purpose-built A3D-2Qs/EA-3Bs) and air refuelling (the last 41 A3D-2s/A-3Bs being delivered as tanker-configured aircraft with hosereel unit mounted, when needed, in the rear of the bomb bay) to its

Left: Add some warts and a tactical grey scheme, and an aircraft designed in 1949/50 does not look out of place on a 1990 apron. No replacement is in sight for the FEWSG's two squadrons of ERA-3Bs, which fly the EW 'aggressor' mission.

Above: The A-3 was designed as a bomber, and it saw considerable action as such during the early days of the Vietnam War, ending bombing operations in 1967. Since then, specialist variants like this ERA-3B have carried the Skywarrior's career to even greater heights.

operational assignments. In addition, 12 A3D-2Ts/TA-3Bs were built as bombardier/navigator trainers.

During the early 1960s, the A-3As were assigned to replacement training squadrons and the A-3Bs lost their nuclear strike *raison d'être* – not, as might have been expected, to their intended carrier-based successors, North American A3J-1s/A-5As, but to submarine-launched Polaris missiles. However, these Skywarriors gained a new lease of life during the Vietnam War when 90 were rebuilt as KA-3B dedicated tankers and EKA-3B tanker and countermeasures strike support (TACOS) aircraft.

Deployments end

With the end of the war and hence the availability of enough Grumman KA-6D tankers and EA-6B electronic support aircraft, active duty air wings no longer had a need for KA-3Bs and EKA-3Bs. Consequently, regular Skywarrior deployments aboard carriers ended on 10 October 1974 when the EKA-3Bs of VAQ-134 Det Four returned to NAS Alameda after a cruise to West-Pac aboard the USS *Ranger* (CVA-61). Not quite

four years earlier, however, KA-3Bs had been assigned to two reserve squadrons, and Skywarrior tankers went on to be operated by these two squadrons for almost two decades, going back to sea regularly for carquals.

Although RA-3B detachments from VAP-61, VAP-62, and VCP-63 occasionally operated aboard carriers during the 1960s and early 1970s, the RA-3Bs were quickly overshadowed in the carrier-based reconnaissance role by supersonic North American RA-5Cs. After their shore-based duty ended during the summer of 1974, surviving RA-3Bs became available for modification as testbeds (as NRA-3Bs) or electronic warfare platforms (as ERA-3Bs). Decreasing requirement for navigator training also led to the modification of five TA-3Bs into VIP-configured transports.

Conversely, with the exception of a single airframe that had been modified early on as the sole VA-3B transport, the EA-3Bs retained their usefulness for over three decades.

When, in October 1987, the tightly-knit A-3 community gathered at NAS Key West for a 35-year reunion hosted by VAQ-33, the last VIP-configured TA-3Bs had just been replaced by Grumman C-20Bs but 48 Whales were still operated by four active squadrons, two reserve squadrons, the Naval Weapons Center, the Pacific Missile Test Center and the Army's White Sands Missile Range. By then, however, the writing was on the wall as the loss of two EA-3Bs earlier in the year was drawing much negative attention from congressmen and senators, the press and the public. Neither of these accidents was attributed

'Whales' are best known for their electronic and test work, particularly the regularly-reconfigured aircraft of the Pacific Missile Test Center. Once a bastion of the A-3 community, only this aircraft and one other survive on the PMTC trials fleet.

VQ-2 'Batmen'

Fleet Air Reconnaissance Squadron Two is the Atlantic Fleet's signals intelligence (Sigint) gatherer, flying the EA-3B Skywarrior and Lockheed EP-3E Orion from its base at Rota in Spain. With the squadron's wide tasking, the aircraft are often deployed to other bases in Europe, the Mediterranean and the Middle East.

to the aircraft or its systems, although the loss of the crew of an EA-3B from VQ-2 during night carrier operations aboard the USS *Nimitz* (CVN-68) was partly due to the fact that the Whale had always been a demanding aircraft during night carrier landings. Nevertheless, yielding to external pressure even though it did not yet have a replacement for the EA-3Bs, the Navy decided to restrict the A-3 to shore-based operations. VAQ-33 ended carqual training immediately and stopped sending 'nuggets' to trap in TA-3Bs. VQ-2 ended carrier operations on 2 November, and an EA-3B of VQ-1 made the last 'trap' aboard the USS *Ranger* (CV-61) during night operations in the South China Sea on 21 November 1987.

Squadrons disband

The ban on carrier operations, as well as the increasingly difficult and costly maintenance of airframes that had been exposed to the rigours of carrier-based duties and were at least 27 years old, led within two years to the disestablishment of two squadrons and to the withdrawal of A-3s from a third. First to go were the 'Griffins' of VAK-308, which were disestablished on 30 September 1988 at NAS Alameda. Two months later, the 'World Watchers' of VQ-1 at NAS Agana, Guam, ended 32 years of EA-3B operations, as the 'Queer Whales' lacked the range necessary to cover areas of interest in the vast Pacific and Indian Oceans when operating from the few available land bases. Finally, the 'Jockeys' of VAK-208 stood down on 30 September 1989 (in 1970, 'Jockeys' and 'Griffins' had been commissioned in the Naval Air Reserve as VAQ-208 and VAQ-308 respectively, and nine years later they were redesignated VAK-208 and VAK-308 to become the only specialised tanker squadrons in the US Navy; regardless of their designations, the two reserve squadrons flew KA-3Bs on tanking and pathfinding missions.

VAQ-33 'Firebirds'

In early 1970, VAQ-33 was established at NAS Norfolk as the flying component of the Fleet Electronic Warfare Support Group, a role in which it continues today although with responsibilities only extending to the Atlantic Fleet. Skywarriors were among its first equipment (A-3Bs) and the type figures prominently today. In October 1977 it was assigned the A-3 support role for the entire fleet, adding crew training and maintenance support of the 'Whale' to its tasks. Shortly after, in 1978, it moved to NAS Oceana, Virginia, before transferring to its current base at NAS Key West, Florida, in 1980.

Before its current incarnation, VAQ-33 and its predecessors flew electronic missions with the Grumman TBM-3E and Douglas AD. It undertook the Skyraider's last carrier deployment in 1969.

Above: To undertake the A-3 fleet training role, VAQ-33 have five TA-3Bs, identified by the lack of electronic equipment and fuselage cabin windows. Useful for training pilots, the TA-3B's main priority was training navigators/ bombardiers, with two pilots, one instructor and five students on board, one of the latter sitting on the flight deck for celestial navigation training. Wing pylons were originally fitted for the carriage of practice bomb dispensers.

Left: VAQ-33 has three ERA-3Bs for its primary EW 'aggressor' role, augmented by a single EP-3A Orion and Grumman EA-6As. A single KA-3B tanker is also in service. The unit's aircraft wear the 'GD' tailcode of the Fleet Electronic Warfare Support Group.

VAQ-34 'Flashbacks'

In addition to its ERA-3Bs, VAQ-34 operates single examples of the UA-3B (ex-TNRA-3B above), KA-3B (below) and EA-3B.

With the increasing requirement for electronic warfare 'aggressors', the US Navy established a second squadron at NAS Point Mugu on 1 March 1983 to cater for Pacific Fleet requirements, allowing VAQ-33 to concentrate on the Atlantic Fleet. Tactical Electronic Warfare Squadron 34 was originally known as the 'Electric Horsemen', and carried the FEWSG's 'GD' code on the fin. Aircraft now wear a more appropriate red star.

The last Whale squadrons

Today, Whales equip only three squadrons, VQ-2 at NS Rota, VAQ-33 at NAS Key West, and VAQ-34 at NAS Point Mugu, and continue to be operated as RDT&E platforms at NAS China Lake, NAS Point Mugu, and Holloman AFB. Established as Electronic Reconnaissance Squadron Two at NAF Port Lyautey, Morocco, on 1 September 1955, VQ-2 obtained its first two carrier-capable A3D-1Qs in September 1956 to supplement its land-based Lockheed P2V-5FE Neptunes. The squadron exchanged these early electronic reconnaissance Skywarriors for A3D-2Qs soon after moving to NS Rota in early 1959 and was redesignated Fleet Air Reconnaissance Squadron Two on 1 January 1960. Hard to predict at a time when US Naval Aviation had yet to celebrate its 50th anniversary, 'Queer Whales', Fleet Air Reconnaissance (FAIRECON) designation, and Spanish basing were to be the lot of the 'Batmen' for more than three decades.

Following the termination of EA-3B operations by its sister squadron in the Pacific Fleet at the end of 1988, VQ-2 picked most of the Whales previously assigned to VQ-1 and stepped up its activities as availability of numerous friendly bases enabled its EA-3Bs to keep a thorough electronic watch over the Med, the Adriatic, the Aegean Sea, the Black Sea, the Arabian Sea, and the Persian Gulf, as well as deep into countries bordering these waters. Thus, in the spring of 1990, the 'Batmen' had nine EA-3Bs, including two aircraft that have been cocooned for later use, to supplement their Lockheed EP-3Es. It is now expected that VQ-2 will phase out its EA-3Bs in late 1991 or early 1992 after carrier-capable Lockheed ES-3As become operational with Fleet Air Reconnaissance Squadron Six (VQ-6).

Specially developed for use in the TASES (Tactical Signal Exploitation System) role, the EA-3Bs of VQ-2 have a crew of seven consisting of pilot, navigator, and DECM (defensive ECM) operator in the cockpit, and an ECM evaluator and three ECM operators in the pressurised fuse-lage compartment. The GTE-Sylvania AN/ALR-40 multiple-band reconnaissance and collection system with antennas in the 'Seawing' ventral canoe is the key piece of TASES equipment and is supplemented by a variety of countermeasures and radar receivers, pulse and signal analysers, ELINT gathering and threat analysis systems, communications intercept and analysis systems, and recording equipment.

Coming under the operational control of the

Above: The recent crop of 'Whale' squadron disbandments claimed the electronic reconnaissance EA-3Bs of VQ-1 'World Watchers' (above right) and the KA-3B tankers of VAK-208 'Jockeys' and VAK-308 'Griffins' (above). The two latter squadrons were the only dedicated tanker squadrons in the Navy, flying as part of the Reserve on deployment support duties. For a year only VAK-208 existed, before final disbandment at Alameda in September 1989.

Right: A chisel-nosed ERA-3B stands on the Point Mugu ramp, flanked by VAQ-34's EA-7L Corsairs, also used for the EW 'aggressor' role.

Pacific Missile Test Center

PMTC (previously known as the Naval Weapons Center) at Point Mugu has over 30 years' experience with the 'Whale', having received its first A3D-1 in 1959. Fourteen aircraft have been used over the years for a variety of missile, ECM and radar tests. By 1985, five aircraft were still in use, but the number has now shrunk to just two, although these still perform valuable work alongside Orions and tactical types. The unit's Skywarriors have been the most radically altered of any, with a variety of 'lumps and bumps' added for various test programmes.

Above: 'Big Nose' seen in happier days. In late 1989, a standard A-3 nose was fitted to the aircraft for further service with PMTC.

Left: PMTC's second aircraft is NRA-3B '71'. It is unusual in having a front fuselage stores pylon and modified tailcone installation.

In keeping with other Navy aircraft, the active Skywarrior fleet is slowly adopting the Tactical Paint Scheme. Unlike the Orion force, the squadrons retain full, if toned-down, markings. This is a TA-3B of VAQ-33.

Fleet Electronic Warfare Support Group (FEWSG), VAQ-33 and VAQ-34 have operated ERA-3Bs since 1972 and 1983 respectively, to provide electronic warfare training for units of the Atlantic and Pacific Fleets (LANTFLT and PACFLT), as well as for naval units from NATO and Pacific Rim nations. Supplemented by EA-7Ls (and, in the case of VAQ-33, by an EP-3A and EA-6As), their ERA-3Bs provide stand-off jamming, chaff laying, and communication and deception jamming; they also simulate a variety of surface- and air-launched missiles. By using known adversary tactics realistically to simulate today's threat, the 'Electric Whales' of the FEWSG squadrons enable shipborne and airborne radar operators to receive invaluable 'hands-on' training in the operation of their equipment in a realistic electronic warfare environment.

Modified from RA-3B airframes, the ERA-3Bs have a crew of five consisting of pilot, navigator, and plane captain in the cockpit, and two ECM operators in the pressurised fuselage compartment. They are fitted with a large capacity chaff dispenser in an enlarged tail cone and with the canoe-mounted AN/ALT-40 FEWSG Airborne Electronic Warfare System (FAEWS),

Naval Weapons Center

The NWC (previously Naval Ordnance Test Station) is based at China Lake in the Mojave desert. The unit is concerned with researching and testing weapon systems and sensors. It received A-3B BuNo 142404 to assist in its work during the 1960s, but this aircraft was converted to a KA-3B and reassigned to fleet duties in 1969. Its replacement was NA-3B BuNo 142630, which still flies with the unit today, resplendent in an all-white scheme.

Many of the test Skywarriors have featured bizarre nose modifications, often mounting new radars or, as here, seeker heads of missiles on a bluff nose profile. Often, associated sensors are also mounted with the missile head to allow testing of a complete weapon system. NWC's NA-3B has had several of these fitted throughout its working life, this example being seen in 1988 at its China Lake base.

Graphically illustrating how it acquired its nickname, the 'Whale' must have been an awe-inspiring sight for a young carrier deckhand. The narrow-track undercarriage and wide wings made it a handful during deck landings. Behind the nosewheel is the lowered crew access hatch.

which consists of a high-power jammer, a direction finder, a receiver, and a computer controller. In addition, they can carry externally AN/AST-4 threat simulation pods, AN/ALQ-167 Multiple Environment Threat Emitter (METE) pods, and AN/ALQ-76 ECM jamming pods. To provide the electrical power required to run the additional electronic equipment with which they are fitted, the ERA-3Bs have four ram-air turbines (RATs), two on each side of the fuselage.

The ERA-3Bs of VAQ-33 and VAQ-34 have long proved to be valuable assets, notably by providing training for naval units deploying to such hot spots as the Persian Gulf and the Gulf of Sidra, but they are becoming increasingly difficult and costly to maintain. Unfortunately, no other airframes suitable for conversion as heavy airborne jamming platforms are currently in the inventory and funds for the acquisition of specialised aircraft, such as proposed versions of the Gulfstream C-20, could not be made available in recent years when the military budget was relatively unlimited. Now that reduced military budgets are the order of the day, replacements for the ERA-3Bs may not become available for several years.

Training support

Having assumed the responsibility of A-3 Fleet Replacement Squadron (FRS) and being responsible for the A-3 Fleet Replacement Aviation Maintenance Program (FRAMP), the 'Firebirds' of VAQ-33 supplement their three ERA-3Bs with five TA-3B trainers and one KA-3B tanker. The 'Flashbacks' (initially nicknamed 'Electric Horsemen') of VAQ-34 do not have such collateral responsibilities but nevertheless supplement their four ERA-3Bs with an EA-3B, a KA-3B, and a UA-3B. (The only aircraft to have received the UA-3B designation, BuNo 144834 had been delivered in 1959 as an RA-3B and modified as an NRA-3B in 1974 for use at the Pacific Missile Test Range. In 1985 all mission equipment was removed prior to its assignment to VQ-2 as the sole TNRA-3B; this designation was later changed to that of UA-3B, and VAQ-34 now uses this aircraft as a less delicate 'bounce bird' for touch-and-go training and as a utility transport.)

US Army

Wearing Army titles, RA-3B BuNo 144843 supports Patriot and other SAM tests at the White Sands Missile Range in New Mexico. The aircraft retains the fuselage side camera fairing but the camera bay is replaced by a systems operator cabin with portholes.

A pair of VAQ-34's ERA-3Bs share the ramp with the KA-3B tanker, complete with open bomb bay doors which in this version cover the tanker package. The unit has a UA-3B, used for continuation training and general 'hack' missions, acquired from VQ-2.

Whales do not die . . . they just test away

Having acquired its first two Skywarriors in 1959 when it was designated the Naval Missile Center, the Pacific Missile Test Center (PMTC or PACMISTESTCEN, according to the alphabet soup for which the USN has a special affinity) has over the years operated no fewer than 14 of these aircraft (NA-3A, NEA-3A, KA-3B, NA-3B, NRA-3B, RA-3B, and TA-3B) on a broad range of development activities including captive flight testing of missile weapon systems (complete missiles being mounted on wing or fuselage pylons or

Seen with a conventional nose fitted, the 'White Whale' of NWC has had a chequered career. In addition to Navy trials units, Skywarriors were bailed to manufacturers for development work, notably Hughes, Raytheon and Westinghouse.

guidance systems being faired into the nose of the aircraft), ECM threat simulation for the Fleet (prior to the commissioning of the co-located VAQ-34), and test and evaluation of airborne radar, laser devices, and electronic warfare (ECM, ECCM, and ESM) systems.

In the spring of 1990 only two of these long-serving, specially configured test aircraft were still operational at NAS Point Mugu, side number 71 (BuNo 142667) and side number 75 (BuNo 144825). Distinguished since 1960 by its unusually large nose (originally fitted by Grumman to house the pulse-Doppler radar and Eagle missile control system being developed by a Bendix/Grumman team for the Douglas F6D Missileer), side number 75 now has a standard Whale nose, that from a KA-3B (BuNo 138944, side number 73) having been mated to BuNo 144825 by Chrysler Technology Airborne Systems during a refit in 1989.

Great White Whale

Painted all white and appropriately nicknamed the 'White Whale', BuNo 142630 has had a long and diversified career since being delivered by

Douglas as an A3D-2 in May 1958. After serving with Heavy Attack Squadrons (notably with VAH-8 aboard the USS *Midway*, CVA-41), it was modified as an NA-3B prior to being assigned to the Naval Parachute Test Range at NAF El Centro, California. Transferred to the Naval Weapons Center at NAS China Lake, California, in the late 1960s, this NA-3B has been fitted over the years with a variety of nose configurations to test guidance systems and serve in the development of numerous missiles and weapon systems. Still without equivalent in the naval inventory, BuNo 142630 remains a useful test platform and is lovingly kept in immaculate shape in spite of its age.

The largest aircraft currently flying with US Army markings, BuNo 144843 has been operated far from the sea for more than a decade but may well become the last Whale to be 'beached'. Based at Holloman AFB, New Mexico, this RA-3B continues to be flown in support of Army missile test and development activities at the White Sands Missile Range. No plans have yet been announced for its retirement and this Skywarrior may well prove that desert air is more conducive to long life than sea air – a rather controversial and unexpected ending for one of the greatest aircraft ever flown from the deck of a carrier.

Skywarrior fleet on 1 May 1990	
VQ-2, NS Rota	9×EA-3B
VAQ-33, NAS Key West	1×KA-3B
	3×ERA-3B
	5×TA-3B
VAQ-34, NAS Point Mugu	1×KA-3B
	3×ERA-3B
	1×UA-3B
	1×EA-3B
PMTC, NAS Point Mugu	2×NRA-3B
NWC, NAS China Lake	1×NA-3B
US Army, Holloman AFB	1×RA-3B
	Total 28

Powerplant
The ERA-3B is powered by the Pratt & Whitney J57-P-10 turbojet, developing 9,000-lb thrust at normal rating and 10,500 lb at military rating. Now long in the tooth and increasingly difficult to support, the J57 is nevertheless noted for its great reliability and strength.

Wing pylons
ERA-3Bs carry additional electronic equipment on the Aero 7A wing pylons. AN/ALQ-76 ECM pods are the usual store, each fitted with its own ram air turbine (RAT) to power the jammers. AN/AST-4 and AN/ALQ-167 threat simulators are alternative stores.

Crew
A crew of five fly the ERA-3B, consisting of pilot, navigator and plane captain on the flight deck, and two ECM evaluators in the pressurised cabin. The latter sit side-by-side along the starboard side of the aircraft, facing the equipment consoles on the port side. Entry is gained from the main crew access, behind the main flight deck.

RATs
Four ram air turbines are located along the fuselage sides to provide power for the onboard electronic equipment.

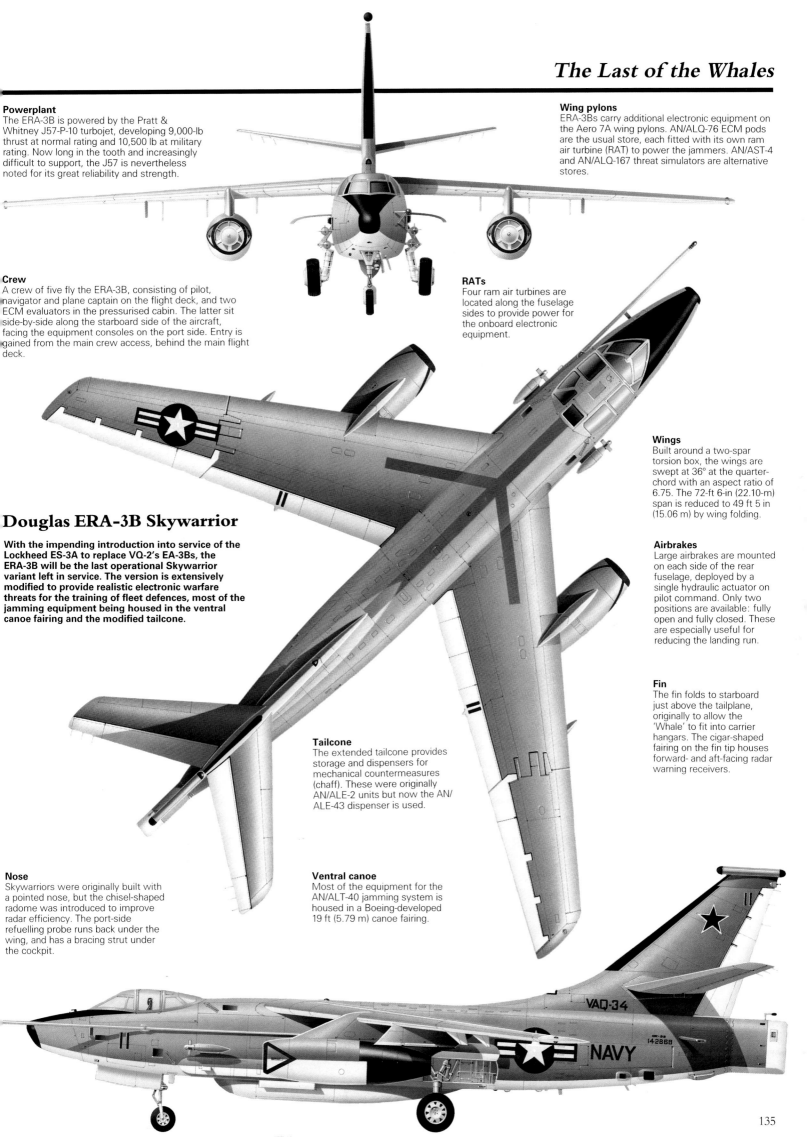

Wings
Built around a two-spar torsion box, the wings are swept at 36° at the quarter-chord with an aspect ratio of 6.75. The 72-ft 6-in (22.10-m) span is reduced to 49 ft 5 in (15.06 m) by wing folding.

Airbrakes
Large airbrakes are mounted on each side of the rear fuselage, deployed by a single hydraulic actuator on pilot command. Only two positions are available: fully open and fully closed. These are especially useful for reducing the landing run.

Fin
The fin folds to starboard just above the tailplane, originally to allow the 'Whale' to fit into carrier hangars. The cigar-shaped fairing on the fin tip houses forward- and aft-facing radar warning receivers.

Douglas ERA-3B Skywarrior

With the impending introduction into service of the Lockheed ES-3A to replace VQ-2's EA-3Bs, the ERA-3B will be the last operational Skywarrior variant left in service. The version is extensively modified to provide realistic electronic warfare threats for the training of fleet defences, most of the jamming equipment being housed in the ventral canoe fairing and the modified tailcone.

Tailcone
The extended tailcone provides storage and dispensers for mechanical countermeasures (chaff). These were originally AN/ALE-2 units but now the AN/ALE-43 dispenser is used.

Nose
Skywarriors were originally built with a pointed nose, but the chisel-shaped radome was introduced to improve radar efficiency. The port-side refuelling probe runs back under the wing, and has a bracing strut under the cockpit.

Ventral canoe
Most of the equipment for the AN/ALT-40 jamming system is housed in a Boeing-developed 19 ft (5.79 m) canoe fairing.

VAQ-34

142B6B

NAVY

The Warsaw Pact Air Forces

Pictured at its 1989 public unveiling in Moscow, the prototype Beriev A-40 'Albatross' jet flying-boat is officially for SAR, but may have an anti-submarine role.

Since it was signed in 1955, the 'Warsaw Pact' has been a convenient label for the integrated armed forces of the Soviet Union and its Central European allies. In fact, it is the 'Status of Forces' agreements, concluded in the late 1940s between Moscow and the communist governments forced upon nations freshly liberated from Nazi occupation, which have provided the military cohesion that focussed the collective mind of NATO.

Now the cement has dissolved. The War-Pac's only military triumphs have been the earlier suppression of democratic movements in East Germany, Hungary, Czechoslovakia and Poland. President Gorbachev's courageous decision not to shore up unpopular and often corrupt dictatorships by threat of invasion has released a flood tide of democratic aspirations which drenched the Soviet satellites during 1989

and lapped at the steps of the Kremlin itself.

Glasnost has also come to aviation. Where once small, grainy black-and-white photographs sufficed to illustrate the Soviet air force's front-line equipment, the hardware now performs daily before the crowds at Farnborough, Paris, Abbotsville and Moscow. Behind the tattered remains of the 'Iron Curtain', satellite air forces hold open days where visitors freely photograph the participants.

Though still far from complete, information on organisation and equipment has filtered out to provide a more reliable basis on which to assess the strengths and weaknesses of WarPac air arms. Increased international trust and decreased internal financing make it unlikely that these air forces will ever again reach the size and destructive power described on the following pages.

Blackjack is white. The new Tu-160 strategic bomber – a parallel to the Rockwell B-1 – was shown in detail to the US Defense Secretary in Moscow during August 1989.

SOVIET UNION

Soviet Military Aviation

Sukhoi's 'Frogfoot' is a robust ground attack aircraft similar in concept to the US A-10A Thunderbolt. First seen in 1989 was the Su-25UB/Su-28 two-seat trainer.

In spite of the upheavals in Soviet society since Mikhail Gorbachev came to power, the powerful armed forces of the USSR have suffered less than most as the chill winds of openness and rationality have blown through an entrenched and formerly privileged bureaucracy. Though military aircraft production has been falling since its 1976-8 peak, the air forces have held their own as the result of Soviet science (or science assisted by industrial espionage), narrowing the technological gap between East and West.

There are those who considered that Gorbachev might be ousted by high-ranking military officers as a result of concluding the INF (Intermediate Nuclear Forces) treaty, which condemned to the scrap-heap what was, in percentage terms, a minute fraction of the Soviet armoury. With the Soviet republics apparently disintegrating, and CFE (Conventional Forces in Europe) negotiations promising large-scale cuts in the armed forces of NATO and the Warsaw Pact, the reaction of the military hard-liners could prove to be Gorbachev's undoing.

Unilateral cuts in aviation announced in 1989 covered 800 aircraft – most in the ground-attack role – by 1991. Naturally, the air forces will do the same as the West: scrap the old machines and keep the most effective operational. If necessary, this will be achieved by passing newer equipment to allies – always assuming that they want it. The independence in matters of defence policy which many Warsaw Pact members have reclaimed for themselves poses problems for Soviet planners. Until recently, satellites in Central and Southern Europe were closely tied into Soviet military plans, and could be expected to operate in concert with Moscow's air forces.

That can no longer be taken for granted. Furthermore, if political pressure and financial necessity result in withdrawal of air units from their forward bases in Poland, East Germany and Czechoslovakia, 'Mother Russia' will be without the defence in depth which she considers a right earned by the sacrifices of World War II.

For the present, at least, the Soviet air forces remain the second-largest in the world after the US Air Force. Use of the plural is correct in this context, for the armed forces of the USSR are organised on a different basis to those in the West. There are five Services, given a status in the military hierarchy entirely unconnected to their dates of formation. First in order of precedence, the Strategic Rocket Force is the most recently established, coming ahead of the Ground Forces, or army.

Next comes the National Air Defence Forces, comprising manned interceptor and SAM units, followed by the Air Force with its bomber, strike/attack/recce/army-aviation and transport commands. Fifth and last, the Navy includes a sizeable air arm for land- and sea-based operations, plus the force of missile-armed submarines. Clearly, 'air force' duties as performed (say) by the USAF are here spread across three armed Services. In a further indication of military thinking regarding the role of the air arm, the term 'army' is sometimes used in reference to the four elements other than the navy.

Despite a vast, autonomous striking power, the air forces are unable to forget their historic role as a supporting element for the ground forces. At all levels, the two elements are under joint control, with aircraft assigned to Military Districts, or multiples thereof. The High Com-

Shown at Paris in 1989, the Mi-28 'Havoc' attack helicopter demonstrated that military openness means a safer world. Despite persistent Western reports of imminent service-entry, it became apparent that only three prototypes had flown and avionics and sighting systems were far from complete.

Largest aircraft ever built, the An-225 Mriya, lacks a straight-through freight loading facility and is currently used for pick-a-back cargoes.

Glasnost is not universal. A few days after a Kamov spokesman denied it existed, this first photo of a 'Hokum' attack helicopter was released by the USA.

The immense area of the USSR and its satellites is divided into Theatres of War (TVDs), each comprising several Military Districts and/or Groups of Soviet Forces (in Eastern Europe).

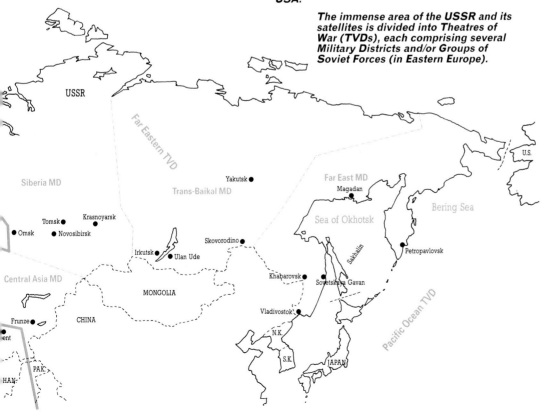

mand has designated four Theatres of War (TV – *Teatr Voyny*) covering the whole USSR and its maritime approaches: Western, Southern, Far East and Strategic Reserve (in the heartland). Theatres of War are divided into one or more Theatres of Military Operations (TVD – *Teatr Voyennykh Destivy*), each comprising a number of Military Districts.

Western TV contains North-Western TVD (i.e. Leningrad MD), South-Western TVD (Odessa MD, Kiev MD and Southern Group of Forces in Hungary), Western TVD (Baltic MD, Byelorussian MD, Carpathian MD, Northern Group of Forces in Poland, Central Group of Forces in Czechoslovakia and Western Group of Forces in East Germany), Atlantic TVD (Baltic Fleet, Black Sea Fleet and Mediterranean Naval Squadron) and Arctic TVD (Northern Fleet).

Southern TV is the Southern TVD (North Caucasus MD, Trans-Caucasus MD and Turkestan MD) and Caspian Sea Flotilla.

Far East TV contains the Far East TVD (Central Asian MD, Siberian MD, Transbaykal MD, Far Eastern MD and Mongolia) and Pacific Ocean TVD (Pacific Ocean Fleet).

High Command Strategic Reserve is equivalent to the Moscow, Volga and Ural MDs and contains the bomber force.

The four Groups of Forces based outside the USSR, plus all Military Districts except four (North Caucasus, Turkestan, Ural and Volga), are assigned one of 20 Air Armies (*Vozdushnaya Armiya*) of tactical aircraft, these varying in size according to location. The units – part of the Air Force proper – were once known as Frontal Aviation, and designated by numbers, but are now known by the more cumbersome title of 'Air Force of the (Leningrad) Military District' or 'Air Force of the (Western) Group of Forces'. Commanders of these Air Forces have two deputies responsible for tactical attack and air defence. If heavier support is required, they can call upon the large bombers and interdictors of the Strategic Reserve, some of whose units are already based in the satellite countries.

Aviation units are organised on army lines. Districts are responsible for one or more Aviation Divisions (*Aviatsionnaya Diviziya*) in their area, each being approximately equivalent to an RAF Group, in that they command an average of 12 squadrons. Divisional HQ is normally located at one of the three air bases under its command and possesses a liaison flight with one or two helicopters and light aircraft. Each air base supports a single Aviation Regiment (*Aviatsionniy Polk*), equivalent to a Wing, comprising the usual supply, security and organisational elements, a communications flight, plus an Aviation Wing (*Aviatsionniy Divizion*) and a Technical Support Wing (*Tekhnicheskiy-Eksplutatsionniy Divizion*).

During the 1970s, the number of flying squadrons in the Aviation Wing was increased from three to four, and a further technical squadron correspondingly added. Each Squadron (*Eskadril*) draws aircraft from the Wing's pool, which would comprise 45 single-seat fighter-interceptors or 42 combat-capable strike aircraft, plus between four and eight trainers. Naturally, the latter are normally 'two-stick' versions of the former, but in cases where none

Air Power Analysis

exists – such as during the early career of the Su-25 'Frogfoot' – other types are used.

Squadrons are divided into Flights (*Zveno*) of four aircraft, while the normal tactical formation is – as the world over – a Pair (*Para*) comprising leader and wingman. On-hand reserve aircraft increase the complement of a typical air base to about 60, allowing a fifth squadron to form in an emergency with a staff of pilots taken from training and administrative duties. It is expected that at least 50 of the wing's aircraft would be ready for action on Day 1 of a conflict, given sufficient warning. Some of these might be flown from reserve bases, where the standard of facilities is reduced – for example, no hardened shelters. In practice, wing strength varies from three to five squadrons in some cases, whilst reconnaissance aircraft are normally assigned to oversize, independent squadrons each containing up to 20 aircraft.

RVSN has a formidable force of 1,600 ICBM launch silos, the oldest, but still most numerous, occupant being the 10000-13000 km range SS-11 'Sego', of which 375 remain.

Strategic Rocket Forces (Raketnyye Voyska Strategischeskovo Naznacheniya)

For political reasons, the RVSN takes precedence over all other components of the Soviet armed forces, although in Western terms it is equivalent to only part of a part of the USAF. Comprising six Rocket Armies – divided into divisions, regiments, battalions and batteries (the last-mentioned with a single missile silo each) – the RVSN is limited by international treaty to 1,618 land-based silos, including 1,096 reserved for SS-17, SS-18 and SS-19 weapons. Additionally, the force began deploying mobile weapons, which have greater immunity from pre-emptive attack, in 1985, when the SS-25 took to the roads. Two years later, the rail-mobile SS-24 was introduced as a partial replacement for SS-18. Some SS-11 silos are being dismantled in compensation for these new weapons, while an SS-26 and SS-27 (at least) are under development.

The inventory of ICBMs is approximately 375 SS-11 'Segos', 60 SS-13 'Savages', 125 SS-17 'Spankers', 308 SS-18 'Satans', 330 SS-19 'Stilettos', 24 SS-24 'Scalpels' and 150 SS-25 'Sickles'. Silo-based weapons are located at the following missile fields:

Organisation

EQUIPMENT	BASE
SS-18	Aleysk

SS-19	Derazhnaya
SS-18	Dombarovskiy
SS-11	Drovyanaya
SS-11	Gladkaya
SS-18	Imeny Gastello
Trials	Kapustin Yar
SS-18	Kartaly
SS-17	Kostroma
SS-11 and SS-19	Kozelsk
SS-11	Olovyanaya
SS-11	Perm
SS-19	Pervomaysk
Trials	Plesetsk
SS-11	Svobodnyy
SS-19	Tatishchevo
SS-11	Teykovo
Trials	Tyuratam
SS-18	Uzhur
SS-25	Verkhyaya Sada
SS-17	Yedrovo
SS-13 and SS-25	Yoshkar Ola
SS-25	Yurya
SS-18	Zhangiz-Tobe

In December 1987, the US-USSR INF Treaty agreed the destruction of 64 SS-4 'Sandals' and 405 mobile SS-20 'Sabers' – plus 365 of these weapons in storage – as well as some SS-12s, SS-23s and SSC-4s assigned to the army. All are due to have been scrapped by the end of 1990. Sites are, or were: Chita, Kaliningrad, Yedrovo and others for SS-4s; and Aleysk, Barnaul, Derazhnaya, Kansk, Kopu, Novosibirsk, Olovyanaya, Omsk, Pervomaysk, Tapa, Tyuratam, Uzhur, Verkhyaya Sada, Yurya and Zhangiz-Tobe for SS-20s.

SS-1 'Scud' is a mobile battlefield missile mounting a nuclear, chemical or conventional warhead. Large numbers have been issued to army units.

The FROG (Free Rocket Over Ground) series of tactical missiles is being replaced by the more accurate Tochka (SS-21 'Scarab'), illustrated here on its launcher.

Ground Forces (Sukhoputnyye Voyska)

Strictly speaking, no aircraft are operated by the Red Army, although in practical terms the Ground Forces are closely supported by the Air Force. This assistance includes the transport and combat helicopters over which many Western armies have complete control. About 1,500 nuclear missiles with ranges under 1000 km (621 miles) are below the criterion for inclusion in RVSN and so are termed tactical weapons and assigned to the army. Of these, 136 SS-12 'Scaleboards' and 167 SS-23 'Spiders' are being destroyed under INF provisions, leaving 620 SS-1C 'Scuds', 120 SS-21 'Scarabs', 110 FROG 3/5s and 550 FROG 7s.

Army intermediate missile units are located at the bases listed below. FROGs are being replaced by SS-21s; SS-1s by SS-23s, until halted by INF.

Organisation

EQUIPMENT	BASE
FROG/SS-21	Bruntal, Czechoslovakia
SS-1/SS-23	Budapest, Hungary
FROG/SS-21 and SS-1/SS-23	Dresden, East Germany
SS-1/SS-23	Eberswalde, East Germany
SS-22	Finsterwalde, East Germany
FROG/SS-21	Grossborn, Poland
FROG/SS-21	Jenna/Namburg, East Germany
SS-1/SS-23	Magdeburg/Juteborg, East Germany
FROG/SS-21	Milovice, Czechoslovakia
SS-21	Mirow, East Germany
FROG/SS-21 and SS-1/SS-23	Mlada Boleslav, Czechoslovakia
FROG/SS-21	Neuruppin, East Germany
FROG/SS-21	Neustrelitz, East Germany
FROG/SS-21	Ohrdruf, East Germany
SS-1/SS-23	Olmütz, Czechoslovakia
SS-1/SS-23	Pardubice, Czechoslovakia
FROG/SS-21	Perleberg, East Germany
FROG/SS-21	Riesa/Grimma, East Germany
FROG/SS-21	Rosslau, East Germany
FROG/SS-21	Szekesfahervar, Hungary
FROG/SS-21	Templin/Bernau, East Germany
FROG/SS-21	Vyskoe Myto, Czechoslovakia
FROG/SS-21	Zvilen, Czechoslovakia

The army also has a tactical air defence force which is integrated with the national air defences. These have twice been reorganised during the 1980s, as detailed below. Currently, the Troops of Troop Air Defence are assigned those SAMs designated as tactical in their deployment, both to protect armies in the field and fixed installations. These are 1,350 SA-4 'Ganefs', 840 SA-6 'Gainfuls', 800 SA-8 'Geckos', 425 SA-9 'Gaskins', 250 SA-11 'Gadflys', 45 SA-12A 'Gladiators' and 930 SA-13 'Gophers'.

Escorted by an Alaskan-based F-15 Eagle, a Su-27 'Flanker' enters US air space on its way to an air show. Two years ago, the presence in America of the Soviets' top-of-the-line fighter would have been unthinkable.

Troops of Air Defence (Voyska Protivovozdushnoy Oborony)

Voyska-PVO is the third most senior formation in the Soviet armed forces, performing a role with no direct parallel in the West. Recognising the waste and inefficiency of a system which duplicated some of the functions of army air defences and the interceptor aircraft attached to the tactical air force, the USSR attempted to rationalise the PVO in 1980 by adding some army missiles and radar, while assigning some fighters in border areas to the Air Force. The name of National Air Defence (*PVO-Strany*) was changed in January 1981 to the present title, implying a role outside the Soviet Union's geographical confines. The anticipated improvements in performance failed to materialise, and by 1986 the army's AA guns had been returned to the Troops of Troop Air Defence. At about the same time, up to 1,000 fighter aircraft reverted to V-PVO operational control, strength now being 2,150.

These manned interceptors form Fighter Aviation of Air Defence (*Istrebitel'naya Aviatsiya PVO*), alongside the Zenith Rocket Troops with their SAMs (*Zenityye Raketnyye Voyska*); Anti-Space Defence (*Protivokosmischeskaya Oborona*), Anti-Rocket Defence (*Protivoraketnaya Oborona*) and the radars and reporting centres of the Radio-Technical Corps (*Radiotekhnicheskiye Voyska*).

Numerically, the MiG-23 'Flogger-B/G/K' is the principal aircraft of V-PVO, armed with two AA-7 'Apex' and four AA-8 'Aphid' AAMs. The latter weapon is infra-red (IR) seeking, whereas – like most Soviet AAMs – AA-7 multiplies its chances by being deployed in IR and semi-active radar homing (SARH) forms. AA-11 'Archer', a new short-range weapon, has been seen on 'Flogger-K'.

The MiG-25 'Foxbat-A/E' mounts two of each version of AA-6 'Acrid', or two AA-7s plus four AA-8s or AA-11s. 'Foxbat-E' has a limited look-down capability, whereas the MiG-31 'Foxhound' is a revised airframe which includes the USSR's first true look-down/shoot-down fighter radar and four associated AA-9 'Amos' missiles. A further four AA-8s are carried for close work, but the Mach 2.4 'Foxhound' is normally assigned to beyond-visual-range interception from its bases near Arkhangelsk and Dolinsk (on the Sakhalin Peninsula).

Numbers are rapidly dwindling of the ageing Sukhoi Su-21 'Flagon-E/F' and remarkable Tupolev Tu-28P/Tu-128 'Fiddler' interceptor which sought long range by being the same size as a bomber. A more effective solution to the range problem is Sukhoi's Su-27 'Flanker-B' – a fighter with an impressive thrust:weight ratio and manoeuvrability, armed with a combination of up to 10 AA-10/AA-11 missiles. With abilities comparable to the F-15 Eagle, 'Flanker' is an all-weather, all-altitude interceptor with great potential for further development. Some additional effectiveness is being obtained from it and its fellows by subtle changes in the management of air interceptions noted during recent years. The rigid system of ground control is being relaxed to give pilots greater latitude to use their judgement in combat,

MiG-31 'Foxhounds' entered service in 1983 as the A-PVO's first true look-down/shoot-down, multi-target-tracking fighter.

'Flanker' on finals. An over-fuselage airbrake stresses similarities of this large but manoeuvrable interceptor to the USAF's Eagle.

A-PVO has some 350 MiG-25 'Foxbats', each equipped with up to three AAMs of both semi-active radar homing and heat-seeking types.

Long-range air defence of the sparsely-populated Arctic wastes is partly entrusted to diminishing numbers of the massive Tu-28P 'Fiddler'.

Designed to confront the North American B-70 (which was cancelled), the MiG-25 'Foxbat' was produced in the best 'rough and ready' traditions of the Soviet arms industry. With old but effective valve-technology radar, it has the creditable maximum 'clean' speed of Mach 3.2, or Mach 2.87 with weaponry.

although it will be some time before the full beneficial effects of this change are felt throughout the entire V-PVO.

Of equal importance to the Su-27, an improved AEW system is now being deployed in the form of the Ilyushin Il-76 'Mainstay', which supplants the Tu-126 'Moss' of limited effectiveness. The role of a smaller such aircraft, the Antonov An-74 'Madcap', which is still under development, has yet to be revealed. The Radio-Technical Corps provides the majority of some 10,000 warning systems (including satellites) available to air defence forces.

Moscow has the world's only anti-ballistic missile defence system ranged around its perimeters. Limited to 100 missiles by treaty – the USA having decided not to deploy its allotment – the force comprises 16 old ABM-1 'Galosh' missiles and 84 of the hypersonic ABM-3 'Gazelles'. It is claimed by some Western sources that the SA-5 'Gammon' SAM also has an anti-ICBM – or, more precisely, an anti-warhead – capability, as does the new SA-12B

'Giant'. Zenith rocket troops have 1,750 obsolete SA-1 'Guilds', 2,400 SA-2 'Guidelines', 1,100 SA-3 'Goas' and 1,500 SA-10 'Grumbles' throughout the USSR.

Aircraft types and quantities operated by V-PVO are as follows:

EQUIPMENT	QUANTITY
Interceptors	
MiG-21bis 'Fishbed-N'	40
MiG-23MF/ML/- 'Flogger-B/G/K'	900
MiG-25/M 'Foxbat-A/E'	350
MiG-31 'Foxhound'	235
Sukhoi Su-21 'Flagon-E/F'	475
Sukhoi Su-27 'Flanker-B'	150
Tupolev Tu-28P 'Fiddler'	15
Airborne Early Warning	
Ilyushin Il-76 'Mainstay'	12
Tupolev Tu-126 'Moss'	3

Air Force (Voyenno-Vozdushnyye Sily)

Three major components form the VVS, operating bomber, transport and tactical aircraft. Of these, only the last-mentioned is closely integrated with Military Districts and Groups of Forces abroad, the transport force operating autonomously and the bombers and some interdictors forming the Strategic Reserve under operational control of the High Command. In 1980, the three Air Armies of medium and heavy bombers forming Long-Range Aviation (*Dal'nyaya Aviatsiya*) were augmented by two new Armies with interdictors – notably 450 Su-24 'Fencers' taken from the tactical arm of the VVS. Currently, the Irkutsk, Legnica, Moscow, Smolensk and Vinnitsa Air Armies have some 1,100 aircraft forming the Strategic Reserve Air Armies.

A typical example is the 46th Air Army at Smolensk, which comprises four Divisions divided into 12 Regiments: seven with Tupolev Tu-16 'Badgers', three of Tu-22 'Blinders' and two of Tu-26 'Backfires'. Support is provided by three independent reconnaissance Regiments and a few transport aircraft. The 46th AA is of particular interest to Western analysts, as it would re-deploy to Polish bases in wartime and operate in support of tactical forces on the Central Front.

Other bombers would be tasked with long-range attacks as far afield as the USA. Prime inter-continental systems are the Tu-95 'Bear' and Tu-160 'Blackjack' bombers of the Moscow Air Army. 'Bear-B/C' versions of this turboprop bomber are armed with a single AS-3 'Kangaroo' stand-off missile, but have now largely given way to the dual bomber/ECM 'Bear-G' with two AS-4 'Kitchen' missiles (and based entirely with the Irkutsk AA in the 1theatre-nuclear role), and the revised Tu-142 'Bear-H' design carrying six AS-15 'Kents' internally and up to eight externally. 'Kent', the ground-based SSC-4 version of which is being scrapped under INF, has a range of 3000km (2,864 miles). The main 'Bear-H' base is

Dolon, where initial operating capability was achieved in 1988 by the first squadron of 'Blackjacks'. Similar to the Rockwell B-1, but 20 per cent larger, the 'Blackjack' carries six AS-15s but will employ the new, supersonic AS-19 when it becomes available, possibly also adding the 3200-km (1,988-mile) BL-10 weapon to its own 7300-km (4,536-mile) combat radius.

Smolensk and Irkutsk AAs hold the majority of medium-range Tu-16, Tu-22 and Tu-26 bombers – as mentioned above – all relying on AS-2, AS-4 or AS-6 stand-off weapons to strike their targets. Old Myasishchev Mya-4 'Bison' bombers, now functioning as tankers, are partnered by converted Tu-16s, but both types are being replaced by the more suitable Il-78 'Midas'. A disconcerting event for the West has been the sight of training flights in which bombers are escorted all the way to their missile-launch points by Su-27 'Flankers'.

Such protection is also afforded to the Su-24 'Fencer' interdictors assigned to the remaining two Strategic Reserve Air Armies: 4th AA at Vinnitsa and 24th AA at Legnica, in Poland. Closest to NATO, the 24th has four Regiments at bases including Legnica and Tukums. The other two, constituting 128th Bomber Division, were previously at Brand and Grossenhain, East Germany, until they began to pull back to Soviet territory in August 1989, to be replaced by less overtly-offensive Regiments of fighter-bomber MiG-29 'Fulcrums'. 'Fencers' of the 4th AA are located in Regiments at Dubno, Gorodok, Starokonstantinov and Vinnitsa, plus Kunmadaras in Hungary. One further Regiment is based in the Far East.

Tactical components of the VVS comprise dedicated ground-attack aircraft as well as a sizeable force of interceptors to provide protection and double-up in the attack role if circumstances permit. In all, some 2,250 attack and 1,550 interceptor machines form the main force of the close-support element, backed by 600 in the reconnaissance and ECM roles, and 4,400 helicopters. As might be expected, some 2,950 jet-powered aircraft are in the Western Theatre, facing NATO: 2,000 in the Western TVD (or European Central Front), 150 in the North-

MiG-29 units are issued with a few two-seat 'Fulcrum-Bs' for converting new pilots. Note that the trainer lacks search radar and is thus non-operational.

A valuable and widely-used variable-geometry attack aircraft, the Su-17 'Fitter' was developed – in typical Soviet style – from the fixed-geometry Su-7.

Regarded as jet successors to the legendary Shturmovik, Su-25 'Frogfoots' saw considerable use in the Afghanistan war, taking punishment from small arms and SAMs.

MiG-27 versions of 'Flogger' are used for strike/attack missions throughout the VVS. A transonic, low-altitude aircraft, it lacks the MiG-23's variable air intakes.

Strategic transport, including airlift of the now-outlawed SS-20 ballistic missile, is the responsibility of a small number of An-124 Ruslan ('Condor') freighters.

Western TVD and 800 in the South-Western TVD.

Attack forces include some 300 Su-24s not assigned to strategic duties, plus MiG-27 'Flogger-D/Js' and Su-17 'Fitter-C/D/Hs'. A few MiG-21 'Fishbeds' remain, but the prime mud-mover is the Su-25 'Frogfoot' equivalent to America's A-10A Thunderbolt II, the squadrons having gained ample experience of their trade in Afghanistan. A recent and somewhat unlikely addition is the MiG-25 'Foxbat-F', a high-altitude interceptor turned 'Wild Weasel' with AS-11 'Kilter' missiles with which to attack radar and SAM sites.

Interceptors are mainly the types included in the V-PVO inventory – MiG-21, MiG-23 and Su-27 – but with the addition of the MiG-29 'Fulcrum' carrying six AAMs which are usually a mixture of AA-10 and AA-11 weapons. Reconnaissance is the responsibility of converted fighters such as the MiG-21R 'Fishbed-H', Su-17 'Fitter', Su-24 'Fencer-E' and MiG-25R 'Foxbat-B/D'. Yakovlev's Yak-28 has been adapted for recce in its 'Brewer-D' form and as an escorting jammer aircraft as the 'Brewer-E'.

The importance of the helicopter in transporting troops and providing fire-support is reflected in the large number of armed rotorcraft assigned to the army. All the 1,900 Mil Mi-8/17 'Hips' and 1,400 Mi-24 'Hinds' are capable of carrying weapons, 1,200 of them being the heavily-equipped, gunship-standard 'Hip-E' and 'Hind-D/E/F' serving in 20 attack regiments – half of them opposite NATO. 'Hinds' would also be expected to operate autonomously, seeking out and destroying enemy armoured vehicles and helicopters. The giant Mi-26 'Halo' forms a numerically small but specialised airlift force, alongside more substantial numbers of Mi-6 'Hooks' and a few Mi-10 'Harke'. Second-line duties, including training, are the lot of the ageing Mi-2 'Hoplite'. The last few Mi-4s are 'Hound-C' jamming helicopters to be used against enemy air defences, their role having largely been assumed by the Mi-8 'Hip-J/K'. A purpose-designed combat helicopter, the Mi-28 'Havoc', has been longer in development than expected and will not enter production until 1991 at the earliest.

Transport Aviation, with a force of 600 aircraft, is allocated to strategic airlift of supplies and troops. Replacement is well advanced of the Antonov An-12 'Cub' by the jet-powered Il-76 'Candid' which now forms the mainstay of the force. Specialist heavy-transports are the 80-tonne capacity An-22 'Cock' and 150-tonne An-124 'Condor'. Not included in the above are 300 more 'Cubs' and 150 lesser types of aircraft assigned to various types of unit for shorter-range and executive transport. Nor should be forgotten the 1,655 Aeroflot airliners and heavy transports which may be called upon by the VVS at any time. The airline is also used as a thin cover for intelligence-gathering aircraft such as 'Cub-B', although the jamming 'Cub-C' flies in military markings. The ELINT Il-20 'Coot-A', Il-22 development and COMINT Il-14 'Crate' are more transports converted for other purposes.

Training of aircrew begins prior to entry into the armed services through the DOSAAF paramilitary youth sport-flying organisation. These

The 'Flogger-G' was a new MiG-23 version when it made a courtesy visit to France in 1978. Three years earlier, 'Flogger-B' had become operational as the first Soviet aircraft able to track and engage targets at lower altitude than itself, using 'High Lark' nose radar.

Above: The 'duck-nosed' MiG-23BN and MiG-27 'Floggers' perform vital battlefield air interdiction and close air support tasks with Frontal Aviation.

Once the backbone of both offensive and defensive Soviet aviation, the venerable MiG-21 'Fishbed' now serves only in limited numbers.

'Backfire' was the first Soviet variable-geometry strategic bomber, and may be armed with cruise missiles for a longer reach.

Long predicted in the West is the 'Mainstay' airborne early warning and control aircraft, based on Ilyushin's Il-76 'Candid' transport.

Tupolev 'Bears' fly ultra-long-range reconnaissance and ELINT sorties.

are replacing their Yak-18 'Max' trainers with the similar, but more modern Yak-52 and aerobatic Yak-53. Once in the VVS, prospective pilots fly Czech-built Aero L-29 and L-39 basic jet trainers at one of the Higher Military Aviation Schools at Balashov, Barnaul, Borisoglebsk, Chernigov, Kacha, Khar'kov, Orenburg, Saratov, Syzran, Tambov and Yeysk. Helicopter trainees fly the Mi-2 'Hoplite', which is expected to give way in the 1990s to Mil's Mi-34 'Hermit', whilst interceptor pilots pass through the Fighter Aviation Schools at Armavir and Stavropol – the latter also training navigators.

Types and quantities of aircraft assigned to the VVS are:

EQUIPMENT	QUANTITY
Strategic bombers	
Su-24 'Fencer-A/B/C/D'	450
Tu-95 'Bear-B/C'	70
Tu-95 'Bear-G'	40
Tu-142 'Bear-H'	50
Tu-160 'Blackjack-A'	12
Tu-22 'Blinder-B'	120
Tu-16 'Badger-G'	220
Tu-26 'Backfire-B/C'	175
Interceptors	
MiG-21PFMA/SMB/bis/bis 'Fishbed-J/K/L/N'	200
MiG-23MF/ML/- 'Flogger-B/G/K'	875
MiG-29 'Fulcrum-A/C'	450
Su-27 'Flanker-B'	135
Ground attack	
MiG-21PFMA/SMB/bis/bis 'Fishbed-J/K/L/N'	130
MiG-25 'Foxbat-F'	45
MiG-27 'Flogger-D/J'	855
Su-7 'Fitter-A'	50
Su-17 'Fitter-C/D/H'	700

Su-24 'Fencer-A/B/C/D'	300
Su-25 'Frogfoot-A'	225
Tankers	
Mya-4 'Bison'	40
Tu-16 'Badger-A'	20
Il-78 'Midas'	40
Strategic reconnaissance/ECM	
Tu-16 'Badger-D/E/F/K'	70
Tu-22 'Blinder-C'	15
Tu-95 'Bear-E'	4
Tactical reconnaissance/ECM	
MiG-21R 'Fishbed-H'	60
MiG-25 'Foxbat-B/D'	130
Su-17 'Fitter-H/K'	150
Su-24 'Fencer-E'	100
Yak-28 'Brewer-D/E'	160
Strategic transports	
An-12BP 'Cub'	150
An-22 'Cock'	55
An-124 'Condor'	15
Il-76 'Candid'	390
Helicopters	
Mi-2 'Hoplite'	550
Mi-4 'Hound'	15
Mi-6 'Hook'	435
Mi-8/17 'Hip'	1,920
Mi-10 'Harke'	10
Mi-24 'Hind'	1,400
Mi-26 'Halo'	55

Miscellaneous transports
An-2 'Colt', An-8 'Camp', An-12 'Cub', An-24 'Coke', An-26 'Curl', Il-14 'Crate', Il-18 'Coot', Il-62 'Classic', Tu-134 'Crusty', Yak-40 'Codling'
Total 1,450

Trainers
Aero L-29 Delfin, Aero L-39 Albatros, Mi-2 'Hoplite', MiG-15UTI 'Midget', Yak-28U 'Maestro', Yak-52, Yak-53. Total 1,500, not including dual-control versions of combat types: MiG-21U 'Mongol', MiG-23UM 'Flogger-C', MiG-25U 'Foxbat-C', MiG-29UB 'Fulcrum-B', Mi-24 'Hind-C', Su-7U 'Moujik', Su-15 'Flagon-G', Su-17 'Fitter-E/G', Su-25UB 'Frogfoot-B', Su-27UB 'Flanker-C', Tu-22U 'Blinder-D'.

Some 1,400 Mil Mi-24 'Hinds', most of them the heavily-armed D, E and F versions, form a formidable attack helicopter force for army support.

Another Russian giant, Mil's Mi-6 'Hook' transport helicopter can carry 12000 kg (26,455 lb) of internal payload loaded through clamshell rear doors.

Able to mount armament for close-support, the 'Hip' is a highly versatile helicopter heavily committed to airlift for the army in the battlefield.

Naval Aviation (Aviatsiya Voyenno-Morskoyo Flota)

Possessing 1,745 aircraft, AV-MF is not the world's largest naval air arm, but its fleet of 290 nuclear-armed bombers makes it the most powerful. AV-MF has traditionally been responsible for coastal surveillance, anti-submarine missions in local waters and long-range reconnaissance and strike against enemy submarines and surface vessels. In 1976, it entered the new sphere of small aircraft-carrier operations with the V/STOL Yak-38 'Forger' and is now about to make a further advance with the deployment of aircraft aboard the USSR's first full-sized carrier. Naval Air Forces are assigned to each of the four Soviet navy fleets, the Northern Fleet having 420 aircraft in the area of the Kola Peninsula; Baltic Fleet, 280 around Leningrad and the Baltic Republics; Black Sea Fleet, 500; and Pacific Fleet, 545 in the region of Vladivostok.

'Forgers' fly from the four 38,000-tonne ASW-cruisers *Kiev, Minsk, Novorossisk* and *Baku*, normal ship's complement being a dozen, plus up to 19 Kamov Ka-27 'Helix'

ASW helicopters. A developed version, the Yak-41 (provisional name 'Ram-T' indicating discovery by US satellites overflying Ramenskoye test centre), will be deployed aboard the new fleet of aircraft-carriers – but not the first, *Tbilisi*, because of development delays with this, aviation's first supersonic V/STOL aircraft.

The 60,000-tonne *Tbilisi* began sea trials in 1989, fitted with only a 'ski-jump' bow ramp and no catapults. Following dummy deck trials at Saki aerodrome, a navalised Su-27 'Flanker' was undertaking landing trials by November 1989, and a similarly modified Su-25 'Frogfoot' and MiG-29 'Fulcrum' had also been tested. *Tbilisi* and the second vessel, *Riga*, will have a 60-aircraft complement, also expected to include the Kamov Ka-41 'Hokum' attack helicopter currently in the prototype stage, as well as 'Helix' for ASW. Third off the slipway will be the 75,000-tonne *Ulyanovsk* with a further 15-20 aircraft, this and the *Riga* probably having a catapult.

Helicopter-carrying vessels have replaced many of their Ka-25 'Hormones' with the more capable 'Helix-A' for ASW and 'Helix-D' for carrier plane-guard. These include the cruisers *Moskva* and *Leningrad* with up to 20 helicopters each; plus single helicopters deployed on the

Flown in the same year (1952) as the Vulcan and Victor, the 'Badger' continues to have an operational naval role as a carrier of large, anti-ship missiles.

The long-fuselage Tu-142 version of 'Bear' patrols the world's oceans from bases such as Cuba and Angola as well as from the Soviet mainland.

stern platforms of seven *Kara*, four *Kresta I*, 10 *Kresta II*, four *Kynda*, two *Slava* and eight *Sverdlov* cruisers, plus the single *Krivak III* frigate. Three are assigned to each of the three *Kirov* cruisers, and two to each of eight *Udaloy* destroyers. Two *Ivan Rogov* landing ships have four helicopters, and it was aboard the nameship in 1987 that the first Ka-29 'Helix-B' armed, commando-carrying helicopter was observed.

Inshore searches for submarines are conducted by the land-based Mi-14PL 'Haze-A', whilst Mi-14BT 'Haze-Bs' are equipped for detecting mines and the Mi-14PS 'Haze-C' is an SAR helicopter. Working a little farther out are Beriev Be-12 'Mail' amphibians and Il-38 'Mays', possibly to be augmented in the future by the graceful Beriev A-40 Albatros jet-powered amphibian. Undisputed masters of maritime patrol are the Tu-142 'Bear-Fs' which cover large swathes of the Atlantic and Pacific Oceans within their 8300-km (5,157-mile) un-refuelled radius of action.

Attacks on opposing maritime surface forces are the responsibility of the naval bomber force comprising Tu-26 'Backfires' armed with AS-4 'Kitchen' nuclear missiles; Tu-16 'Badger-C/Gs' carrying AS-2 'Kipper' and AS-5 'Kelt', respectively – but sometimes AS-6 'Kingfish'; Tu-22 'Blinder-As' using free-fall bombs; and Su-17 'Fitter-C/Ds' carrying the conventional-warhead AS-7 'Kerry'. More 'Badgers' and 'Bears' function as tankers and reconnaissance/ELINT aircraft.

Two 'Backfire' Regiments are assigned to the Northern Fleet, and one to each of the remaining three, including the Pacific Fleet base at Alekseyeva. Attack 'Fitters' are only with the Baltic Fleet, whilst the 'Blinder-C' reconnaissance bomber flies from Ukrainian and Estonian bases to cover the Black Sea and Baltic. Semi-permanent overseas deployments include 'Bears' at San Antonio de los Banos, Cuba, covering the North Atlantic and Gulf of Mexico; Luanda, Angola, for the South Atlantic; and Cam Ranh, Vietnam, for the South China Sea; and 'Mays' on the South Yemeni island of Socotra for surveillance of the Indian Ocean.

Naval aviation assets are:

Though a poor Sea Harrier substitute, the Yak-38 'Forger' attack aircraft was a crucial step in development of Soviet carrierborne air power.

Some 300 'Badgers' are retained by all four fleets of the Soviet navy as bombers, tankers and reconnaissance/Elint aircraft.

The Beriev Be-12 Tchaika ('Mail') amphibious twin turboprop undertakes inshore patrols around the Soviet coastline.

Towed MAD equipment is carried by this Mi-14 'Haze' for anti-submarine missions in coastal waters.

Some medium-size Soviet warships have provision for an anti-submarine helicopter, such as the Kamov 'Hormone' (illustrated) and later Ka-27 'Helix'.

Medium-range maritime patrol aircraft is the Ilyushin Il-38 'May', fitted with MAD and undernose radome. Some are detached to Yemen.

Ka-29TB 'Helix-B' is a troop-carrying and close support Ka-27 variant.

EQUIPMENT	QUANTITY
Bombers	
Tu-16 'Badger-C/G'	150
Tu-22 'Blinder-B'	25
Tu-28 'Backfire-B'	90
Tu-28 'Backfire-C'	30
Fighter-bombers	
Su-17 'Fitter-C/D'	70
Yak-38 'Forger-A/B'	75
MiG-23 'Flogger'	10
Tankers	
Tu-16 'Badger-A'	45
Reconnaissance and ECM	
An-12 'Cub-B/C/D'	12
Ka-25 'Hormone-B'	20
Su-24 'Fencer-E'	10
Tu-16 'Badger-H/J'	60
Tu-16 'Badger-D/E/F'	55

Tu-22 'Blinder-C'	5		Mi-14 'Haze-A'	50
Tu-95 'Bear-D/E'	45		Tu-142 'Bear-F'	60
Anti-submarine			**Support helicopters**	
Be-12 'Mail'	90		Ka-29 'Helix-B'	30
Il-38 'May'	45		Mi-14 'Haze-B/C'	35
Ka-25 'Hormone-A'	100		**Transport and trainer**	588
Ka-27 'Helix-A'	50			

POLAND

Polish Air Force (Polskie Wojska Lotnicze)

Poland, though not in the front line of forces facing NATO, has been regarded as an important base and marshalling point for reserves – notably theatre-nuclear bomber units locally based (Su-24 'Fencer') and brought forward from their Soviet peacetime stations (Tu-16 'Badger', Tu-22 'Blinder' and Tu-26 'Backfire'). Combat strength is officially 480 aircraft (of which 108 are strike-capable) and 43 helicopters, but many of these are of limited effectiveness. Poland only continues to maintain the largest air force of the Soviet satellites by sacrificing quality in order to keep up numbers. Many divisions are, effectively, two-wing units, with the third component either existing as a flight or operating downgraded equipment. The same sometimes happens at regimental level – for example, Su-22 'Fitter' regiments have aged MiG-17s (locally-built Lim-6 versions) as 'padding'. Local names for these units are *dywtzion* (division), *pulk* (regiment) and *eskadra* (squadron).

As Poland was leading the Eastern European battle in 1989 against total communist rule, its air force was simultaneously receiving the first MiG-29 'Fulcrum-As' and re-organising the air force administration. Under the previous system, a separate National Air Defence Force, the *Wojska Oborony Powietrznej Kraju*, existed to assist Soviet fighters to defend their rear areas. This has now been absorbed into the PWL with the status of three Corps (*Korpus-Oborony Powietrznej Kraju*) and taken control of the smaller tactical air defence force. The enlarged air force remains divided on regional lines: 1 Corps in the Warsaw Military District; 2 Corps at Bydgoszcz for the Pomeranian MD in the north-west; and 3 Corps at Wroclaw for the Silesian MD in the south-west and south.

Soviet units resident in Poland include those assigned to the Northern Group of Forces: an attack regiment of MiG-27 'Flogger-D/Js' at Osla; a fighter division of a MiG-29 'Fulcrum' and two MiG-23 'Flogger' regiments at Chojna, Kolbrzeg and Stargard; a reconnaissance regiment of MiG-25R 'Foxbat-B/Ds' and MiG-21R 'Fishbed-Hs' at Brzeg; and an Mi-24 'Hind' and Mi-17 'Hip-H' combat helicopter regiment which is in the process of being withdrawn to the USSR. Also present, at Szprotawa and Zagan, are two regiments of Su-24 'Fencer' interdictors which come under the Strategic reserve unit, 24th Air Army at Legnica (also controlling the Su-24s currently withdrawing from Germany). Departure of all of these is only a matter of time.

Having withdrawn its early F-13 and PF models of MiG-21 (and sold some abroad to avid 'warbird' collectors in the USA and elsewhere), the PWL retains some 350 MiG-21PFM/M/MF/bis 'Fishbed-F/J/J/N' versions with 4½ national interceptor regiments and up to three assigned to tactical defence. One further defensive wing equipped between 1981 and 1986 with 45 MiG-23MF 'Flogger-Bs', and a start was made in June 1989 with the transfer of one MiG-21 wing to MiG-29s. A halt to further deliveries has been called, however. SAMs in their air defence element are 300 SA-2 'Guidelines' and SA-3 'Goas' at 50 bases.

Attack forces have fared a little better, in that of six 'Fitter' wings (three interdictor; three fighter-bomber), only one remains with the fixed-geometry Su-7 'Fitter-A'. The others have progressed to the export variant of Su-17 in the form of Su-20 'Fitter-Cs' and Su-22M-4 'Fitter-Ks', most of the 170 in service being the 'K' variant. The 'Fitter' regiments also share 40 Lim-6 and Lim-6bis fighter-bombers. Reconnaissance squadrons number six, comprising three designated tactical units with 40 MiG-21R 'Fishbed-Hs' and three forming a bomber-recce regiment of Su-7 and Su-20R 'Fitters'. Two Combat Helicopter Regiments share up to 60 Mi-24 'Hind-D/Es' and some of the 100 locally-built Mi-2 'Hoplites' in service, and may have begun to receive the armed Mi-17 'Hip-Hs' recently noted. 'Hoplites' are the Mi-2US armed model, carrying AT-2 'Swatter' or AT-3 'Sagger' anti-tank missiles. Three heavy-lift Mi-6 'Hooks' were obtained from a civilian organisation in 1987.

Main transports are 20 An-12 'Cubs', six An-24 'Cokes' and 12 An-26 'Curls'. Two Tu-134 'Crustys' are used for VIP work, and 20 Yak-40 'Codlings', 10 An-2 'Colts' and five Mi-8S 'Hips' are among the communications fleet. Poland builds the An-28 'Cash', so it is not surprising that five are in service for light transport. Furthermore, Polish industry provides training aircraft, so instead of L-39s, the WSK is the only WarPac air force with the Iskra light jet. A few of the new piston-engined Orlik trainers partner Iskras at the Deblin-based Officers' School, but it is the turboprop version of Orlik which is expected to receive the main production order. It will be joined by the new I-22 Iryd jet trainer, a prototype of which flew in 1985.

Poland's navy is responsible for defending the Baltic coastline with Mi-14 'Haze' anti-submarine helicopters of the Naval Aviation Force (*Obrona Przeciwlotnocza*). There is also reportedly an attack regiment of MiG-21s (which may be a naval-dedicated unit of the air force), some An-2 and Sokol liaison aircraft and Mi-2 SAR

Three Polish fighter-bomber regiments are equipped with Sukhoi 'Fitters', this Tumanskii-engined Su-22M-4 version serving with the 1 Eskadra of 6 PLM-B 'Oposkie' at Pila.

'Fitter' armament includes 57-mm rocket pods (as here), FAB 100 and FAB 250 bombs (100/225 kg) and two 30-mm cannon.

Air defences include just one regiment of MiG-23MF 'Flogger-B' fighters, the 28 PLM-OPK at Slupsk.

Mil's Mi-24 'Hind-D' forms the backbone of the assault helicopter forces, armament including a 12.7-mm nose turret, four UV-32-57 rocket pods and four wingtip 'Swatter' ATMs.

Initial deliveries to Poland of the variable-geometry 'Fitter' were of the Su-20 'Fitter-C' version, powered by the Lyul'ka AL-21 turbojet.

Most numerous defender of Polish skies is the MiG-21MF 'Fishbed-J', this example wearing the ancient knight badge of the 41 PLM at Malbork.

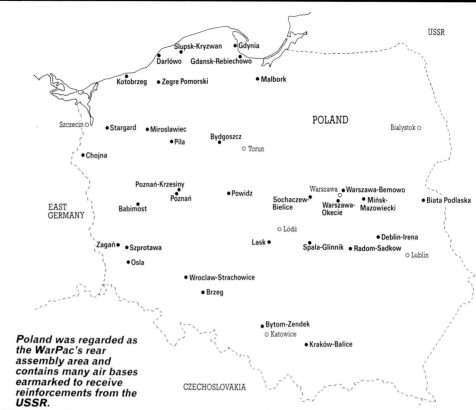

Poland was regarded as the WarPac's rear assembly area and contains many air bases earmarked to receive reinforcements from the USSR.

Previously grey, Polish 'loggers' have recently adopted tactical camouflage.

Up to 350 MiG-21s of various types remain in Polish service. Extended range is bestowed by 490-litre (108-Imp gal) drop tanks on this MiG-21MF 'Fishbed-J'.

The venerable Antonov An-2 'Colt' was produced in Poland as well as the USSR. Several serve as 'hacks' but have been partly replaced by the Polish-built An-28 'Cash'.

Although outclassed by more modern machines, 'Fishbeds' continue to shoulder the main burden of air defence, serving seven regiments, including three in tactical roles.

Pre-production PZL-130 Orlik primary trainers serve the Air School Squadron.

Unique in the Warsaw Pact, Poland does not use Czech basic jet trainers, preferring its own PZL TS-11 Iskra. The only export sale has been to India.

Poland uses the Mil Mi-14 for both mine countermeasures and SAR. Tasked with the latter duty is this Mi-14PS 'Haze-C' from the naval aviation force base at Darlowo.

The Ilyushin Il-14 remains in Warsaw Pact service in small numbers, for miscellaneous support tasks. This one wears Polish air force insignia.

Unit badge and cockpit detail of a Polish MiG-23MF 'Flogger-B' of 28 PLM-OPK.

helicopters. The army has 51 FROG and 36 SS-1 'Scud' SSM launchers.

Order of Battle

UNIT	EQUIPMENT	BASE
Air Fighter Regiments *(Pulk Lotnictwa Myśliwskiego)*		
2 PLM 'Krakow'	MiG-21M/MF 'Fishbed-J'	Goleniow
9 PLM 'Torun'	MiG-21 'Fishbed'	Zegrze-Pomorskie
41 PLM	MiG-21MF 'Fishbed-J'	Malbork

Above units constitute 4 *Pomorska Dywizja Lotnictwa Myśliwskiego* (Pomoranian Fighter Air Division) at Malbork

Air Fighter Regiments – Air Defence Force *(Pulk Lotnictwa Myśliwskiego – Oborony Powietrznej Kraju)*		
1 PLM-OPK 'Warszawa'	MiG-29 'Fulcrum-A', MiG-21PF 'Fishbed-D/E'	Mińsk-Mazowiecki[1]
10 PLM-OPK	MiG-21PFM 'Fishbed-F'	Lask[1]
11 PLM-OPK 'Brandenburski'	MiG-21 'Fishbed'	Wroclaw[3]
28 PLM-OPK 'Koszalin'	MiG-23MF 'Flogger-B', Lim-6 'Fresco'	Slupsk-Krzywan[3]
34 PLM-OPK	MiG-21 'Fishbed'	Gdynia[2]
62 PLM-OPK 'Poznań'	MiG-21 'Fishbed'	Poznań-Krzesiny[3]

[1]comprise 1 National Air Defence Corps *(Korpus-Oborony Powietrznej Kraju)* at Warsaw
[2]comprises 2 KOPK at Bydgoszcz
[3]comprise 3 KOPK at Wroclaw

Air Defence Artillery Brigades *(Brygada Artilerii Oborony Powietrznej Kraju)* and Regiment		
1 BAOPK	SA-2, SA-3	Bytom
3 BAOPK	SA-2, SA-3	Warsaw
4 BAOPK	SA-2, SA-3	Gdynia
26 BAOPK	SA-2, SA-3	Gryfice
79 SamPAOPK	SA-?	Poznań

Interdictor Air Regiments *(Lotniczy Pulk Szkolno-Bojowy)*		
3 LPSz-B	Su-7 'Fitter-A'	Bydgoszcz
45 LPSz-B	Su-22 'Fitter-K', Lim-6 'Fresco'	Babimost
61 PLSz-B	Su-? 'Fitter'	Biala Podlaska

Fighter-Bomber Air Regiments *(Pulk Lotnictwa Myśliwsko-Bombowego)*		
6 PLM-B 'Oposkie'	Su-22M-4 'Fitter-K' Lim-6 'Fresco'	Pila[1]
8 PLM-B	Su-22M-4 'Fitter-K' Lim-6 'Fresco'	Miroslawiec
40 PLM-B	Su-22M-4 'Fitter-K' Lim-6 'Fresco'	Swidwin-Smardsko[2]

[1]constitutes 2 Fighter-Bomber Air Division *(Dywizja Lotnictwa Myśliwsko-Bombowego)*
[2]constitutes 3 DLM-B

Bomber Reconnaissance Air Regiment *(Pulk Lotnictwa Bombowo-Rozpoznawczego)*		
7 PLBR	Su-20 'Fitter-C' Su-22M-4/U 'Fitter-K/G'	Powidz ('Fitter' OCU)

Tactical Reconnaissance Air Regiment *(Pulk Lotnictwa Rozpoznania Taktycznego)*		
32 PLRT	MiG-21R 'Fishbed-H'	Sochachew-Belice

Special Air Regiment *(Pulk Lotnictwa Specjalnego)*		
7 PLS	not known	Siemirowice

Combat Helicopter Regiments *(Pulk Smiglowcow Bojowych)*		
49 PSB	Mi-24 'Hind-D/E' Mi-2US 'Hoplite'	Pruszcz-Gdański
59 PSB	Mi-24 'Hind-D/E' Mi-2US 'Hoplite'	Inowroclaw

Air Transport Regiment *(Pulk Lotnictwa Transportowego)*		
13 PLT	An-2, An-12, An-24, An-26	Kraków

Transport Helicopter Regiment *(Pulk Smiglowcow Transportowych)*		
37 PST	Mi-2, Mi-6	Leczyca

Special Air Transport Regiment *(Specjalny Pulk Lotnictwa Transportowego)*		
36 PLT	Tu-134, Yak-40 , Mi-8, Mi-17	Warsaw

Air School Regiment *(Lotnicza Pulk Szkolny)*		
58 LPSz	Iskra, Lim-6, An-2, Mi-2	Deblin
60 LPSz	Iskra	Radom
66 LSz	Iskra, Lim-6	Tomaszów Mazowiecko

Air School Squadron *(Lotnicza Eskadre Szkolna)*		
23 LESz	Orlik	Deblin-Irena

Attached to *Wyższs Oficerska Szkola Lotnicza*

Experimental Air Squadron *(Lotnicza Eskadra Doświadczalna)*		
45 LED	various	Modlin

Helicopter Air School *(Szkolny Pulk Smiglowców)*		
47 SzPS	Mi-2 'Hoplite'	Nowe Miasto

Naval Aviation Force *(Morskie Lotnictwa Wojskowe)*		
	Mi-14 'Haze'	Darlowo

Army SSM units		
Brigade	SS-1 'Scud-B'	Boleslawiec
Brigade	SS-1 'Scud-B'	Choszczno
Brigade	SS-1 'Scud'	Poznan
Brigade	SS-1 'Scud'	Szczecin
Brigade	FROG	Elblag
Brigade	FROG	Koszalin
Brigade	FROG	Legionowo
Brigade	FROG	Lubiechów
Brigade	FROG	Lubin
Brigade	FROG	Opole
Brigade	FROG	Rzeszow
Brigade	FROG	Szczecinek

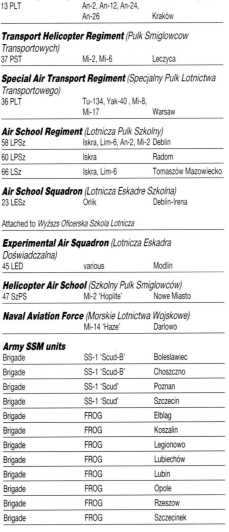

EAST GERMANY

National Army Air Force and Air Defence – Luftstreitkräfte und Luftverteidigung der Nationalen Volksarmee

On 3 October 1990, the two Germanies were unified, the new nation being part of NATO. The Luftwaffe will not adopt any Soviet types, most of which will return to the USSR or be destroyed. However, what follows is a review of East German air forces before unification.

East German air assets were organised on the Soviet pattern with interceptor and SAM forces in a separate organisation *(Luftverteidigung)*. The latter had been the major element since formation in 1956, but the past few years saw the emphasis passing to the attack component *(Luftstreitkräfte)*. Official data listed 269 fixed-wing combat aircraft (65 of them strike-configured) and 74 combat-capable helicopters, plus 24 naval combat aircraft. This omitted 50 MiG-21MF 'Fishbed-Js', which were scrapped in 1989 when the 7th Air Defence Wing at Drewitz was disbanded in a unilateral disarmament gesture.

Although the LSK/LV ranked in size after Poland and Czechoslovakia, it was dwarfed by the Air Force of the Soviet Western Group of Forces (HQ: Zossen-Wünsdorf), stationed in

WarPac workhorse, the 'Hip' is used by Poland in both Mi-8 (illustrated) and improved Mi-17 guise. Several are equipped with armament for offensive roles.

The TS-11 Iskra, shown here, has suffered a high accident rate and will eventually be replaced by the I-22 Iryd – flown in 1984 but still not in service.

Showpiece of the East German air force was the MiG-29, 24 of which were received by JFG 3 at Preschen, including four trainers. A further 32 on order have been cancelled.

Prominent in the inventory was the Sukhoi Su-22M-4 'Fitter-K' attack-fighter. This JBFG 77 example is carrying two 800-litre (176-Imp gal) drop tanks.

Over 100 Mi-8/17 'Hips' of various types served with Luftstreitkräfte combat and transport helicopter regiments, including a few dedicated to SAR.

Prime PWL executive aircraft is the *Tupolev Tu-134A 'Crusty'*, which operates as 'air force one-zero-one' with *Special Air Transport Regiment 36*. The serial number was previously used by two different *Ilyushin Il-18 'Coots'*.

Short-range transport of VIPs is entrusted to a fleet of *Yak-40 'Codling'* twin-jets based at *Warsaw* and flown by the *Specjalny Pulk Lotnictwa Transportowego*.

Left: Taking off over a 'Hind', this Mi-17 *Hip-H'* carries UB-32-57 rocket pods and is fitted with an IR jammer atop the fuselage.

Right: The indigenous PZL W-3 Sokol turbine-powered helicopter is used in small numbers by naval aviation.

Antonov's *An-26 'Curl'* tactical transport was delivered to the PWL in 1972 as the main means of dropping parachutists of the 6th Pomeranian Airborne Division.

One combat wing, the 37th fighter-bomber, named for *Klement Gottwald* and based at *Drewitz*, was equipped with MiG-23BN *'Flogger-Fs'* and (here illustrated) *'-Hs'*.

Right: East German bases are augmented by unmarked motorway strips.

Q' (Quality Maintenance) symbols denote efficient ground crew.

An *Aero Albatros* in L-39ZO armed configuration. In addition to Dayglo patches, a serial number below 300 confirms the aircraft's instructional role.

One whole and one part-equipped regiment flew the *MiG-21MF 'Fishbed-J'* on air defence duties in East Germany. All are likely to be withdrawn after German re-unification.

Close-up of a *MiG-21MF* reveals details of safety markings for ejection seat and canopy release, plus the rear-view mirror fairing on top of the canopy.

Half mounted knight; half jet fighter – the badge of Su-22-equipped JFG 77.

East Germany with up to 900 fixed-wing combat aircraft and 400 helicopters. The Soviet VVS had seven divisions in East Germany: three air defence (the 307th, 308th and 309th Fighter Divisions); two attack and interdiction (421st and 427th Attack Divisions); one Reconnaissance (15th Division); and one (previously 128th Bomber) converting from Su-24 'Fencers' to MiG-29 'Fulcrums'. The last-mentioned had only two regiments, at Brand and Grossenhain, but the others all had three. Of these, the fighter regiments were based at Alt Lonnewitz, Altenburg, Finow, Juteborg, Kothen, Merseburg, Putnitz, Wittstock and Zerbst – three with MiG-29s, three with MiG-23s and three with MiG-21s.

Attack regiments in the Soviet forces in East Germany were based at Brandenburg-Briessen, Finsterwalde, Grossenhain, Mirow, Neuruppin and Templin, equipped with MiG-21s, MiG-27 'Flogger-D/Js' and Su-17 'Fitters'. The reconnaissance force of MiG-25 'Foxbats', Su-22M-4 'Fencers' and MiG-21RFs was found in three regiments at Allstedt, Welzow and Werneuchen. 'Hind' and 'Hip' types formed the 16th Combat Helicopter Regiment at Stendal and 16th Independent Transport Helicopter Regiment at Parchim. Logistic support aircraft were assigned to the 29th and 33rd Transport Regiments.

East Germany used the term *Geschwader* for its regiments, these having 10 combat-ready aircraft and up to three dual-control versions of the same type in each of their three squadrons. Wing complement was thus some 39 jet aircraft and a handful of piston-engined Zlin Z.43 liaison aircraft. The *Luftverteidigung* (Air Defence) was divided on geographical criteria into the 1st and 3rd Divisions, at Cottbus (south) and Neubrandenburg (north) respectively. After recent cuts in strength, each division had two interceptor regiments and three or four SAM regiments – the latter totalling 200 launchers at 30 bases. The 'showpiece' regiment was the 3rd at Preschen, where the first non-Soviet MiG-29 'Fulcrum-As' in the War-Pac began arriving in May 1988. There were 60 MiG-23MF/ML 'Flogger-B/Gs' and 100 MiG-21s (mostly MF/bis 'Fishbed-J/Ns') in 1 and 3 Divisions, plus 24 MiG-29s, of which four were tandem-seat trainers.

The *Luftstreitkräfte* had its HQ at Eggersdorf, its main component being the *Kommando der Front-und Transpostfliegerkrafte* (KFT-Tactical and Transport Command) with fixed-wing and helicopter combat wings, including those assigned to naval duties. Newest of these was at Laage, where 23 Su-22M-4 'Fitter-Ks' and a pair of two-seat 'Fitter-H' trainers arrived in 1985 to replace 50 attack-configured MiG-21PF/PFM 'Fishbeds'. A 'Flogger-F' wing at Drewitz had 28 MiG-23BNs and two autonomous tactical reconnaissance squadrons each operated a dozen MiG-21Rs. Front-line helicopters were 48 Mi-24 'Hind-Ds' and 80 Mi-8TB/TBK/TBK 'Hip-C/E/Fs' with two combat regiments under *Armeefliegerkräfte* (army) control at Basepohl and Cottbus supported by a transport unit at Brandenburg with 24 Mi-8 'Hips'. Mainly fixed-wing transport units include a VIP squadron (shortly to be disbanded) at Strausberg, another at Dresden and a liaison squadron at Strausberg.

The utility division, or *Fliegerübungsdivision*, was responsible for providing training, notably on 40 L-39 Albatroses at Bautzen for pilots attending the school named after Otto Lilienthal. Most were L-39ZO versions, but there were two L-39Vs used for target towing. After qualifying on the L-39, pilots specialised at one of three satellite schools: at Rothenburg flying 24 MiG-21PFMs and 30 two-seat MiG-21Us; at Kemenz, where there were 12 An-2s and eight L-410s for transport training; or at Brandenburg for helicopter training on 18 Mi-2 'Hoplites' and 18 Mi-8 'Hips'. A few of the Mi-2s were *Schnellemedizinhilfe* (emergency medical) versions. The two remaining services operated missiles and aircraft, including 24 FROG and 18 SS-1 'Scud' SSMs assigned to the army. A helicopter wing dedicated to the *Volksmarine* (People's Navy) used the Mi-14PL 'Haze-A' as a land-based ASW helicopter, eight in this configuration being partnered by four Mi-14T 'Haze-B' mine-hunters and four Mi-14PS 'Hip-C' SAR variants. An anti-shipping attack wing at Laage employed 23 Su-22M-4 'Fitter-Ks' and two 'Fitter-H' trainers for operations in the Baltic – these a recent arrival first reported in 1988.

Order of Battle

UNIT	EQUIPMENT	BASE
Luftverteidigungs fighter wings		
1 Luftverteidigungsdivision:		
Jagdfliegergeschwader 1	MiG-21MF 'Fishbed-J'	Holzdorf
Jagdfliegergeschwader 3	MiG-29 'Fulcrum-A'	Preschen
	MiG-21bis 'Fishbed-L/N'	
Jagdfliegergeschwader 8	MiG-21bis 'Fishbed-L/N'	Marxwalde
3 Luftverteidigungsdivision:		
Jagdfliegergeschwader 2	MiG-21MF 'Fishbed-J'	Neubrandenburg
Jagdfliegergeschwader 9	MiG-23MF/ML 'Flogger-B/G'	Peenemünde
Zieldarstellungskette	L-39ZO/V	Peenemünde
Luftverteidigungs SAM wings		
Flugabwehrraketenregiment 13	SA-2 'Guideline'	Parchim
Flugabwehrraketenregiment 14	SA-2 'Guideline'	Strassgräbchen
Flugabwehrraketenregiment 15	SA-	Trollenhagen
Flugabwehrraketenregiment 16	SA-3 'Goa'	Ladeburg
Flugabwehrraketenregiment 17	SA-3 'Goa'	Uhlenkrug
Flugabwehrraketenregiment 18	SA-	Sanitz
Flugabwehrraketenregiment	SA-	
KFT attack wings		
Jagdbombenfliegergeschwader 37	MiG-23BN 'Flogger-F/H'	Drewitz
Jagdbombenfliegergeschwader 77	Su-22M-4 'Fitter-K'	Laage
KFT reconnaissance squadrons		
Taktischeaufklärungsstaffel 47	MiG-21R 'Fishbed-H'	Preschen
Taktischeaufklärungsstaffel 87	MiG-21R 'Fishbed-H'	Drewitz
Armeefliegerkräfte helicopter wings		
Kampfhubschraubergeschwader 5	Mi-8TB/TBK 'Hip-C/F' Mi-24 'Hind-D', Mi-2	Basepohl
Kampfhubschraubergeschwader 3	Mi-8TB/TBK 'Hip-C/F' Mi-24 'Hind-D', Mi-2	Cottbus
KFT helicopter wings		
Transporthubschraubergeschwader 34	Mi-8T/TB 'Hip-C'	Brandenburg
KFT transport units		
Lufttransportstaffel 44	Il-62, Tu-134, Tu-154, Mi-8S	Strausberg
Transportfliegergeschwader 24	An-26	Dresden
Verbindungsstaffel 14	An-2, L-410	Strausberg
Fliegerübungsdivision schools and OCUs		
Offizierflugzeugführerschule 'Otto Lilienthal' (Bautzen):		
Fliegerausbildungsgeschwader 25	L-39ZO/V Albatros	Bautzen
Fliegerausbildungsgeschwader 15	MiG-21PFM 'Fishbed-F' MiG-21U/UM/US 'Mongol-A/B/B'	Rothenburg
Hubschrauberausbildungsgeschwader 35	Mi-8, Mi-2B	Brandenburg

Anti-submarine patrols along the Baltic shores were undertaken by Mil Mi-14PL 'Haze-A' amphibious helicopters equipped with towed MAD at the rear of the cabin.

First non-Soviet unit to operate Sukhoi Su-25K 'Frogfoots' was the Czechoslovak Ostrava Regiment, based at Pardubice with 35 aircraft.

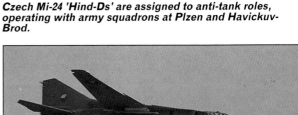

Czech Mi-24 'Hind-Ds' are assigned to anti-tank roles, operating with army squadrons at Plzen and Havickuv-Brod.

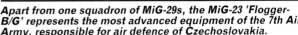

Apart from one squadron of MiG-29s, the MiG-23 'Flogger-B/G' represents the most advanced equipment of the 7th Air Army, responsible for air defence of Czechoslovakia.

The two-seat Su-25UB trainer was first revealed in Czech markings in 1989. The raised rear seat gives a distinctly hump-backed appearance.

Imported from Czechoslovakia, this Let L-410 Turbolet served in the communications and light transport role with Verbindungsstaffel 14 at Strausberg.

East Germany had remarkably few cargo aircraft in military service. Antonov An-26 'Curls' flew from Dresden with TFG 24.

Farewell 'Fitter' – a fixed-geometry Su-7 'Fitter-A' attack aircraft (nearest) is escorted by its replacement Su-22M-4 'Fitter-K' some time in the late 1980s.

Transportfliegerausbildungsstaffel 45		
	L-410, An-2, Z.43	Kamenz

KFT naval attack wing

Marinefliegergeschwader 28	Su-22M-4 'Fitter-K'	Laage

KFT naval helicopter wing

Marinehubschraubergeschwader 28	Mi-8 'Hip', Mi-14 'Haze'	Parow

Volksarmee (People's Army) SSM brigades

3 Brigade	SS-1 'Scud'	
5 Brigade	SS-1 'Scud'	Demen
–	FROG 7	Dresden
–	FROG 7	Eggesin
–	FROG 7	Halle-Erfurt
–	FROG 7	Potsdam

NOTE: Named regiments are 1 'Fritz Schmenkel', JFG 2 'Juri Gagarin', JFG 3 'Wladimir Komarow', JFG 8 'Herman Matern', JFG 9 'Heinrich Rau', JFAG 15 'Heinz Kapelle', JFAG 25 'Leander Ratz', TFG 27 'Arthur Pieck', MFG 28 'Paul Wieczorek', THS 34 'Werner Seelenbinder', HAG 35 'Lambert Horn', JBFG 37 'Clement Gotwald', TFS 44 'Arthur Pieck', JBFG 77 'Gebhard Leberecht von Blucher', KHG 57 'Adolf von Lutzow' and KHG 67 'Ferdinand von Schill'

CZECHOSLOVAKIA

Czechoslovak Air Force (Ceskoslovenske Letectvo)

Of the WarPac satellite states, Czechoslovakia ranks second after Poland in size of air force, contributing an officially-quoted total of 407 fixed-wing combat aircraft (including 137 strike/attack) and 101 combat helicopters to Pact forces. This indicates a substantial expansion after the CL was virtually disbanded in the wake of the 1968 Soviet invasion, when an embryonic democratic movement was crushed. Now, however, a 'Prague Spring' is spreading to almost all of Eastern Europe, bringing with it defence economies which are sure to affect the air force in the 1990s. Czechoslovakia is urging Moscow to make a speedy withdrawal of the Central Group of Forces which was imposed on the country post-1968 as a thinly-disguised deterrent to further liberalisation during the Brezhnev era.

Soviet air elements in Czechoslovakia include an interceptor regiment of MiG-23M 'Flogger-Bs' at Milovice; a nuclear strike regiment of MiG-27 'Flogger-D/Js' at Mimon; and a fighter-bomber regiment at Sliac equipped with Su-22M-3 'Fitter-Hs' – 130 combat-capable aircraft in all. A sizeable army support component consists of five mixed 'Hind-D/F' and 'Hip-C' regiments at Milivic, Mimon, Olomouc and Sliac-Zvolen (two) with an overall total of 120 of each type. A transport regiment at Milovice flies 11 Tu-134s, 13 An-12s and three An-26s, whilst a radar calibration squadron with four Il-28 'Beagles' is at Sliac.

The 1990s have begun for the CL with a swing of the pendulum. During the previous decade, tactical air support forces of the 10th Air Army (HQ: Hradec Kralove) were the principal beneficiaries of new equipment. However, in 1989, deliveries began of the first MiG-29 interceptors to a Regiment of the 7th Air Army (HQ: Prague) – the independent force assigned to air defence. In total, the 7th comprises nine regiments, including six sharing about 250 launch systems for SA-2 'Guideline' and SA-3 'Goa' SAMs spread over 40 sites. The MiG-29s have gone to the Zatec-based regiment, where replacement of MiG-21 'Fishbed-D/Fs' is a priority. Two squadrons totalling 35 'Flogger-B/Gs' serve here and elsewhere, but the re-

Left: Used by an attack regiment at Caslav is the MiG-23BN 'Flogger-H'.

South-west Czechoslovakia shares a short border with West Germany, but is otherwise surrounded by neutral or WarPac territory.

maining five squadrons have 'Fishbeds'. The inventory of the latter is 80 'Fishbed-D/Fs', 60 'Fishbed-Es' and 165 'Fishbed-Js'.

Since 1985, the 10th Air Army has been operating Su-25K 'Frogfoot-As' in a 35-aircraft regiment at Pardubice – the first WarPac member outside the USSR to do so. Two further regiments, equipped with 35 'Flogger-Hs' and 35 'Fitter-Ks' have an interdiction role, whilst three more with 'Fishbeds' are tasked with close-support – one of them in the process of receiving the 'Fitter'. 'Fitters' arrived with the CL in 1984, initially for a reconnaissance regiment at Kralove, where 45 have SLAR (side-looking airborne radar) sensors. A co-located squadron has a pair of Tu-134 'Crusty' transports modified for ELINT missions. Two-seat trainer versions of front-line types include 60 MiG-21U 'Mongol-Bs'.

In one of the few examples of a 'two-way street' between Moscow and its allies, Czechoslovakia is the provider of basic jet trainers to the entire WarPac, except Poland. Not surprisingly, therefore, the Aero L-39 Albatros is employed at the Kosice air force training school *Vysoká Vijenksá Letecká Skola Slovenského Národniho Povstáni*, where 30 serve. Future jet pilots fly 280 hours on L-39s over a four-year course before conversion to fighters at the Prerov MiG-21 OCU, but prospective helicopter pilots fly some of the 60 ancient Mi-1 'Hares', first at Kosice, then at Piestany for the advanced stage. Transports include a VIP Tu-154, a pair of An-12 'Cubs', 15 An-26 'Curls' and a half-dozen An-24RV 'Cokes'. 'Hack' aircraft are the inevitable An-2 and the locally-designed Let L-410M Turbolet light twin – about 15 of each.

Ground forces have army aviation (*Vojskove Letectvo*) to provide transport and armed support. There is one regiment with the 10th Air Army at Prostejov and three smaller units operating a total of 45 'Hind-Ds', 25 'Hip-Cs', 20 'Hip-Hs', four ECM 'Hip-Ks' and 32 'Hoplites'. Helicopters at Plzen are assigned to the 1st Army and those at Havlickuv-Brod to the 4th Army. Army SSM units operate SS-1 'Scuds' and are converting from FROGs to SS-21s.

Order of Battle

UNIT	EQUIPMENT	BASE
7th Air Army interceptor units		
Squadron	MiG-29 'Fulcrum-A'	Zatec
Squadron	MiG-23M 'Flogger-B'	Zatec
Squadron	MiG-21MF 'Fishbed-J'	Zatec
Squadron	MiG-23ML 'Flogger-G'	Budejovice
Squadron	MiG-21PF/PFM 'Fishbed-D/F'	Budejovice
Squadron	MiG-21MF 'Fishbed-J'	Budejovice
Squadron	MiG-21PF/PFM 'Fishbed-D/F'	Brno
Squadron	MiG-21PF/PFM 'Fishbed-D/F'	Brno
Flight x40	SA-2 'Guideline' SA-3 'Goa'	various bases
10th Air Army attack units		
Regiment	Su-25K 'Frogfoot-A'	Pardubice
Regiment	MiG-23BN 'Flogger-H'	Caslav
Regiment	Su-22M-4 'Fitter K'	Námest
Regiment	MiG-21MF 'Fishbed-J'	Pardubice

Regiment	MiG-21MF 'Fishbed-J'	Dobrany
Squadron	Su-22M-4 'Fitter-K'	Prerov
Squadron	MiG-21MF 'Fishbed-J'	Prerov
Squadron	MiG-21MF 'Fishbed-J'	Prerov
Squadron	MiG-21 'Fishbed-E'	Bechyne
Squadron	MiG-21 'Fishbed-E'	Bechyne
Squadron	MiG-21MF 'Fishbed-J'	Bechyne
Squadron	MiG-21PF/PFM 'Fishbed-D/F'	Bechyne
10th Air Army reconnaissance units		
Regiment	Su-22M 'Fitter-H/K'	Králove
Flight	Tu-134 'Crusty'	Králove
10th Air Army helicopter units		
Regiment	Mi-24 'Hind-D', Mi-8 'Hip-C', Mi-2 'Hoplite'	Prostejov
Transport units		
Regiment	An-2, An-12, An-24/26, L-410M, Tu-134, Tu-154, Yak-40	Mosnov
Training units		
School	L-39 Albatros Mi-1 'Hare'	Kosice
School	Mi-1 'Hare', Mi-2 'Hoplite'	Piestany
School	MiG-21 'Fishbed-E', MiG-21U 'Mongol-B'	Prerov
Army aviation units		
Squadron	Mi-24 'Hind-D'	Plzen
Squadron	Mi-17 'Hip-H'	Plzen
Squadron	Mi-8 'Hip-C/K'	Bechyne
Squadron	Mi-24 'Hind-D'	Havlickuv-Brod
Squadron	Mi-8 'Hip-C/K'	Havlickuv-Brod
Army SSM units		
Regiment	FROG/SS-21 'Scarab'	Szlany
Regiment	FROG/SS-21 'Scarab'	Budejovice
Regiment	FROG/SS-21 'Scarab'	Tabor
Regiment	FROG/SS-21 'Scarab'	Havlickuv-Brod
Regiment	FROG/SS-21 'Scarab'	Susice
Regiment	FROG/SS-21 'Scarab'	Topolcany
Regiment	FROG/SS-21 'Scarab'	Karlovy-Vary
Regiment	SS-1 'Scud'	St Boleslav
Regiment	SS-1 'Scud'	Hranice

HUNGARY

Hungarian Air Force (Magyar Lègierö)

A large-scale reduction is in prospect for combat aircraft based in Hungary as the local armed forces undergo a 17 per cent cut in funding imposed by the new government, which has also requested the departure of the Air Force of the Soviet Southern Group of Forces (HQ: Tokol). Hungary officially possesses 113 fixed-wing combat aircraft and 96 combat helicopters, to which may be added the Soviet total of 190 front line aeroplanes, 80 helicopters and 20 transports (An-12s and Il-76s).

Of the Soviet equipment, the MiG-29 'Fulcrum-A' regiment at Tokol is being withdrawn during 1990, leaving two interceptor regiments with 45 MiG-21 'Fishbeds' and 45 MiG-23 'Floggers' at Sarmellek and Kiskunlachàza; an attack regiment of Su-17 'Fitters' at Kunmadaras; a mixed ECM/ELINT squadron; a tactical reconnaissance squadron of Su-17s, also at Kunmadaras; and two helicopter regiments with a total of 50 Mi-8 'Hips' and 20 Mi-24 'Hinds'.

Here in the markings of its home air force, the Aero L-39 Albatros is used for basic jet training almost throughout the whole Warsaw Pact.

Long-range flights on behalf of the Czech government are flown by Tu-134 (illustrated) and Tu-154 aircraft, operated by the transport regiment at Mosnov.

Right: A dramatic picture of an afterburning Hungarian MiG-23MF 'Flogger-B' with decompression vapour above the wings.

Situated to the west of neutral Austria, Hungary has been regarded by the Warsaw Pact as a less important sector of its front line – hence comparatively few air bases.

Above: Mi-8TB 'Hip-Cs' are generally used as transports, but may carry light armament externally. Two squadrons partner 'Hinds' in the 'Bakony' combat regiment.

In the absence of a Soviet rival, Let's L-410 has been adopted by some Warsaw Pact air forces as an An-2 replacement. The Czechs have about 15 L-410M versions.

A Mi-8T 'Hip-C' in standard central European camouflage prepares for take-off. A SAR winch is above the cabin door.

No Warsaw Pact nation can rival the mighty Soviet transport fleet. Czechoslovakia, for example, has only a pair of Antonov An-12 'Cubs'.

The Czech transport regiment is based at Mosnov, with a twin-engined fleet including An-24 'Cokes' and (as here) An-26 'Curls'.

Two regiments of 'Fishbeds' – such as this MiG-21MF – form the majority of the Hungarian National Air Defence Command, operating from Kecskemét and Taszar.

Some 12 Antonov An-26 'Curl' rear-loading tactical freighters are operated by the 'Szolnok' and 'Hari Laszlo' regiments.

Hungarian Mi-24 'Hind-Ds' are early production versions which lack the infra-red jammer behind the engine bay. UV-32-57 rocket pods are fitted.

Becoming a rarity, the Mil Mi-2 'Hoplite' is used in Hungary for SAR, fitted with a hoist above the rear door.

Hungary's air force – which is actually attached to the army – is principally a defensive organisation with three interceptor (*vadász*) and three SAM regiments, but only one squadron of attack aircraft. The two first-mentioned are administered by *Orszàgos Lègvédelmi Parancsnoksàg* (National Air Defence Command) and include one *szàzad* (squadron) of 10 MiG-23MF 'Flogger-Bs' (armed with AA-2 'Atoll' and AA-8 'Aphid' AAMs) and one of MiG-21s at Pápa and two further wings, of two squadrons each, at Kecskemet and Taszar, or some 65 MiG-21s in all.

The attack aircraft of *Csapatrepülö Parancsnoksàg* (Troop Air Command) were reduced to one *vadasz-bombazo* (fighter-bomber) squadron in 1980, this unit now having 10 Su-22M-3 'Fitter-Hs' and three Su-22U trainers. Since 1985, there have been repeated reports of Su-25 'Frogfoots' flying from Dombovar, but these are visiting Soviet aircraft. Helicopter support is provided by 50 Mi-8/17 'Hips' (including two squadrons within the 'Bakong' Regiment), 26 Mi-24 'Hinds' and 25 Mi-2 'Hoplites' used for SAR at Szekesfehervar and elsewhere. The transport arm includes a pair of An-24V 'Cokes', 12 An-26 'Curls' and a few L-410s.

Unusually for Warsaw Pact air force, no L-39s have been received, as training of new pilots is undertaken at Kosice, Czechoslovakia, once students have been selected at light aircraft schools operated by the pre-service training organisation, *Magyar Honvédelmi Szövetség*. Type conversion is undertaken at regiment level, except for helicopter training on Mi-8s at Szolnok.

Order of Battle

UNIT	EQUIPMENT	BASE
Orszagos Legvedelmi Parancsnoksag air defence units		
Regiment	MiG-23MF 'Flogger-B', MiG-21bis 'Fishbed-L/N'	Pàpa
Regiment	MiG-21MF, 'Fishbed-J'	Kecskemét
Regiment	MiG-21MF/bis 'Fishbed-N'	Taszar
Regiment	SA-2 'Guideline', SA-3 'Goa'	
Regiment	SA-2 'Guideline', SA-3 'Goa'	
Regiment	SA-2 'Guideline', SA-3 'Goa'	
Csapatrepülö Parancsnoksag attack/recce unit		
Squadron	Su-22M-3 'Fitter-H'	Taszar (part of 'Kapos' Regiment)
Csapatrepülö Parancsnoksag support units		
'Bakony' Regiment	Mi-8TB 'Hip-C'	Veszprém
550/550 Squadron	Mi-24 'Hind-D/E'	Veszprém
'Szolnok' Regiment	Mi-8TB 'Hip-C', An-26 'Curl'	Szolnok
'Vitez Hari Laszlo' Squadron	An-24, An-26, L-410, Z.43	Tököl
Training unit		
OCU	Mi-8TB 'Hip-C'	Szolnok
Army SSM units		
Brigade	SS-1 'Scud'	Tapolca
Regiment	FROG 7	Gyöngyös
Regiment	FROG 7	Nyiregyháza
Regiment	FROG 7	Tata

Army SAM units

Regiment	SA-4 'Ganef'
Regiment	SA-6 'Gainful'
Regiment	SA-6 'Gainful'
Regiment	SA-6 'Gainful'

ROMANIA

Romanian Air Force (Fortele Aeriene Romania)

Even before the 1989 revolution, Romania was an unusual Eastern Bloc member, in that it had comparatively many contacts with the West and neighbouring Yugoslavia. As a result, the FAR is the only constituent of the WarPac with French-designed helicopters in its Army support regiments and the only one to initiate joint development of a combat aircraft with a non-Pact member and fit it with Rolls-Royce engines. During the 1980s, defence spending was progressively reduced as 'an example' to the Superpowers – but more likely as a result of deepening financial problems which slowed deliveries of the Romano-Jugoslav IAR-93 attack aircraft and appear to have slowed development of the IAR-99 Soim advanced trainer and IAR-317 Airfox (Alouette III-based) attack helicopter.

Until 1989, the FAR was committed to support Soviet air elements in the neighbouring Odessa Military District. Administration comes from the Romanian Army, of which the Air Force is merely one element, equal in status to the infantry and armour branches. Comprising four Air Divisions centred on the Cluj and Bucharest Military Districts, the FAR has five air defence and four attack regiments, plus a Division of 135 SA-2 'Guideline' SAMs spread over 20 sites.

Only one regiment of 45 MiG-23 'Floggers' may be described as having reasonably modern equipment within the air defence forces, a further four sharing 150 MiG-21s – mainly 'Fishbed-J', but with a significant number of hardly-effective 'C' and 'D' models included. Armament includes the AA-2 'Atoll', AA-3 'Anab' and AA-7 'Apex' missiles, built locally under the designations A91, A90 and A911 respectively.

Attack forces are contained within four regiments which are currently in the process of converting from MiG-17 'Frescos' to IAR-93s. Originally, plans were to build 20 IAR-93As and 165 afterburner-equipped IAR-93Bs, but the total has almost certainly been reduced. However, it is suggested that at least 100 IAR-93s have been built to augment the 90 or so remaining MiG-17s, the former probably fitted with the AS-7 (A921) 'Kerry' ASMs that Romania is manufacturing. Helicopter units have 50 Aérospatiale Alouettes and up to 100 Pumas from local production, supported by 25 Mi-8 'Hips', a few Mi-2 'Hoplites' and Mi-4 'Hounds' and two VIP AS-365N Dauphins. A small transport aircraft force at Baneasa includes 10 An-24 'Cokes', five An-26 'Curls' and 10 An-2 'Colts'.

Training of pilots begins in the state flying clubs on IAR-823s or, on entry to the air force on IAR-28MA graders. Romania appears not

to have modernised its equipment beyond that stage, and so the FAR trains on L-29 Delfins and MiG-15UTI 'Midgets'. The few L-39s delivered are used for advanced weapons training. A small batch of 15 turboprop IAR-823s was delivered in 1983 for evaluation, but planned production of 100 appears not to have begun. An unconfirmed report implies that manufacture of the IAR-99 Soim jet trainer began in the late 1980s.

In the other armed services, the navy has a pair of Alouette IIIs and the army operates 18 SS-1 'Scud' and 30 FROG 3 launchers.

Order of Battle

UNIT	EQUIPMENT
Air defence units	
Regiment	MiG-23 'Flogger'
Regiment	MiG-21 'Fishbed'
Regiment	MiG-21 'Fishbed'
Regiment	MiG-21 'Fishbed'
Regiment	MiG-21 'Fishbed'
Regiment	SA-2 'Guideline'
Regiment	SA-2 'Guideline'
Regiment	SA-2 'Guideline'
Attack units	
Regiment	IAR-93
Regiment	IAR-93
Regiment	MiG-17 'Fresco'
Regiment	MiG-17 'Fresco'
Support units	
Regiment	Puma, Alouette III
Regiment	An-2, An-24, An-26, Mi-8, Puma, Alouette III, Dauphin
School	IAR-28, IAR-823, IAR-825, L-29 Delfin
School	L-39ZA Albatros
Naval aviation	
Flight	Alouette III

Hungary is defended by three under-size regiments, of which two are equipped with MiG-21s, representing 65 aircraft of MF, bis and UM variants.

A single squadron of MiG-23MF 'Flogger-Bs', delivered to the 'Stromfeld' Regiment 10 years ago, represents the most modern equipment in Hungary's Air Defence Command.

Both An-24 and An-26 transports serve the Hungarian 'Hari Laszlo' Regiment at Tököl, lack of a rear loading ramp identifying this An-24 'Coke'.

USSR

HUNGARY
● Satu Mare
● Oradea
● Cluj
● Arad
● Timisoara
ROMANIA
YUGOSLAVIA
● Craiova
● Iasi
● Bacău
Tecuci ●
● Brasov
Galati ●
Buzău ● ● Zilistea
Băneasa ● ● Otopeni
Bucuresti ○ ● Popesti Leordeni
Mamaia ●
● Constanta-Mihai Kogalniceanu
BULGARIA

Until recently the most repressive state in the Warsaw Pact, Romania is located far from the former centre of tension on the East-West German border, behind Hungary and fraternal communist state, Yugoslavia. It has comparatively few major air bases – in part because no elements of the Soviet armed forces are based on Romanian soil.

Using the Alouette III (for which it has a production licence) as a basis, Romania developed the tandem-seat Airfox attack helicopter in the early 1980s, but severe financial problems prevented production for the air force and the programme was abandoned.

Hungarian VIP aircraft include the Defence Ministry's Tu-134 'Crusty'.

Bulgaria's small air force faces NATO members Greece and Turkey, but as a reliable ally of Moscow the country has no resident Soviet forces.

In conjunction with Yugoslavia – a communist country not in the Warsaw Pact – Romania has developed the IAR-93 ground attack aircraft.

Similar to the Anglo-French Jaguar, the IAR-93 suffered long development delays. The Romanian prototype flew in October 1974.

IAR-93s are believed to serve with two regiments of the Romanian air force, first deliveries being of the non-afterburning IAR-93A.

BULGARIA

Bulgarian Defence Forces (Bulgarski Vizdusny Vojski)

Previously one of Moscow's more loyal allies, Bulgaria was regarded as a guardian of the south-eastern approaches to Central Europe until its government yielded to democratic elements in December 1989. Greece and Turkey are Bulgaria's NATO neighbours, but the threat which they pose is not regarded as being particularly high. On Bulgaria's western border is Yugoslavia which, though outside the Warsaw Pact, is a trustworthy fraternal communist state. For the medium-term future, Bulgaria's defensive concerns will centre on preventing an overspill of civil strife as factions within Romania and Yugoslavia fight for autonomy.

No Soviet troops are stationed in Bulgaria, although local air defence forces are believed to be integrated with the V-PVO and tactical air forces committed to operating alongside their equivalents in the Odessa Military District of the USSR. This may change if a stable, liberalised government is able to retain power. One certain fact, however, is that the new rulers have planned a massive 12 per cent cut in defence spending for 1990, implying a significant reduction in all armed services.

SAM forces have their HQ at Sliven. There is one Air Defence Division controlling several regiments operating from some 30 bases, responsibility for control being delegated to the three Army Commands: Eastern at Yambol; Central at Plovdiv and Western at Sofia. Launch systems total 280 for the SA-2 'Guideline' and SA-3 'Goa' SAMs. These two weapons are complementary, the SA-3 with its range of up to 30 km (18½ miles) acting as 'goalkeeper' for the 50-km (31-mile)/25000-m (82,000-ft) SA-2.

Tactical air forces, headquartered at Plovdiv and technically part of the army, are organised into seven regiments, of which four are of manned interceptors, two have attack tasking and the last is a reconnaissance unit. Most, if not all, of the 110 interceptor MiG-21s in service are of the ageing MiG-21PFM 'Fishbed-F' variety armed with AA-2 'Atoll' AAMs and possibly even the obsolete AA-1. More effective are the two squadrons totalling 30 MiG-23MF 'Flogger-Bs' fitted with the 20-km (12.5-mile) AA-7 'Apex' missile. Two varieties are used: heat seeking and radar homing – these having the official Soviet designations R23T and R23R.

Three squadrons of 'Floggers' lead the attack aircraft inventory. These MiG-23BN 'Flogger-H' versions arrived in the early-1980s, the 45 in service seeming to be spread through three bases, suggesting that regiments are either widely dispersed or not homogenous. Retirement of the last 50 MiG-17 'Frescos' was heralded in 1989 on arrival of at least a squadron of Su-25 'Frogfoots'. The targeted Su-25 total is 45 (one regiment) but orders may have been cancelled.

MiG-21R 'Fishbed-H' reconnaissance aircraft fly from Tolbuhin in two squadrons. There have been reports that Bulgaria also uses

MiG-25R 'Foxbat-Bs' and Su-22 'Fitters' for recce, but firm evidence is lacking. A few Ilyushin Il-28 'Beagle' light bombers are retained for jamming and possibly intelligence-gathering.

Turgovishté is the main base for army support helicopters. Routine tasks are undertaken by 20 Mi-2 'Hoplites' and 20 Mi-4 'Hounds', the front-line role belonging to 30 Mi-8 'Hips' and 40 Mi-24 'Hind' gunships. Sofia/Vrajdebna is the principal transport terminal, housing up to a dozen An-12 'Cubs', a similar number of An-24s and -26s and a pair of An-30 'Clank' photo-survey aircraft. The VIP aircraft is a single Yak-40 'Codling', but around 20 An-2 'Colt' biplanes are assigned to several units as utility transports. Training aircraft are the standard WarPac issue of L-29 Delfin and L-39 Albatros, backed by MiG-15UTI 'Midgets'.

To defend the Black Sea coast, the navy includes a small aviation element, principally equipped with 10 Mi-14 'Haze' helicopters for ASW patrols from shore bases. A few Mi-2 'Hoplites' and Mi-4 'Hounds' are used for secondary tasks.

Order of Battle

UNIT	EQUIPMENT	BASE
Air Defence Force SAM units		
Western Army Command	SA-2 'Guideline', SA-3 'Goa'	Sofia, etc
Central Army Command	SA-2 'Guideline', SA-3 'Goa'	Plovdiv, etc
Eastern Army Command	SA-2 'Guideline', SA-3 'Goa'	Yambol, etc
Tactical Air Force fighter units		
Squadron	MiG-21PFM 'Fishbed-F'	Balchik
Squadron	MiG-21PFM 'Fishbed-F'	Khaskovo
Squadron	MiG-21PFM 'Fishbed-F'	Rusé
Squadron	MiG-21PFM 'Fishbed-F'	Yambol
Squadron	MiG-23MF 'Flogger-B'	
Squadron	MiG-23MF 'Flogger-B'	
Tactical Air Force attack units		
Squadron	MiG-23BN 'Flogger-H'	Sofia
Squadron	MiG-23BN 'Flogger-H'	Plovdiv
Squadron	MiG-23BN 'Flogger-H'	Pleven
Squadron	Su-25K 'Frogfoot-A'	
Squadron	MiG-17F/SF 'Fresco'	
Squadron	MiG-17F/SF 'Fresco'	
Tactical Air Force reconnaissance units		
Squadron	MiG-21R 'Fishbed-H'	Tolbukhin
Squadron	MiG-21R 'Fishbed-H'	Tolbukhin
Squadron	MiG-25R/Su-22 – unconfirmed	
Army support units		
Regiment	Mi-24 'Hind-D', Mi-8 'Hip-C'	Turgovishté
Transport units		
Regiment	An-12BP 'Cub', An-24 'Coke', An-26 'Curl'	Sofia/Vrajdebna
Training units		
School	L-29 Delfin, L-39 Albatros	Bozhuristé
Naval aviation		
Squadron	Mi-14PL 'Haze-A', Mi-2 'Hoplite', Mi-4 'Hound'	Burgas & Varna

Picture credits

Front cover: British Aerospace. **5:** Paul Jackson, Peter Gunti, Hendrik van Broekhuizen (two), Tom Ross. **6:** J. Sjoersdsma, Jon Lake, Panavia. **7:** Mike Stroud, Jon Lake. **8:** Robert F. Dorr (two). **9:** Robert F. Dorr (two), No. 111 Squadron. **10:** Boeing Vertol, Bob Archer, Robert F. Dorr. **11:** LTV, Richard Gennis, P. J. Cooper. **12:** Northrop. **13:** Northrop, David Donald (two), P. Sjoerdsma. **14-15:** Saab. **16:** Richard Gennis, MBB (two). **17:** Robert E. Kling via René J. Francillon (four). **19:** via J. W. R. Taylor, Vaclav Jukl via J. W. R. Taylor. **20:** Vaclav Jukl via J. W. R. Taylor, J. W. R. Taylor. **21:** Hendrik van Broekhuizen. **22:** Press Association, Associated Press. **23:** Press Association. **24:** Associated Press, Popperfoto. **25:** US Department of Defense (USDoD). **26:** Associated Press, USDoD. **27:** Associated Press. **28:** USDoD. **29:** David Donald (three), Bob Archer. **30:** USDoD. **31:** Richard V. Rizzo (three). **32:** USDoD, Associated Press. **33:** Associated Press, Jon Lake (two). **34:** Paul Jackson (two), RAF, Terry Senior. **35:** Terry Senior. **36:** RAF (two), Associated Press (two). **38-39:** Andrew Johnson. **39:** British Aerospace. **40:** British Aerospace. **41:** British Aerospace, Panavia. **42:** Panavia, British Aerospace. **43:** British Aerospace. **44:** Panavia, MBB via Paul Jackson. **45:** MBB via Paul Jackson. **46:** Hunting, MoD. **49:** Bob A. Munro, British Aerospace via Mike Stroud. **50-51:** Flt Lt Mike Lumb (No. 14 Sqn). **52:** Panavia, Panavia via Paul Jackson. **53:** Tony Paxton, MBB. **54:** Panavia, Panavia via Paul Jackson. **56:** Panavia via Paul Jackson, Panavia. **57:** British Aerospace via Mike Stroud, Panavia. **58:** British Aerospace (two), No. 20 Sqn. **59:** MBB, British Aerospace. **60:** British Aerospace. **66:** Tony Paxton. **67:** MBB. **68:** British Aerospace via Paul Jackson, Terry Senior. **69:** Tony Paxton, British Aerospace. **70:** Paul Jackson. **72:** Tony Paxton. **73:** Flt Lt Ian Black, via R. L. Ward. **74:** David Donald (three), Robbie Shaw, via Jon Lake, Bob Archer, Terry Paxton. **75:** Jon Lake, David Donald, Robbie Shaw, Bob Archer, Squadron Prints. **76:** Robbie Shaw, Terry Senior, David Donald, Jon Lake. **77:** Robbie Shaw. **77:** Jon Lake (three), Terry Senior via Jon Lake (two), Geoff Lee ARPS, Terry Senior, David Donald. **78:** No. 16 Sqn, David Donald (three), Robbie Shaw, via Jon Lake, Bob Archer, Terry Paxton. **79:** Ian Black, Jon Lake (two), David Donald (three), Bob Archer, Jonny Bonny, No. 13 Sqn. **80:** Jon Lake (five), Terry Senior (three). **81:** Bob Archer, Jon Lake (five), Terry Senior via Jon Lake, Tony Paxton. **82:** Paul Jackson, Jon Lake (two), No. 11 Sqn, Tony Paxton via Jon Lake. **83:** Tony Paxton, Jon Lake (two), Terry Senior, Flt Lt P. Lightbody. **84:** Paul Jackson, via Jon Lake, Richard Gennis. **85:** Bob Archer, Robbie Shaw, MBB, Jon Lake, H.J. van Broekhuizen. **86:** David Donald, Jon Lake, Robbie Shaw, Paul Jackson (two), Jon Lake, Paul Jackson. **87:** David Donald, Bob Archer, Jon Lake, Jonny Bonny, Paul Jackson. **88:** David Donald, Bob Archer, Robbie Shaw (two), Mike Stroud, Federico Anselmino, Paul Jackson. **89:** British Aerospace, Jon Lake. **90:** Peter R. Foster, General Dynamics, New Jersey ANG. **91:** General Dynamics, New Jersey ANG. **92:** Robert F. Dorr, 174th TFW via Warren E. Thompson, General Dynamics. **93:** Ken Shuffield via Warren E. Thompson, New Jersey ANG, General Dynamics, James Benson. **94:** Peter R. Foster, Warren E. Thompson (two), MSgt David Saville via Warren E. Thompson. **95:** General Dynamics, Warren E. Thompson (two). **96:** Peter B. Mersky, Lockheed. **97:** US Navy (two), RAAF. **98:** Peter B. Mersky, Robbie Shaw, Peter B. Lewis via René J. Francillon. **99:** RAAF, René J. Francillon, Lockheed. **100:** Jim Dunn via René J. Francillon (RJF), US Navy via Peter B. Mersky, Lockheed. **101:** René J. Francillon, R.F. Kling via RJF, P. J. Cooper. **102:** via Peter B. Mersky, Lockheed-California. **103:** Carl E. Porter via RJF, Peter B. Lewis via RJF, US Navy via Peter B. Mersky, Robbie Shaw. **104:** Lockheed-California, Hideki Nagakubo via Peter B. Mersky, Lockheed-California. **105:** Robbie Shaw, R.E. Kling via RJF (two). **106:** R.E. Kling via RJF (two), Robbie Shaw, Peter B. Lewis via René J. Francillon. **107:** Robbie Shaw. **108:** Peter B. Lewis via RJF, René J. Francillon, Lockheed. **109:** via Peter B. Mersky, Hideki Nagakubo via Peter B. Mersky, Lockheed-California. **110:** R. E. Kling via RJF (two), Military Aircraft Photographs, David Donald (two), Jim Dunn via RJF, Lindsay Peacock. **111:** Peter B. Mersky, Lindsay Peacock, D. Yount via Marty J. Isham via RJF. **112:** Lockheed-California, Robert E. Kling via RJF (two), Wayne Whited via RJF (three). **113:** R. E. Kling via RJF (two), Lockheed-California. **114:** US Navy via René J. Francillon, Robbie Shaw, via Peter B. Mersky (two), RJF. **115:** René J. Francillon (five), Robbie Shaw (two), R. E. Kling via RJF (three), David Donald, B. Rys via Marty J. Isham via RJF. **116:** Jilly Foreman, Peter B. Lewis via RJF, RAAF via RJF, Robbie Shaw (four), René J. Francillon, Masanori Ogawa via RJF. **117:** Toyokazu Matsuzaki via RJF, Lockheed-California, Robbie Shaw via RJF. **118:** René J. Francillon (two). **119:** René J. Francillon (three). **120-127:** Peter Steinemann. **128:** René J. Francillon (two). **129:** Jim Dunn via RJF, René J. Francillon. **130:** Michael Grove via RJF, René J. Francillon, Richard Gennis. **131:** David Donald (three), Bob A. Munro, US Navy, René J. Francillon. **132:** David Donald, Carl E. Porter via RJF, Daniel Soulaine via RJF, Bob A. Munro (two). **133:** René J. Francillon, René J. Francillon. **134:** David Donald, René J. Francillon. **136:** Soviet Military Power. **137:** Jon Lake, Soviet Military Power. **138:** USDoD (three). **139:** Jon Lake (two), US Navy, USDoD. **140:** Jon Lake (three), Robert J. Ruffle. **141:** Paul Jackson (two). **142:** Jon Lake, Peter R. Foster (two). **144-145:** Graham Napper. **152:** Paul Jackson, David Donald.